A Twice-Taken Journey

Autobiography of Bishop Ray Owen

A Twice-Taken Journey

Autobiography of Bishop Ray Owen

John Wesley Press • San Antonio, Texas

A TWICE-TAKEN JOURNEY

AUTOBIOGRAPHY OF BISHOP RAY OWEN

Copyright©2002

by Southwest Texas Conference of The United Methodist Church

Library of Congress Control Number 2002115535

ISBN 0-9662905-2-6

Printed in the

United States of America

Limited First Printing: December 2002

John Wesley Press

The United Methodist Church

Southwest Texas Conference

16400 Huebner Road

P.O. Box 781149

San Antonio, Texas 78278-1149

MANUFACTURED IN THE UNITED STATES OF AMERICA

Contents

Acknowledgments

The writer of one's own autobiography soon realizes the life story being told is not just the account of the writer. It is also the story of a host of people who shared in, shaped, and contributed to the life that has become a story. William (Bill) Hestwood, a retired pastor and valued friend, reminded me of that. We were sitting around a lunch table with several other retired pastors. When someone asked me how my autobiography was coming along, Bill mischievously inquired if the title would be "Hindsight of a Has-Been."

In that setting with several other longtime colleagues, I realized that my life story as it was being written was not just my story. Indeed, it was the story of countless persons, including those around the table, who had mentored me, encouraged me, and shaped much of what my life's story had become. Bill, then, became the face that represented that host of contributors. I acknowledge with deep gratitude, therefore, not only Bill's friendship but also for his gift of "realization" while eating lunch.

Certainly I want to acknowledge Lavelle with endearing and enduring praise and gratitude for the development of this book. Again and again she has played a critical role as she has deciphered my handwriting, made it legible on the computer, and then gone over my words to correct and edit. She not only made the written text live; she also played the large role in the living of the story for more than 50 years. Obviously, this story could not have been written and would not have been published had it not been for my much-loved wife, best friend, coworker, counselor, and sometimes adviser.

Then there is Doug Cannon, communications director for the Southwest Texas Conference of the United Methodist Church. He has coached and encouraged me to write this autobiography. His efforts began and continued for well over a year before I retired. We enjoyed talking about it many times over a bagel sandwich lunch. The format with which the book is written came from Doug's insights.

My admiration and appreciation for Doug as a communicator as well as a treasured friend is beyond my capacity to express. I hope "Thank you, Doug" again will serve as a feeble start.

> Ray Owen
> Oklahoma City. Oklahoma

Introduction

For some time now, I have sensed a gentle but persistent prodding to recall and relate my life's journey. The idea, therefore, of *A Twice-Taken Journey* was conceived, nurtured, and now lives again on the pages that follow.

These pages do not reveal the life story of some notable or noble person whose life has been lived so remarkably as to demand publishing. Any reader who expects this account to be that of an uncommon person, therefore, will be greatly disappointed. And I will be embarrassed. Quite contentedly and comfortably, I take my rightful place among those far, far back from the ranks of the eminent and renowned.

Simply stated, this story is of one very ordinary human being who grew up in hard times, searched awhile for anchorage, became a Methodist preacher, pursued his call with fervor, and lived life once by experiencing it and twice by writing it. From the beginning as a part-time supply pastor (barely licensed to preach) to the ending as a bishop in the United Methodist Church, I have relished every mile and moment of this grand adventure. Even now, when I reflect on my life's journey, I can be only humbled and grateful for what God, the church, my family, friends, mentors, colleagues, and many others have made of my life.

I realize much of the value of one's recounted story always must be measured on the scales of accuracy and authenticity. That's good! That's also bad! It is *good* in that precision and honesty has had constantly to monitor my motives and govern my pen. It is *bad* in that additional insights gained during recall are apt to have embellished incidents and points being made. Should such embellishments and inaccuracies creep in to suggest errancy, I trust they will be received with forgiving humor regarding my own humanness.

Over these 40-plus years of ministry, I have endeavored to take my calling most seriously. At the same time I have sought not to take myself nearly so seriously. Consequently, I have come to claim kindred spirit with that pastor/mentor who said to me decades ago, "Love yourself, Ray, but don't fall in love with yourself."

So far, I have! And I have not!

1

Journey Through Roots, Heritage, and Culture

In the full grip of this country's greatest economic struggle came the birth of a boy at home in a house near Gleason, Tennessee. The boy arrived April 21, 1932, and was named Raymond Harold. He was the sixth of eight children born to Charlie Emerson Owen (born December 28, 1894) and Lula Adell Owen (born June 26, 1902).

All my life I have heard it said by those who grew up in the era of the Great Depression, "We were poor, but we didn't know we were poor." Certainly that was true for the seven surviving siblings of my parents.

Both my parents came from large families. Dad, the third child of John R. Owen and Norah M. Owen, had eight brothers and eight sisters. All of them grew into adulthood. Mother, the first child of Andrew Jackson Page and Venera Paschall Page, had five brothers and one sister. Large families were commonplace in those days. When family reunions took place, it was a get-together of tribal proportions. Since all our neighbors and relatives were economically depressed, we were not much aware of being poor.

In the early stages of their marriage, my parents lost their firstborn son, J.C., who died in infancy. Dad farmed land in rural Weakley County, Tennessee. As the severity of the Great

Depression bore down, my parents lost the farm. Market prices for their sweet potatoes and other crops fell so low that they were hardly worth harvesting. Indeed, then, like most families living around them, their children were born into a culture of poverty.

Of course, the loss of their farm was a devastating blow to a proud couple who believed in hard work, honest dealings with others, and a strong faith in God. By far, they were more God-loving people than God-fearing people. Not once in all my life was I ever disappointed in either of my parent's behavior, morals, motives, or lifestyle. They set before their children high and honorable values by which to live. They taught us by example and discipline how to live up to those values. Their language might have been deficient in grammar because of limited education, but never did vulgarity or profanity pollute it. They did not practice such language ("blackguarding," as they called it) or allow their children to use it.

Having lost the farm, my father was forced to take work wherever he could find it to keep the family clothed, sheltered, and fed. With a generous jersey cow, two young hogs to slaughter each winter, a huge garden each spring, and several broods of chickens hatched in early summer, they managed to keep food on the table—for which at every mealtime, Dad would offer thanks to God. Food was treated like a sacrament. It was not to be wasted by leftovers on one's plate.

E.W., the oldest surviving sibling, married while he was in his late teens and moved away with Frances, his new wife, to begin their life together. I was but a small boy at the time. For that reason, I never had opportunity to spend time with him and get to know him. Even to his death in 1986, he always called me Little Brother. I considered the name a title of affection.

When E.W. and his family came home for brief visits, he invariably told additional stories of his growing up and how much tougher he had it than the rest of us. Of course, we fiercely disagreed with him.

As an aside, while our three sons were growing up, I found myself telling them how much harder I had it growing up than they did. They never would believe I had to walk two miles each way on a muddy dirt road in the grip of winter each day to attend school. They would laugh and scoff at my exaggerations, saying, "Yeah, yeah, we know. We've heard it a thousand times before!" To which I have responded with a standing invitation for them to go back with me to the Old Dinkins Place, a few miles from Gleason, Tennessee, where I was born. I have offered to show them the other places I have lived and had it tough. So far, they have declined the invitation. Apparently that is the only way I can be exonerated for "stretching things" before I pass off the scene. I still have hopes. I may have to kidnap them, tie them up, throw them in a van, and head out for Tennessee. It would be worth the risk, I think.

Apparently, every generation carries within it a latent need to share with the younger folks just how much more difficult its members had it growing up. It seems to be all a part of the endowment we must bequeath to the next generation, whether or not those youngsters want to hear or believe it.

In 1941 my family moved to McKenzie, Tennessee, in adjoining Carroll County. Within a short time Dad proved his skills as a fine carpenter, house painter, and paperhanger. Soon he decided to establish his own small business as a general contractor. In December of the year, World War II broke out.

By this time P.J., our eldest sibling at home, was in his mid-teens. Of all the children in the family, P.J. was the most colorful and controversial. Because of that, he was the object of more joking and joshing than any of us. As one of the other siblings said to me much later in life, "We loved him—most of the time!" That about said it all!

P.J. also was a right shrewd trader. He would not allow any of us kids to fool around with anything he acquired or arbitrarily determined was his property. He was known to be a bit tight when it came to money—what little he had. He was especially protective of the bicycle he had acquired and kept in tip-top shape. He pampered and polished it and kept it spotless from all foreign material. None of us was allowed even to touch it or move it gently. Certainly we were not to ride it.

If he were leaving the house even for a short while, he would park the bike in the side room of the smokehouse. Then he would warn us that if anyone touched it, he would know it.

On one occasion my brother Doyle and I decided to find out how he would know it. We found the bike looking like it was on display for sale. Very cautiously we inspected it to find any clues that would prove we had touched it. Then we saw it. Leaning up against the front tire was a straw. We decided to have some fun. Very carefully we removed the straw and let it fall just a few inches from the tire. Its location looked like it had fallen off from the bike being moved. Sure enough, P.J. found the straw near the tire. He accused us of not only touching the bike, but riding it as well. "I've done a little detective work," he said, "and I know for sure you have been fooling with my bike and riding it!" We denied his charges simply because we had done neither. He tried to pull Mother into the dispute, but she had a few hundred other things to worry about before she got around to judging the crime of the century.

P.J. proved to be a much better brother than he did a detective. We all loved him, and he loved us kids, even if at times he was accusatory, cantankerous, and bossy over the rest of us. Years later at a family gathering we reflected on such capers as the bike case.

Before World War II ended both P.J. and E.W. were drafted into the Army. At that time E.W. had children. What a surprise it was when both brothers showed up at the same time to take combat training at Fort Blanding, Florida. From there both of them were assigned to a combat unit preparing to fight the Japanese in the Pacific Theater. Just before shipping out from the west coast, E.W. was discharged because he had children. P.J. boarded a ship and headed toward the combat zone. While he was at high sea, Japan surrendered. P.J. was reassigned to Hawaii and remained in the Honolulu area until his time was up.

He returned to McKenzie and soon married Ruth Scott, a truly fine person. The two of them proved successful in business. They were highly regarded in the community for their hard work and impeccable honesty. Even now when I return to McKenzie and meet old friends, I often hear them sigh and say, "I wish P.J. and Ruth were still running the Polar Bar. They always served good food and made us feel they sincerely appreciated our business with them."

Now thoroughly retired, P.J. and Ruth are enjoying the good life they so richly deserve. All their children and grandchildren live in Tennessee. It is always a treat to visit in their home. The feeling of welcome wraps its warmth as sincerely on the day one departs as on the day one arrives.

The third eldest surviving sibling was Virginia Adell. Even after all these years, I find it difficult to name a person I admired and respected more than she. Not only was she my hero, she was the hero of the family. With much affection I called her Shorty because she was indeed short. From early childhood she was afflicted with severe curvature of the spine. She never objected to being called Shorty, simply because she already had faced down her handicap and decided to live above her limitations. She succeeded.

In so many ways Shorty stood tall among her siblings as well as among peers, friends, relatives, classmates, and anyone else who came to know her. She never objected also because she knew her nickname came with much love and respect. Shorty was both feisty and fiery of disposition. She would not tolerate one's feeling sorry for her. Words like pity and sympathy occupied no place in her vocabulary. Her quick retort could chop down anyone who patronized her. She could talk frankly about her circumstance but only so long as she felt the conversation was helpful to her and to those conversing with her.

She also was about the neatest person I ever knew. In public, every hair was in place. Her person was immaculately groomed. Every piece of her apparel coordinated with every other piece of her clothing. Her complexion and facial features actually complimented the makeup she applied. For these reasons and many more, I suspect Shorty inspired and influenced her siblings more than all the rest of us put together.

She was a class person in every sense of the word. I was always honored and proud to be seen with her. It was a special treat for me to walk downtown with her occasionally to see a movie, usually at her expense. Later on she would finance many of my dates with a loan. I always paid her back, sometimes asking her to make me another loan, even as I handed her the payment for the previous one. She never refused, after her usual brief but pointed lecture. I've often said to members of the family that I might never have married had it not been for Shorty financing some of my dates. To this day I am grateful for all the conversations we had and the special relationship we shared. Indeed, she was and still is my hero.

Shorty graduated from high school in 1949 along with Doyle, our brother (more about him later). It was quite evident at her graduation that classmates, faculty, and staff members all held her in high esteem.

A few years later she married a young man in the community. In time she became pregnant. Her physician was more than a little concerned for her being able to bear and deliver the baby. Members of the family reflected the same concern. Apparently, though, no one had checked with Shorty to ascertain how she felt about the whole thing. When time came, she calmly underwent a cesarean section, which she and the baby came through with few complications.

As time passed, her husband seemed not very excited about taking responsibility for his wife and son. He joined the U.S. Air Force. Later, Shorty and he divorced.

Shorty found a job in a technology plant some 20 miles away. She drove those miles each way each day to support herself and her son. As time passed, however, it became obvious her health was deteriorating. That brought on almost constant pain. Still, she was determined to fend for herself and her son.

As months passed, the curvature of the spine was less and less able to support her neck and head. Her stature decreased more as her head and neck began to sink into her chest cavity. That increasingly aggravated her breathing, which in turn increased her lingering and excruciating pain.

Even so, she was determined to endure and overcome. She was hospitalized several times in Memphis, where she had been treated as a little girl. She was now more than 40 years old, and I was pastor of a church in Oklahoma. While at my desk, I received a phone call from Mother. She advised me that Shorty was in the hospital again and that the outlook was not good. When I asked if Shorty was able to talk on the phone, Mother said yes and gave me the number.

I called immediately. When I asked Shorty how things were going for her, she replied with her typical frankness: "Hon, I won't be going home from here this time."

I knew better than to try disputing her conclusion. She knew her state of affairs better than anyone else. So I said to her, "Well, Shorty, you've always had strong faith in God, and you have faced courageously all the challenges you have had to endure. I know you will face all that is ahead of you with that same faith in Christ."

There was a brief silence. Then she said simply, "You can count on it."

I prayed with her. That was our last conversation. She died just a few hours later, as we were already on our way to Tennessee.

Strange as it may seem, when the family had all gathered for Shorty's funeral, there was as much joy expressed as sadness. She had prevailed in her all too brief life of 41 years. We all knew her journey had been made by one who was larger than life. We knew also that Shorty had not only taught us how to live but equally how to die.

Doyle, my immediate older brother, played a large role in my life from childhood through high school. He was so many things—natural born leader, dreamer of big dreams, hard worker toward reaching those dreams, risk taker, football player, popular in high school, entrepreneur, friend maker for life. He was and still is a talker, salesman, churchman, motivator, and communicator. He ultimately became president of Ohio Sound in Cleveland, Ohio, and is now retired. He and his wife, Rosemary, are much involved in the Church of the Savior in Cleveland Heights. They are blessed with a son and daughter and four delightful grandchildren.

Because we were fairly close in age, Doyle was much like a best friend. He was also a role model for me in so many ways. We explored the hills and hollows, the fields, and creek beds all around our home. Being a natural leader, he demonstrated some of the characteristics of leadership. He soaked up current events, which made him well informed on many subjects as we grew up. He was a great storyteller of historical events and characters. He helped me as I made my way into my teen years.

I had not the ability he had to play sports, but he taught me that life was somewhat like a sports game. It was about believing in yourself, preparing yourself to do your best, playing to win, but not quitting or sulking when you lose. These lessons were valuable. We also had a lot of fun growing up.

As a part of a large family, we were assigned the jobs of tending the large garden every year. It seemed our father always insisted on a garden the size of a football field. Rows upon rows of corn, cabbage, potatoes, tomatoes, beans, squash, cucumbers, okra, and onions all beckoned to us for care.

One spring Saturday while we were still quite young, we decided the garden work was taking up too much of our time. We had planted already about three-fourths of a huge onion bed. It was time for some weekend exploring. But that one-forth of a dishpan of onion bulbs was still waiting to be planted. We got the bright idea of burying the rest of the onions in a big hole we dug at the far end of the wide row. Let someone else figure out why there were no onions on the last part of the bed. It would be a long time before anyone would notice, anyway. The hole dug, the bulbs dumped into it, and the hole filled again, we headed for the house. Mother seemed somewhat surprised that we had finished planting all the onions so soon. We were off quickly to discover more of nature.

Much to our surprise a huge clump of onions broke forth later to testify to our wrongdoing. Needless to say, when Mother's response to our grand scheme was over, we knew we never wanted to implement that particular plan again.

Since P.J. was several years older than Doyle and me, he seemed to enjoy telling on us for other boyhood pranks and misbehavior. When I was about 6 and Doyle was 9, a new swimming hole was discovered a short distance from our home. Not only that, it had a diving board from which to make big splashes. Dad warned us not to go swimming there since the water was too deep. Well, one day while we were out exploring, we just happened to come upon that swimming hole. The temptation was too strong to resist on a hot, sweaty summer day. The "diving board" turned out to be a large limb, which had been cleaned off and cut off out a few feet above the water. Indeed, the water was deep. After a nice cooling off, we put our clothes back on and took our time getting home so our hair could thoroughly dry.

Dad and P.J. were doing a bit of repair work on the house as we arrived. Right away, P.J. saw this was an opportunity to get us into trouble with Dad.

"Well," he said, "ya'll have been to that swimming hole, haven't you?"

We didn't respond.

Quickly he turned to me and said, "Raymond Harold, what kind of diving board did it have?"

Now completely rattled, I blurted out, "It was nothing but a stubbed off limb!"

The truth was out. I must have looked pale. I couldn't look at Doyle for having betrayed our agreed-upon secret. Gleefully P.J. then said, "I knew it! You both looked guilty," as if he were some fine two-legged lie detector.

Now found out, I just knew Dad would be taking punitive action for our disobedience, cruelly exposed by P.J.'s tattling and trickery. Instead, Dad was trying not to show his amusement. He turned his head away to keep us from seeing his laughter. For once he didn't discipline us as P.J. had supposed. I guess Dad felt Doyle and I had suffered enough for our misbehavior. He was right on that point, for sure. I don't recall ever going back to that swimming hole. I can't say for sure that either Doyle or P.J. ever went. Even after all the years, however, I want to believe P.J. sometime later tried out that diving board himself. Now in my retirement years, it would do me good to know he too succumbed to the temptation.

Ruby, the next youngest to me, was fun-loving, pretty, and outgoing. Because our birthdays were fairly close, we had several mutual friends. I dated some of her girlfriends, again with the help of Shorty.

I can still recall some of our conversations. Ruby married early, which removed her from our daily lives as older teenagers. Still, when we were together, it was quality time. Ruby laughed easily and had a knack for gathering you into her laughter. She could tell a story in such a way as to rivet your attention, then make you glad you listened so attentively. Sometimes she would get so tickled herself at some funny joke she was telling that I would start laughing at her laughter, often making the punch line seem only incidental.

Ruby had two sons. The untimely death of her younger son, Darwin, in his 30s was a terrible blow to her and to all of us. I flew to Lansing, Michigan, on short notice to be with her and the family for the funeral. It was evident that Darwin was well-known and loved by many people in the Lansing area. He had accumulated quite a reputation for his acting and stage abilities. I knew Darwin when he was only a boy. Even then he showed keen wit and a definite flair for drama.

Ruby and her husband, James, are now retired and make their home in Florida. We are still a scattered family, with each of the surviving siblings living in a different state.

Mayme (Gayle, as she prefers to be called) is the youngest child in our family. Like Adell and Ruby, Gayle was attractive and personable. Yet she probably had the hardest time growing up of any of us. She was rather independent of disposition. Her teenage years came in the 1950s amid the Korean War and a fast-changing world.

As a fully established world power, the United States behaved as if all things were indeed possible for America. The spirit of prosperity wafted sweetly from shore to shore. The entire work force of the nation was mobilized, constructing superhighways, manufacturing automobiles, building new homes, producing big-ticket items for those homes, and then watching television each evening to check on the progress made that day.

Making up for time lost fighting two wars, the nation set itself to the task of forging an economy based on peace. All the while, the ominous clouds of the Cold War hung heavily across the world.

It was into this milieu of forging forces that Gayle came at life with a mixture of "free bird" gusto and independence. Because of our age difference, we spent very little time sharing life and talking about the affairs, hurdles, and hardships she was enduring. Much like my limited relationship with E.W. because of our age difference, my relationship with Gayle was fleeting and irregular.

By the time she was in her teens, the rest of us were married and living with our families in different parts of the country. In many ways I have come to regret not being there for Gayle more regularly as she struggled with her incredibly fast-changing world amid the erosion of our core values as a people. Indeed, it was very likely Gayle had it harder growing up in prosperous times than most of us had growing up in tough times of the Depression years.

Gayle and her husband, Hirch, along with their children and grandchildren, all live in Illinois.

To this point, I have given a few snapshots of our family members and their relationship with one another. Here's a bit more about my own growing-up years, through my teen years in high school and into marriage with Lavelle.

My first clear memories of life came when we lived at the Bandy Place, high on one of several hills. It was here that E.W. left home to marry Frances. At the time I was about 5 years old. The home place offered us boys opportunities to play on the hills, in the nearby woods, in a creek bed, and among the many gullies. In time, we called it Goat Hill because goats seemed most able to thrive on the land.

As the youngest of four boys, I was often baited by my brothers to evoke their planned response. We lived by some strange neighbors. One such person was Miss Willie Brannon, who lived 100 yards or so down the lane from us. In those Depression years, neighbors regularly borrowed items from one another, including foodstuff such as cups of flour or sugar. I remember my mother sending me to Miss Willie's house to borrow a few kitchen matches. We had no electricity, running water, or any modern conveniences. Our house was heated by two wood-burning stoves and lighted by lamps. Matches were a necessity.

I never much liked to go to Miss Willie's house, especially alone. High weeds covered her yard. Her house was unkempt, unpainted, and overgrown with thick bushes that hid every door and window and front porch. To a 5-year-old boy, it was a spooky and scary place.

Reluctantly I obeyed my mother and made my way down the dirt lane. Cautiously I walked up the path from the road to her hidden porch, while head-high weeds brushed my face and hair. Tentatively I called out, "Miss Willie!" I had not seen her sitting on the front porch until she barked, "What do you want?" I nearly jumped out of my skin because she was so close to where I called her. Still shaking, with goose bumps marching quick time up my spine, I stepped forward and told her my mother wanted to borrow a few matches. There she sat, shelling an apron full of peas. Mumbling to herself, Miss Willie gathered up the corner of her apron, got up, and disappeared into the dark house. She returned a few minutes later and counted out into my hand precisely 12 kitchen matches. Then she sternly said, "Tell your mother to return the matches right away!" She acted like those matches cost half the value of Weakley County, when, in fact, 12 matches didn't amount to a penny in the Depression days.

I ran away from her, down the lane, and into the house as fast as I could. Between heavy breaths I told Mother what Miss Willie had said and then pleaded with her to send Doyle to pay back the matches. Mother just shook her head and smiled. I don't know who she sent to return the matches, but it wasn't I. I never went again to Miss Willie's house for any reason.

In mid-spring the following year, P.J., Doyle, and I were enjoying a splash in a shallow pool of water at a bridge near our home. The sun was warm. Spring flowers were in full bloom. We were enjoying our nude frolicking about. From out of nowhere, Miss Willie appeared on the bridge with the sun at her back. She proceeded to tell us to "get out of that water before you catch pneumonia or your death of cold!" I could hardly see her from having to look at her straight into the sun. P.J. and Doyle immediately squatted down to hide their innocence in the water. I just stood there, looking up and squinting at her into the sun and carrying on a brief conversation with her.

My brothers still like to tell that story on me for its embarrassing effect. Having now published the incident, the embarrassment has now been lost. At last!

Though it was an event several years in the past, the kidnapping and death of Charles Lindberg's baby was still the frequent subject of conversation. Especially among imaginative older brothers. I remember one day P.J.'s telling the story in terms of horror (which he made up). Every time he told it I became more scared even to walk to the mailbox a few hundred yards from our home. One day Doyle and I went out to get the mail. P.J. called out to us to "watch out for kidnappers because they are everywhere stealing children for ransom." As we waited for the mail carrier, I would duck behind the bushes at the passing of every infrequent car.

One day I complained to Mother about P.J.'s talk of kidnappers. Amused, she said finally, "Don't worry about being kidnapped. Any kidnapper who made off with you would bring you back quick when he learned we don't have any money to pay him."

I was comforted—I think. On the one hand, I was glad to know kidnappers would bring me back. On the other hand, I was sad to know I wasn't worth keeping. So goes the mind of a small boy growing up through hard economic times. And among baiting brothers.

From those early years I grew up a typical boy who got into trouble about as regularly as other boys. As said earlier, in 1941 the family moved to McKenzie—the town I would come to know as home. That August while attending the annual revival meeting at New Valley Methodist Church, I committed my life to Jesus. It just seemed the thing I wanted to do after the Reverend Herschel Blankenship had preached. I was asked several questions I did not fully grasp but said yes anyway. I was then baptized and received into the church and counted a full member.

New Valley was a small, one-room, framed white church. There were four Sunday school classes. The men sat in one corner in the "Amen" section. The women sat in the choir corner. Married couples sat in another corner, leaving all ages of kids to occupy the remaining corner. Classes sounded like an open meeting with everybody talking at once. Yet no one seemed to notice. I learned the Bible stories from wonderful teachers like Miss Elsie Winsett, who loved each of us. Our family later joined First Methodist Church.

Our home was right next to the high school football field. The field was almost totally enclosed by a tall wooden fence, except for one short section. That section of American wire fence was overgrown with thick honeysuckle vines, rising to about five feet. It was more difficult to scale it than the wooden fence, which had several glaring gaps.

That honeysuckle portion held high appeal to us boys. In early spring while the honeysuckle was in full bloom, we would ride astride the fence while breathing the honeysuckle's sweet aroma. Gene Autry's horse, Champion, was outclassed in the ride we experienced. It would take us two-to-three minutes to go from one end of the honeysuckle to the other.

By summertime, however, the honeysuckle would be infested with ill tempered yellow-striped wasps. When some hotshot newcomer came to the area or some overbearing cousin came for a visit, we would initiate him by playing follow the leader. One of us would serve as leader and quickly pass over the top of the fence, calling the newcomer to follow. By that time the disturbed and angry wasps applied their temper to the victim. It didn't take nearly as long for the newcomer to dismount as it did to climb aboard.

The fun lasted three times on different victims. We abandoned the game quickly when my father got wind of it and applied the sting of his ethical standards to a tender part of my anatomy.

That same summer two of my buddies came over to play on a hot day. In those days a 12-ounce soda pop cost a nickel. We were all sweaty and thirsty and wished we had a cold drink. A small felony began to take shape in my mind. I went into the house and took a dollar bill from Mother's milk money. I then strutted back outside to announce I had money for some refreshments.

We went up the street to Ellis' Community Store, and I bought each of us a soda pop, a package of peanuts, a moon pie and a piece of bubble gum—and still got change back.

We swigged and swallowed, chomped and chewed until the guilt of my sin turned me nauseous. Our appetites satisfied, my two buddies went home without blame.

In the full grip of my guilt, I told myself I would earn enough money to pay back the dollar, and Mother would never know. Well, she did know. Mothers have a way of instantly solving unsolved mysteries. Her ethics were pointedly applied, which didn't pain me half as much as her disappointment in me.

As I said, I was a typical boy who got into trouble about as much and as often as other boys. Life was fun but also dramatically instructive at times.

My high school years were marked with a mixture of best times, worst times, and everything in between. In my sophomore year I worked evenings at the local roller-skating rink with Charles Thompson—my best friend. In our free time we would play a few games of pool downtown. As we were playing one day, we heard that three of our classmates had been killed in a terrible car wreck. Six people in all lost their lives. Speed and beer figured into the terrible tragedy. Only the man in the other car survived. His wife and two sons were killed along with Terry, Peter, and Jim.

Charles and I got to the scene before the scattered bodies were removed. We saw death in its starkest horror. Certainly it was a permanently sobering experience about drinking for all of us.

By our junior year in high school, seven of us classmates had become a very close-knit group. Someone tagged us "The Seven." The name stuck until our senior year, when four of the group joined the Navy. We frolicked and had fun together. We were always doing crazy things together. We never seriously ran afoul of the law. In fact, all of us came from families whose parents demanded we respect law officers and what they represented. (*Note:* For the benefit of my three brothers, our father said that if any of us ever got arrested and thrown into jail, he would not spend a dime to get us out. His statement never had to be tested, but we never doubted his word.)

The closest the group ever came to breaking the law was when one of us suggested we "borrow" a few watermelons one night from a field up the highway and close to the road. Charles owned a car, so we all piled into it, and away we went. He dropped us off at the fence row and promised he would be right back to pick us up as soon as he could find a place to turn the car around.

We crossed the fence, crept quietly through a patch of corn and into the field of melons. We started to inspect the merchandise to determine which we would take. From a thick clump of bushes came an angry shout, "HALT RIGHT WHERE YOU ARE!"

Not one of us did so. We scrambled roadward, knocking down cornstalks and stumbling toward the fence. Then came a shotgun blast that peppered us with birdshot. Had it not been that we were running so fast that the buckshot had to catch up with us, we might have been seriously injured.

Of all the luck, I stepped in a mud hole, which stripped off my moccasin-type shoe. It contained my name, National Guard rank, and serial number. I reeled to keep my balance. By then I had no idea where to look for my shoe in the dark. So I scampered with one shoe on and one shoe off toward the road. As I neared the fence row, I saw one of the group flat on his back, flailing his arms about, trying to break his pants leg free from strands of barbed wire. In stress the fence squeaked and shook for yards in both directions.

He heard me coming and pleaded, "Help me! I'm hung up!"

I had not the time to dally, so I said, "I wouldn't stop for my grandmother!" I cleared the fence in one bound and was making my way quickly toward the car when he zipped passed me and piled into the convertible first. How he broke free, got to his feet, cleared the fence, and beat me to the car as fast as I was running is still a mystery to me. For all our efforts, not one of us brought out a single melon.

We all gathered at the Log Cabin Drive-In to assess the damage of our failed mission. The next day a deputy sheriff came up to me, smiling, and said, "Is this your shoe?"

It was *prima facie* evidence, so I said, "Yes sir, it is."

Having a hard time keeping from laughing, he offered me and the others "a deal we couldn't refuse." The owner of the field said he would forget the whole thing if we each would pay $10 for damages done to his patch the night before by another group. We all agreed, though it was our luck to pay for the sins of another group. Of course the whole town soon knew about the matter and enjoyed a good laugh on us.

Fortunately, we had already shared our mischief with our parents. While they laughed at our expense, they certainly did not approve of our actions. Any mother of the group exercised authority of all the mothers when we were in different homes. Each fed us when we just dropped in unexpectedly. Each also corrected us when we got out of line. My own mother told me years later how all the mothers enjoyed the boys when they happened by for a snack. We were all fortunate to have several "mothers."

At the time of this ordeal, I was working for my father, who paid me by the hour. It was a good deal, which gave me resources to buy my own clothes and to pay my own way in high school. When I sheepishly asked Dad to advance me the $10 I had to pay, he refused.

"Payday is Saturday, not the middle of the week," he said. "I meant what I said about not getting you out of trouble with the law!"

I must have turned pale. I could just see myself handcuffed, arrested, roughly thrown into jail, and stained for life. Desperately I asked Mother to lend me the $10 until the following Saturday. She did! Mothers are like that. I was grateful the whole ordeal was over. Except for one thing.

The owner sent word by the deputy sheriff for us to come to his shop, and he would take us to the field to each select a watermelon we could take with us. It was such an unusual response to our mischief, so we went. He greeted us and chuckled with us. Sure enough, we each selected a melon. He seemed not angry with us. In fact, we felt we had met a man who understood our dumb prank. As luck would have it again, the melon I picked proved to be quite green and unready to harvest. I wasn't about to go back for a trade-in.

The last year and a half of high school was extremely difficult for me. To this day I cannot nail down exactly what had happened to me. I had many good friends. I did my homework. I made decent grades. Yet I was just listless. I began skipping school and having trouble especially with two teachers. Early in my final semester, I dropped out of school altogether.

Billy (my future brother-in-law), Frank, Gordon, and Earl had all joined the Navy. Only two of The Seven remained. Charles became concerned about me. I missed going to classes, but I just didn't want to go back any more. The school counselor kept in touch with me and genuinely encouraged me to return. She said I could still catch up and graduate with my classmates in 1951. By that time I guess I was just too embarrassed from dropping out to drop back in.

Then a good thing happened. Because so many other senior boys had joined the Navy, the senior class did not have enough male actors to put on the annual senior play. Charles came by and said in so many words that the class needed me. One of the male roles was yet to be filled, and I could do it in a fine way. For the first time in my school life, I felt the weight of being asked to do something because my classmates needed me. I went back and took the role of a crook. It turned out to be an enjoyable comedy.

Back in school I buckled down to catch up and graduate. It was tough going for me. I was severely behind in every subject. Yet every teacher, the counselor, many of my classmates, and even the staff were there for me. Especially was Charles there for me. For his deep and abiding friendship I shall always be grateful. Had it not been for him, I suspect I would not have graduated. I have often wondered just what direction my life would have taken had it not been for Charles Thompson.

After graduating I worked for my father before attending food service schools in the National Guard. I met Lavelle at a basketball game where my date and Lavelle's sister were playing on opposing teams. For the first quarter it was nip and tuck in the game. The more I talked to Lavelle in the bleachers, the less I cared about who won the game. I was quite smitten with Lavelle's beauty and engaging personality.

While my date played against Lavelle's sister, I made a date with Lavelle for the following week. After the game I escorted my date to her home. She was a likeable and lovely girl, but I never dated her again. My eyes and heart were focused on Lavelle.

Our very first date was dismantled by Charles' grandfather's death. Since my own two grandfathers died while I was very young, I felt about Charles' grandfather as if he were my own. Also, since Charles had a car, I could not keep my date with Lavelle. Besides, Charles and I decided we should sit with his family the night of the date. I rushed off a letter to Lavelle saying that I could not make the date because of the circumstances. For a long time Lavelle pretended the death of Charles' grandfather was not the real reason I failed to appear. Then I discovered she had already stood me up by leaving with her sister, Minniezell, for another event. She left word for her mother to tell me when I showed up for the date.

In August 1952, Charles married his longtime sweetheart, Betty Sue Wilson. She is a fine person. Her mother and father occasionally entertained the four of us on Sundays with a fried chicken dinner while we were dating.

Lavelle and I married October 4, 1952. Charles and I served as best man for each other. Both of us were married by the same Methodist preacher in Corinth, Mississippi.

After all expenses were paid, Lavelle and I had a total of $5 between us. It didn't take long for us to agree we would never recommend any marriage beginning with such meager means. Yet we survived and prevailed in our marriage for now more than 50 years.

Twelve days after our wedding, I departed for several months of active military duty to attend bakers school at Fort Benning, Georgia. Lavelle lived with my folks and took a job while I was away in a garment factory nearby.

2

Journey of Emerging Family

On my return from active duty at Fort Benning, Georgia, and for the next three years, I worked in restaurants in and around McKenzie. My life was meaningful, yet a bit unsettled. Unknowingly, I was moving onward in the direction my life ultimately would take.

Perhaps it would be of value at this point to say a few things about my own growing family of three sons. That will familiarize you with family names and personalities as we move through the following pages.

Lavelle

For more than 50 years I have been married to a remarkable woman. Mary Lavelle Coburn grew up as a farm girl. She was the third of four daughters of William Isaac and Lucille Archer Coburn. Her birthplace is as fascinating and perhaps as unusual as is her person.

Lavelle was born January 28, 1933, in Frog Jump, a small, rural farming community near Alamo, Tennessee. The identity of that community still centers around a well-kept general store, which is painted green to match the color of its namesake. The surrounding area is known for some of the finest cotton land in West Tennessee.

Lavelle and I were experienced cotton pickers before we ever met. Consequently, we helped out one fall by picking cotton for her father. By the time fall was over, we both knew cotton farming was not our future.

Not only was it hard, backbreaking, finger-pricking, and cuticle-sticking misery, our skills as pickers were not sufficient for us to make a living. We could hardly pick enough in one day to feed ourselves for that day and have more than the value of one sock apiece left over. Every time I "weighed up" with what I felt was at least 100 pounds, the load would tip the scales at about 40 pounds. Or fewer. I was always discouraged at the end of every cotton-picking day.

Over the years of our marriage, Lavelle developed and honed many of her skills and talents. All these she put to use effectively at different times and places to supplement our inadequate income—especially during my student pastorate years. One of the smartest things I ever did was to turn over to her talent the keeping of our budget and checkbook. I never could—and never will be able to—keep a checkbook straight. I am quite certain that, had I taken charge of our checkbook, I would have accumulated a terrible credit rating. Lavelle has the ability for the tedious work of accounting. For that one ability I have given thanks to her many times.

While I preached, pastored, and brought home inadequate income, Lavelle monitored our cash flow and wrestled with how to make ends meet. When on the horizon she saw my income would no longer be adequate, she would find work to fit one of her many skills. And the remarkable thing was that she ably fulfilled the role of true homemaker as well.

Lavelle and I went to Oklahoma City University every school day for two years. I went to get a degree; she went to see that I got it, helping to pay for it by working as the secretary to the director of food services. She loved her work and was loved by everyone on campus who knew her.

Lavelle demonstrated her skills later as a salesperson at a variety store in Texas while I attended seminary. Years later still, she worked as a salesperson in a kids clothing store to eliminate the feeling of empty-nest syndrome. Because it was a clothing store for small children only, more grandparents than parents shopped there. After our first grandchild, Denae, was born, that grandparent shopping rubbed off on Lavelle to the point that we really did have the cutest and best-dressed granddaughter in public. At least *we* thought so. Lavelle's easy-to-talk-to personality and her engaging conversation contributed to her success as a salesperson.

When I became a district superintendent, I asked Lavelle to be my secretary, office manager, and bookkeeper for district funds. She started out at the awesome sum of $50 a month. She performed all aspects of the work with excellence and expertise. During that time Lavelle typed, edited, and made ready for publication three books I wrote. Thus she demonstrated several additional skills related to the tedious perfection of manuscripts, sermons, and lectures.

Because of her ability to talk easily with people—especially when I was in a state of frustration with a certain pastor—I would ask her to call for me and convey the message I wanted to communicate. I am sure she prevented injury to several of my relationships with pastors. When district family members called the office, they always enjoyed Lavelle's cheerful and helpful manner. They saw her not as the district superintendent's wife but as an endearing friend. When I left the district, everyone regretted her leaving more than mine.

When Lavelle stopped working at the clothing store, she went to work as a volunteer in the Jane Phillips Hospital in Bartlesville, Oklahoma. Her multifaceted responsibilities included everything from managing the visitors and information desk to getting incoming patients checked in and settled comfortably into their assigned rooms and escorting outbound patients to their point of pickup. Even in those brief moments with attendant family members, she managed to endear herself to each one.

All the above skills were demonstrated again as Lavelle served as volunteer receptionist at the United Methodist Center in San Antonio. Her spirit of helpfulness and brief conversations always made visitors feel good about being in the building.

Perhaps Lavelle's most rewarding natural talent is that of caretaker. Any time a family member was ill, she was there to render care. She didn't mollycoddle us but cared for us. She saw that family members got their prescribed medication on time, even when they objected. When any of us was ailing and was at our worst, she was there at her best to offer hope, care, and cure.

Lavelle worked for two different physicians as doctor's assistant, and her skills at dealing with older persons became apparent. She convinced such persons that she truly cared. She communicated with aging people so easily that she immediately won their confidence and cooperation.

Many people have noticed Lavelle's fun-loving way, which often erupts in a quick comeback to someone's comment. I have said many times that only once was I ever able to respond quickly to her and leave her temporarily speechless. It came as we sat at the breakfast table soon after I arrived as bishop of the San Antonio Area. I was dressed in shirtsleeves for the warm day ahead, so I pinned my bishop's crest onto my collar. She looked at the crest and asked, "Why are you wearing that?"

I replied, "That's to let you know who's the boss." Immediately I thought I saw wisps of steam curling upward out of her ears. Quickly, I added, "and *you* are the boss!" The steam subsided.

It was in the home, however, that Lavelle radiated all the qualities mentioned above—plus one more. That is the quality of unselfish sacrifice. She literally sacrificed whatever dreams she had personally for the sake of seeing her husband and sons educated and well established in their vocations. While all the rest of the family was preparing for our calling to ministry, she went about sacrificing herself to making our ministry a prepared one.

Being of strong will, Lavelle held high standards for morality and behavior—at home and away. As husband and wife, and as parents, we have not always agreed. In such instances, we worked around our differences to the good of the family.

As my wife and the mother of our three sons, Lavelle had always been outnumbered sex-wise but was never outdone or outclassed. She could and did hold all of us males within the bounds of her expectations. Even now when she speaks, the menfolk listen and usually concur. But not always. With so many fine clergymen close at hand, she has had ample opportunity to receive pastoral counseling and guidance—all free of charge, of course. She has never once taken advantage of that benefit. None of us has asked her why. I strongly suspect she feels she has more reason to counsel the three of us than the other way around.

On January 26, 2002, the family, along with Jack and Bobbie Lyons as witnesses, bestowed upon Lavelle our honorary "Doctor of Selfless Service and Sacrifice" degree. We awarded her the degree in recognition of the enormous debt each of us owes her. Naturally, she objected to the whole idea. We did it anyway. Certainly she deserved the distinction and a great deal more.

Dana Carnell

Dana Carnell, our first son, burst upon the scene of life October 28, 1953. He was baptized at New Valley Methodist Church by the pastor, the Reverend Wheatley. Twelve years earlier I had stood at that same chancel as a boy of 9 and received my baptism at the hands of the Reverend Herschel Blankenship. It hardly seemed possible that so much had happened in those in-between years from my baptism to Dana's. I guess it was my first inkling of how rapidly life had a way of slipping by. No wonder, then, that Dana's baptism was such a memorable occasion for all of us—but especially for me.

Naturally, to Lavelle and me Dana was special. In time he would prove himself so. He was an obedient child and mature beyond his years as a youth. He liked sports in high school and played football. Early in his second season a knee injury requiring surgery put an end to all contact sports for him.

Dana held himself to high moral standards and was liked by both his peers and adults. He made good grades in his studies and got along well in all sorts of situations. He had no difficulty finding and holding jobs that kept him in spending money plus savings. His two younger brothers looked up to him as their big brother and role model.

Because Dana was a responsible youth, we gave him my old Pontiac, which had served me so faithfully while I was in seminary. Under his ownership that car had its best care and upkeep. When it finally gave up the ghost, we helped him pay the trade-in costs for a smaller but newer Pontiac. That one he drove to Oklahoma City University, a United Methodist institution, where he enrolled. He chose law enforcement as his major.

Dana had a dream. On several occasions he commented to Lavelle and me how drugs were killing his generation. His dream, therefore, was to work with some federal agency, preferably the FBI, to fight drug use and drug trafficking. At the end of his first year in college he made preliminary inquiry as to how to proceed.

His inquiry was processed but rejected because he did not have 20/20 vision without glasses. He was advised, however, that if he could accumulate prior government service, like a term in the armed forces, that requirement could probably be waived.

He immediately enlisted in the U.S. Army for three years, choosing the Army Security Agency as his branch. It was a wise as well as a practical decision. Not only would he be working to waive the eyesight requirement in a related field. He also would be entitled to educational benefits to help pay for his college degree when his enlistment was finished.

In a matter of months, Dana departed for Fort Leonard Wood, Missouri, for basic training. Eight weeks later he was granted a three-day pass for being the only recruit ever to ace all phases of basic training. The citation from the commanding officer was quite impressive.

Following his three days at home, he returned for a second eight weeks of advanced training. From there he was assigned to Vent Hills Farm in Virginia, near the Pentagon. There he received top-secret clearance and proficiency in coded radio communications.

Dana spent a few days with us in Oklahoma City before departing for Virginia. He and I had a brief conversation the day before he left. He said to me, "Dad, you spent several years in the Army. Would you have any advice for me on how to get along and to do my best?"

Such a request was so much like him. I think my reply was born more of inspiration than wisdom. I said to him, "Dana, the Army offers you equal opportunity to set the example for your peers to follow or to follow the example your peers set for you. I hope you will always set the example."

He hugged me and said, "I'll do my best to set it."

On his way to Virginia, he made a stopover visit at "Papa's house" (Lavelle's parents) in Tennessee. The next day he would continue to his destination. On every occasion when any of Papa's children departed after a visit, he would always say as we left, "Ya'll be particular on the highway!"

Those were the words he likely said to Dana as he started to leave. If so, they might well have had some bearing on Dana's strange response that he might not see Papa again. Nevertheless, Dana arrived safely at his new duty station in Virginia.

Darryl Ray

While I was between enlistments in the military, our second son, Darryl, was born February 10, 1958, in Jackson, Tennessee. We considered him special, too. As he grew up, everyone thought he looked like me and would take my features. He soon passed me, though, in height and body frame to become a husky and larger man.

Darryl was the reserved, contemplative, and freehearted type. He read books—all kinds of books. Many of them, we thought, beyond his years. Though he was somewhat intimidating in size, he was not a bully or arrogant. He displayed no desire to play sports. Certainly he did not seek the spotlight or "front page" status. He did well in school. Unlike Dana, Darryl never talked much about his inner thoughts and dreams.

As he moved into his early teen years, I was appointed to Epworth Church in Oklahoma City. We were there only 29 months before I was appointed to New Haven Church in Tulsa. Because he never talked much about his feelings, I did not realize until years later what a profound effect the move from Epworth had upon Darryl. So suddenly he had been uprooted from a school and teachers he loved and moved into a world of strangers and a different environment. By his second year he began to show signs of not liking the new school in Tulsa.

On his 16th birthday, we gave Darryl Dana's car. In his junior year Darryl became headstrong and somewhat belligerent. Though he worked at several part-time jobs, he seemed to have no direction as to future career. In 1976 he graduated from high school in Tulsa.

At that time I was a delegate to the World Methodist Conference, which was to be held in Dublin, Ireland, that summer. Also at that time Mr. and Mrs. Don Myers of New Haven Church were home on furlough as missionaries in Kenya, East Africa. When Don learned of my planned trip to Ireland, he suggested I take a side trip to Africa. He assured me he could get the airline tickets much cheaper on his side of the world and could send them to me in plenty of time for my trip.

Darryl had just graduated and was definitely unsettled, if not troubled about his life in general. So I invited him to take the trip with me. It would give us some extensive quality time together. With his typical nonplussed reserve he accepted my offer.

When I received the tickets from our friends, I discovered we were to enter Africa at Johannesburg, South Africa. Some side trip it was turning out to be. We arrived in Johannesburg after a night's stopover in London. Immigration and Customs officials delayed us when the officials noticed I was a United Methodist clergyperson. It was not a pleasant delay, as I had to answer question after question about why I was coming to South Africa. I got some idea of how the apartheid system worked. Finally the authorities admitted us. The person waiting to pick us up at the airport was a bit worried at our delay.

For several days we visited churches, attended a breakfast at which an American astronaut spoke, and visited sights in and around Johannesburg. The final visit we made was to a black settlement where thousands of families were segregated because of apartheid.

After an enlightening few days it was time for us to head for Nairobi, Kenya, an independent black African country. Shortly after takeoff from Johannesburg, we were advised we might have a bit of difficulty entering Kenya because of increasing tension between Kenya and segregated South Africa. Since we had gone through a rigorous interrogation at Johannesburg, we were more than a little anxious about being allowed to enter Kenya. We could just imagine being held in detention for more questioning.

About midnight we landed in Nairobi. As we taxied toward the terminal, we saw a parked Israeli El Al airliner with bright lights shining on it from all sides. Guards with all sorts of weapons were walking around it. Our hearts sank. We just knew we would be delayed, but our concern was unfounded. We passed quickly through immigration.

Don Myers and his wife picked us up at the airport and informed us about the El Al plane. It had been only a short time since Israeli commandos had raided Entebbe Airport in Uganda and rescued a large number of hostages. The Kenyan government had allowed the raid to be staged from Nairobi. The guards were fully prepared for any terrorist attack upon the plane as an act of revenge.

The beauty of Kenya, its people, and its culture captured our hearts. For more than a week we visited animal parks, museums, shops, and mission stations.

One special moment for both Darryl and me came as we were at the Rift Valley near Nukuru. It was a spectacular view. We gazed down into the valley and spotted a family compound in a large clearing. One huge thatch-roofed structure was surrounded with several smaller thatch-roofed huts. We were told the large structure was the family community center for gatherings and business sessions. Each of the smaller structures was a home for a different head of household and his family. Still looking down, Darryl said quietly, "Someday I just might come back here as a missionary."

I was deeply touched and inspired by his words. That comment was his first signal as to what direction his life might take.

Having spent a week in Kenya, we boarded a plane to Dublin. We passed over Switzerland and saw the Matterhorn sticking up majestically into the sunlight above the clouds below. What a sight! We stopped in Frankfurt, Germany, and then flew on to London. We changed planes and arrived in Dublin the next afternoon. We were tired but excited about being a part of the upcoming World Methodist Conference

We attended the sessions and were deeply inspired by the messages of Bishop Prince Taylor and Bishop Earl Hunt. Joe Hale was elected general secretary of the World Methodist Conference. In our spare time we visited many wonderful attractions— parks, museums, cathedrals, and statues of famous persons. We thoroughly enjoyed the three weeks we had with each other.

Upon our safe return to Tulsa, Darryl enrolled at Oklahoma City University in September 1976. Like his older brother, he chose law enforcement as his major. The following year he dropped out of school and went to stay with Lavelle's sister and husband, who owned a thriving lumberyard in Jackson, Tennessee. He worked there for about three months. In June, Lavelle, Dyton and I went to Tennessee to visit our parents and to see Darryl at his aunt's home. There Darryl said he wanted to talk to me before I went back to Oklahoma. The last night in Tennessee we stopped by Lavelle's sister's house for dinner. Darryl and I had a long conversation, during which he told me he wanted to explore the possibility of ministry.

Later he was granted a license to preach and appointed to a small church for the summer and fall. The following January he returned to Oklahoma City University and continued his study in law enforcement. While getting his degree, Darryl met Denise—a lovely and talented student majoring in music performance in piano. In July 1981 they were married at Asbury United Methodist Church in Tulsa. I had the privilege of conducting the ceremony. In time, they would present to us two beautiful granddaughters—Denae Rachelle and Deandra Elise. They are as special as their names.

Darryl stayed in school, finished his degree, and graduated from the police academy. Then he was accepted into the traffic division of the police force in Oklahoma City. We assumed Darryl at last had made his career choice. Later, he and I were discussing police work compared to the ministry. Somewhere in our conversation I observed that in police work officers regularly had to deal with people at their worst. In the ministry, on the other hand, one worked mostly with people trying to live at their best.

Darryl's decision to buy a motorcycle understandably gave us grave concern. A few weeks later he totaled the motorcycle as it rammed into a car that had run a red light at a busy intersection. He was thrown tumbling through the air across the car's hood, landing on his hands and knees on the pavement. It was a good position from which to pray and to give thanks for not being permanently injured. The experience was quite sufficient for him never to want another motorcycle.

While Darryl enjoyed most of his work as a policeman, he did not like having to deal with inebriated, foul-mouthed drivers who had been stopped and possibly arrested for dangerous driving.

Late one evening Darryl called me and said without any ado, "Dad, I am going into the ministry!"

Just like that! His words rang out with finality. I was quite surprised, yet somewhat pleased.

"What made you change your life's work so quickly and so emphatically?" I asked him.

He related how he had chased down and finally stopped a thoroughly drunk driver. From the start the driver was unruly, nasty-talking and furious for being stopped. "He yelled about police brutality when all I was trying to do was save his life and perhaps someone else's, too!" Darryl said. He added, "While I was writing out his ticket and waiting for assistance to arrive, I heard a voice inside me ask, 'Darryl, is this what you really want to do the rest of your life?'"

A bit amused, I asked Darryl, "Well, what was your answer?"

"I said no, I'm going into the ministry," he replied.

He continued his work on the police force until June. At the Oklahoma Annual Conference he was assigned to a student charge in El Reno, Oklahoma, and entered Phillips Theological Seminary in Enid, Oklahoma. He graduated from seminary and was ordained as elder in full connection in 1988. I had the awesome joy and privilege of participating in his ordination by adding my hands on his head to those of Bishop John Wesley Hardt and several other elders.

It wasn't until sometime later that I realized how Darryl's struggle and being unsettled were in many ways a replay of my own life in search of direction and purpose.

Denise earned her master's degree in music at Oklahoma City University. She is now a public school teacher—and a fine one.

Dyton Lee

Though mysteriously so, it is still true that no matter how many children are born to the same parents, each one will be distinctly different. Dyton Lee, our third son, arrived in the midst of the shock and sadness of President John F. Kennedy's assassination. On the examining table in the doctor's clinic in Oklahoma City that day in November 1963, Lavelle kept hearing the doctor saying, "I can't believe it! I can't believe it!" The doctor's words referred to the assassination of the president. Lavelle's thoughts were that things must be going wrong with the impending delivery. That particular moment her mind was not focused on anything except the business at hand. Both she and her doctor had a good laugh about it later.

Dyton Lee's arrival came November 23, 1963, in the full flush of the assassination's aftermath. That alone served as an omen about the drama of his life. He was the only native-born Okie in the family. I suppose that made him special, too.

By the time he had reached the ripe old age of one week, Dyton Lee had managed to turn himself over from his stomach onto his back. There he lay, bright brown eyes looking up at this whole new world. He's been looking up ever since. Lavelle and I mused "that this kid is going to be different!" Our observation was not lost.

He grew into a happy, well-adjusted, and high-spirited child. Unlike Dana, who was observant and a dreamer, Dyton was quick-witted and playful. Unlike Darryl, who was contemplative and deliberate in decision, Dyton tended to move on, make decisions, and settle questions as they became relevant. That made him somewhat adventurous.

About the only similarity among the three sons was their eagerness to work, do a good job and earn money for their own use. Even in the use of money, however, they were all different. Dana spent some and saved some. Darryl treated money as if it were a coal of fire to be spent before it burned his hand. Dyton tended to save more than he spent.

While in junior high school, Dyton and his classmates were in a science lab class. Their assignment was to melt wax and make a candle with the wick properly installed. In that time drugs and pill popping had begun to invade the junior high level of school. Lavelle and I on regular and frequent occasions talked to our sons about drug use and pill popping.

As Dyton went about his project of making a candle, a

classmate came to him and opened his hand. There Dyton saw several pills. In a hushed tone the classmate asked if Dyton would like to have one. Without hesitancy Dyton said yes. He took one and plopped it into a pot of boiling wax at his station—to the astonishment and anger of his would-be friend. His quick assessment of what was going on was matched with his equally playful wit. His words to the classmate were, "I don't need it!"

Never again was he approached by classmate pill peddlers who had been recruited for the sinister service by adult drug suppliers. We were more than a little proud of Dyton. From our perspective, he was turning out to be some kind of kid, indeed.

Most of Dyton's teenage years came while I was the superintendent of the Bartlesville District. Dyton literally loved to accompany me to charge conferences in the local churches of the district. That was just one more indication that this boy was different.

In the course of my tenure as a superintendent, Dyton probably accumulated more experience at charge conferences than most ordained elders have in a 40-year career. He was familiar with every question asked and every report given. He jokingly told his mother he believed he could conduct a charge conference if I ever needed him to.

Dyton got to know the leaders of every church, which endeared him to the members of the congregations. At times it seemed the people were more pleased to see Lavelle and him than to see me. In some instances I know they were, when it was necessary for their superintendent to remind the church of its evangelistic growth and its support of the church's worldwide responsibilities.

Dyton graduated from Bartlesville High School in 1982. He remembered the trip Darryl and I had taken to Africa when Darryl had graduated. Being the adventurous one, he broached the subject of equal opportunity.

"Well, Dad," he said, "where are you going to take me to celebrate my graduation?" There was no avoiding his assumption. I asked him where he would like to go. He said, "I'd like to go to the Holy Land."

We went to Jordan, Israel and Egypt for two weeks. We

visited tombs, shrines, and ancient cities. We rode camels, visited the pyramids, and saw a sound and light show at the Sphinx. We saw Mount Sinai and Mount Nebo. We spent most of one day visiting the Cairo museum that holds the treasures of King Tut's tomb. We even added a stop in Athens on the way over and Vienna on the way back.

What a trip we had! What quality time we shared! Looking back, I am sure that trip played a pivotal part in Dyton's decision later to enter the ministry.

In the fall of 1982 Dyton enrolled at Oklahoma City University. He planned on majoring in stagecraft, though he didn't know just where that would take him. Here again was an indication of his getting on the road before he had settled questions and answers about destination. Yet his major seemed to make some sense in that it issued out of his flair for drama.

Because there were 10 years between Dana's age and Dyton's, Dana really had very little interplay with Dyton as he grew up. Both Darryl and Dyton adored their older brother, but it was Darryl and Dyton who had time to grow up with each other.

Even now, when the two of them get together, their differences make for the family a bit of havoc, hilarity, and heaven. Darryl is of light complexion with brownish hair and scanty beard that can't seem to produce a decent mustache. Dyton's complexion is darker, with thick black hair and beard. All that is to set the stage for acting out who they are.

While at Oklahoma City University, Dyton worked on the staff of a church in Oklahoma City. The congregation put on a seasonal production that had the character of Jesus in it. Dyton's thick black hair and beard got him that role. He grew an impressive beard and played the part well. The production received rave revues from the community. Mission accomplished!

Shortly thereafter, Dyton shaved off his beard. Some have said that in growing the beard and playing Jesus, Dyton got to thinking he might *be* Jesus. When Darryl pointed out to Dyton that he definitely didn't measure up, Dyton shaved. A bit later he let his beard grow again, and he tediously shapes and grooms it to this day. Rumor has it that he let it grow out permanently just in case it is discovered he really is Jesus after all.

Such are the antics and erupting conversations when the two of them get together, and their distinguishing traits begin to play themselves out in family gatherings.

While Dyton worked at the church and hoped for an encore performance of Jesus, Darryl was serving Ellison Avenue United Methodist Church in El Reno. He was also attending seminary at Enid. One day Lavelle and I had occasion to travel through the Oklahoma City-El Reno area. We invited Dyton and Darryl to join us for lunch. They were both available.

Right away at the lunch table the banter between them began. After a bit, Lavelle and I managed to get a word in between their laughing and joking. Lavelle asked Dyton how school was going. He casually replied, "I've changed my major to religion! I'm going into the ministry!" Just like that! Again! We were surprised but had learned long before that our sons' decisions were somewhat like a Superball. They could bounce at any time to any height and in any direction at the most unexpected moment.

Darryl asked, "What convinced you to change your mind?"

In his usual playful way Dyton replied, "Well, I was walking across the campus one day, and God thumped me on the head and said, 'This is it, boy! I want you in the ministry!'"

You can imagine the roar of our laughter that brought questioning glances to our dark corner booth in the restaurant.

Dyton's way of explaining his call certainly reflected no shallow commitment to his sincerity and determination to follow through in the ministry.

While he was in college, Dyton was appointed pastor of Luther United Methodist Church, just north of Oklahoma City. It was his first pastoral appointment. By that time, Dyton had already met Deena Burger, a talented student from Kansas. They fell in love, and on October 20, 1985, I had the happy honor of joining Dyton and Deena in marriage at the campus chapel of the university. Following the ceremony, Deena sang a special and beautiful love song to Dyton. I must say, I joined several other teary-eyed guests looking on. In time Dyton and Deena would present to us two more grandchildren—Dana LaRae and Dustin Michael. They, too, are lovely children who bless our lives in so many ways.

In 1986 Dyton graduated from Oklahoma City University and headed out for the Chatfield-Barry charge in the Central Texas Conference. He would spend four years there while attending Perkins School of Theology at Southern Methodist University in Dallas.

Like Denise, Deena received her bachelor's degree and credentials to teach in the public school system. Both Deena and Denise are fine vocalists and pianists. In 1995 Deena was invited to participate in a choral group in Carnegie Hall. Later she participated in a tour to Vienna and other European cities. In 2002 she was chosen by her peers as Teacher of the Year for the Bartlesville School District.

Lavelle and I feel our two sons did especially well in selecting their life's partners. Of course we feel our two daughters-in-law did equally well in selecting their partners for life.

In 1990 Dyton graduated from seminary. In 1992 he was ordained an elder in full connection at the Oklahoma Annual Conference session. Again it was a joy for me to add my hands to those of Bishop Dan. E. Solomon and other elders, including the hands of Darryl.

"Church" is an unavoidable conversation topic when the family is together. So is sorting through the names—all starting with the letter D. Any of us at times is likely to say da, de, duh, and perhaps dad-gummit as we search for the name of Darryl, Denise, Dyton, Deena, Denae, Dana, Deandra or Dustin. It is easy to understand why Lavelle and I chose to be called Grams and Papaw.

3

Journey of Flashback ... and Forward

Our two sons, Darryl and Dyton; their wives, Denise and Deena; and their children, Denae and Deandra, Dana, and Dustin, were gathered at the episcopal residence in San Antonio. They had come to be present with us for a brief but special event. The next day, August 4, 2000, proved to be a day with a mingling of many emotions.

At 6 p.m. the entire family was limousined to the Hyatt Regency Hotel in downtown San Antonio. Awaiting our arrival were more than 600 friends and well-wishers to greet us and celebrate the evening together. The Southwest Texas and Rio Grande conferences had arranged for an areawide fiesta in appreciation of my eight years as bishop of the area and in recognition of my August 31 retirement.

We dined on a sumptuous meal, listened to choral and instrumental music, viewed videos, and heard many accolades showered upon us. We were deeply moved, especially by the keynote address of Bishop John Wesley Hardt. At the same time, we were a bit saddened at the abruptness of our upcoming retirement.

Forty-one years, less eight days, it had been since I had said "yes" to God's call to ministry. We had served eight congregations, a stint as district superintendent, and eight years as a bishop of the church. I've said "we" intentionally because Lavelle was there every step with me. Now it was time to let go and to take hold of retirement and all it held in store.

As we sat there drinking into our souls all the events of the evening, I was gripped with a strange awareness of a gift, one unique to all human beings. We refer to it as flashback. In a nanosecond my thoughts traveled back across thousands of miles into four decades of "ago." Flash by flash there appeared on the screen of my mind 41 years of ministry, with all its activity, clarity, and pulsating energy.

The first flash took me back to my hometown of McKenzie, Tennessee. To that point I had served seven years in the Tennessee Army National Guard. I liked the military. Its training, travel, and discipline had a way of extending the boundaries of one's life. It also aided in focusing one's life and career.

While in high school I worked as a short-order cook at a popular drive-in restaurant. By the time I was 18, I had advanced to night manager. My National Guard years afforded me opportunity to attend cooking school, baking school, and food service supervision school. Each school required active-duty service.

I enjoyed preparing and serving food and had no difficulty, therefore, in working at several restaurants in the area. In time I was promoted to food service supervisor at Regimental Headquarters in Jackson, Tennessee. By that time I had become known locally as quite a chef.

My mind flashed again to age 24, when I was on a military troop transport ship to Germany. The year was 1956. Lavelle and I had been married four years and had our first son, Dana. They were to join me later as military housing became available.

My assignment in Germany was to head up the food preparation and service unit at the Eighth Evacuation Hospital in Landstuhl, Germany. On board that ship I had no idea of the size or capacity of a 500-bed hospital. I would learn in a hurry just what that hospital could do.

It was a field hospital fully equipped for every medical capability needed in a theater of combat—including our responsibility to serve 500 meals three times a day, seven days a week. The serving line was never closed. To get the job done, I supervised five able and hard-working teams of six members each.

As luck would have it on board that ship, we found ourselves in the full fury of a North Atlantic storm. Immediately I was stricken with seasickness. Without a doubt seasickness was the most awful affliction I ever endured, before or since. Seasoned sailors would look at our pitiful state, grin, and shake their heads. In the throes of my agony, one smart-aleck sailor said to me, "Take heart, Sergeant. It's all in your head. It will pass in two or three days!"

I wasn't inspired by his words or even encouraged. In the first place, my seasickness definitely was not "in my head." In the second place, I wasn't sure I'd still be around to greet the passing of my ailment in two or three days. What's more, I didn't much care if I weren't. I just wanted to go somewhere in utter seclusion to feel sorry for myself and to die alone, if it came to that.

I found a remote stairwell and slid down into a corner to brace myself on two sides. For a long while I just sat there trying to read my pocket New Testament and praying intermittently. I prayed my time in Germany would honor God and be a good experience for me. Quite unexpectedly, and as if to confirm my prayer request, I had a profound sense that God was with me in that stairwell. I must have dropped off to sleep. When I awoke my seasickness had subsided, though the storm raged on for another day.

It would not be until later that I would realize that stairwell experience was my first awareness that God's spirit was subtly and quietly calling to me. Had there been someone to help me understand that experience, I think that right there and then I would have settled the matter of God's call upon my life.

We arrived in Germany after nine days at sea. I took up my responsibilities at the hospital. Several weeks later Lavelle and Dana joined me. We enjoyed our 19 months in Germany. We made many new friends. I grew a lot, learned a lot, and enlarged my competence. As far as I can remember, I never gave further thought to that stairwell experience while we were in Germany.

Upon receiving a discharge from active duty, we returned to Jackson, Tennessee, where I was assigned again as food service supervisor at Regimental Headquarters. A few weeks later Lavelle gave birth to our second son, Darryl. I had already found civilian employment preparing food at the prominent downtown restaurant in Jackson. It had been in business for decades. I enjoyed my work but stayed only a few weeks. The clinging sense of being "unsettled" seemed to grip my life.

Two months after my discharge from active duty, I decided the military life was to be my future. Lavelle and I have often agreed that we got out of the Army just long enough to pay all the medical costs for Darryl's birth. We supposed that again made Darryl special.

Within a few days I found myself at Fort Sill, Oklahoma, on duty in the base hospital food service unit. But not for long. Within a month or so, I was assigned to an Army light air transport unit, which was being newly organized. My job was to get the unit's kitchen and dining facilities up and running. We did that with a great deal of efficiency, pride, and morale. Having stated publicly that the military would be my career, I was encouraged to apply for a direct commission from the Secretary of the Army. Since I was bound to stay in the military, I might as well become an officer and enjoy some of the privileges and advantages a commission afforded. I was tested, then interviewed by a board of officers, and recommended for a commission.

I waited and waited for so long I forgot about it. Now, looking back, I know even that waiting period was serving a valuable purpose.

In the meantime, Lavelle and I united with Highland Park Methodist Church in Lawton, Oklahoma. A small congregation near where we lived, it was a church with numerous struggles and challenges situated on an out-of-the-way site. Someone had donated the land on a dead-end gravel street. The front entrance of the church faced the garbage cans behind the houses across the street. Adjoining the north side of our property was a trailer park. The west side had served as an overgrown dumping ground for the community. On the south was a railroad track, where trains regularly drowned out all sounds of worship. To say the very least, the church had problems. Yet the membership was loyal and welcomed us with genuine love and friendship. The church couldn't survive, but it refused to die. In spite of everything, we had found our church home.

The church was being served by the Reverend Herman Snodgrass, who at 84 was serving his fourth time as a retired pastor. As the founding pastor, he was much loved by the entire community. His short stature and booming baritone voice certified him as an uncommon servant of the Lord.

Regular opportunities were always available for gathering during the week. Prayer groups, study groups, choir, youth meetings, and work crews drew interest for every level of membership. We painted pews and walls and did repair work, which was always needed. Little did any of us know or even suspect just how much our lives as a church family would change so dramatically in the near future.

On September 8, 1958, one of our boys was ill. Lavelle suggested I go on to church services while she stayed home with the boys. I went with some reluctance. The worship service was well attended. Reverend Snodgrass delivered a message in his usual eloquent way.

Toward the end of the sermon, his voice abruptly changed. As if a bit frustrated, he announced that he was going to retire *again* at the end of the conference year. He stated emphatically he would not be serving as pastor again. His fourth time to retire would be his last time.

Then, with seeming passion, he raised his hand and moved his finger across the congregation and asked, "What I want to know is who will take my place?" By that time his finger seemed to have come to rest squarely on my nose. Without hesitation, I heard myself say softly but audibly, "I will!" In that instant I knew at last what I was really to do with the rest of my life. There were no claps of thunder. No audible voice from God. No notice of the other people concerning myself. I just knew within. The matter was settled, and that was it.

I delayed leaving the church until the entire congregation had greeted Reverend Snodgrass. As I shook his hand I asked, "Brother Herman, would you have time to talk with me for a few minutes this afternoon? I could come by any time it is convenient for you."

Gripping my hand and smiling, he replied, "Ray, come over at 2 p.m. I've been expecting it."

I was puzzled. What did he mean he has been expecting me? He must be thinking of someone else or something else.

On my way to the car, it suddenly dawned upon me that I had to explain a few things to Lavelle when I got home. I became a bit anxious at the decision I had made. "How will she respond to what I have done?" I mumbled to myself. The rest of the few blocks between the church and home were taken with my hurried prayers for God's help and Lavelle's understanding.

I think it was at the lunch table that I blurted out to Lavelle an awkward question about how would she feel if I became a Methodist preacher. There was a slight pause. Then she replied, "I'd not be surprised!" I was relieved to hear her supportive response and filled with gratitude for her. I still am. Seems no one was surprised by it all, except me.

At 2 p.m. I knocked on the door of Reverend Snodgrass' home. He greeted me before I could speak. He then pointed to a small table near the door where the *Book of Discipline*, three other books, and some forms to fill out were waiting. Again, before I could speak, he said, "Here is what you must do, Ray, to become a Methodist preacher." He went on to explain the disciplinary requirements and the three books I had to master before I could be interviewed and properly licensed as a supply pastor. My head was spinning. I stood there trembling and mystified.

"How could he have known what I wanted to speak to him about?" I asked myself once more. Only Lavelle, God, and I knew why I wanted to speak to him—and neither Lavelle nor I had told him. Since then I have come to believe that God indeed had already spoken to Brother Herman. Maybe even before his question fell on my ears and his finger pointed to my nose.

A few weeks later I received notification that I had been commissioned as a second lieutenant by the Secretary of the Army, Wilbur Brucker. I was called to report to the battalion commander to be sworn in as an officer. I was received with courtesy by the commander and given a reserve commission. I was then ordered to report to my company commander for further instructions. When I arrived, I found the entire company standing at attention, waiting for my arrival. I reported to the company commander, who subsequently read the order from Secretary Brucker. The commander then shook my hand and congratulated me. The whole company let out a roar of approval. To say the least, I was stunned beyond words.

Though gratified at having been commissioned, I knew the Army no longer was my destiny. When later the company commander inquired if I wished to enter training for active duty as an officer, I replied, "Not at this time!"

In December 1958 the district board of ordained elders interviewed me, processed me, and licensed me to preach as a supply pastor in the Methodist Church. I was received with joy and sincerity.

The following Sunday Reverend Snodgrass informed the congregation that I was to be his associate without pay. That was fine with me. I knew I would be paid great dividends by what I would learn from him. I was not disappointed. Besides, I was still in the military receiving a salary for the family.

According to my records, I preached my first sermon to the congregation October 19, 1958. I worked so long and so hard that I just knew it would take at least a full hour to get it all preached. In fewer than 15 minutes I had said all I had written. I was thoroughly through. The people were merciful. Reverend Snodgrass was complimentary and encouraging. I was exhausted. I muttered all the way home about what would I preach the next time since I had covered already all the major themes of the Bible.

At the Oklahoma Annual Conference session in May 1959, I was appointed pastor of Highland Park. Brother Snodgrass was so pleased and proud of me that I asked him to be my associate— without pay, of course. He said yes. I was joking. He was not. I had already reached distinction in that I was the only "supply pastor" known ever to have had an associate pastor in his first appointment.

Since our church attendance was about 50, Reverend Snodgrass and I could split up the pastoral work into a manageable size of 25 each. The truth is, I did all the work, and he did all the advising and counseling of me—which he knew I needed most assuredly.

Though small, the congregation grew. We were all excited and proceeded to dream dreams and to develop visions for the church. All summer long we worked on the church building and small house that served as space for Sunday school classes and as a small fellowship hall.

New faces began to show up for various church activities. From July to November we had received 28 new members, 18 of which came by profession of faith and baptism.

Never in my entire life had I been happier, at peace with myself, and more productive with my work at Fort Sill. I had only 13 months left on my enlistment. Soon I would be discharged and get on with my education and ministry. Then the unexpected happened.

4

Journey of Ministry in Far Away Land

Having just enough time remaining on my enlistment for a tour of duty in South Korea, I was ordered to report to Oakland, California, for processing and debarkation in December 1959. What a disappointment. Just when things were going so marvelously well at the church, Uncle Sam ordered me elsewhere. Some members were angry. Others openly expressed their sadness. Unbeknownst to me, several leaders in the church appealed to Congressman Victor Wickersham of Mangum, who represented Oklahoma's Sixth District in the U.S. House, to help the church keep its pastor. He tried but to no avail.

When I was told of the effort made and its results, it was to me a signal that I was being obedient to a higher authority as well. Goodbyes were difficult for all of us, but we departed believing God was in it with us. This time the family would not be joining me. It meant 13 months of hardship duty in a country still devastated by the war that had ended some six years earlier.

A cross-country train trip took me to Oakland on schedule. Sailing time required 19 days to reach Korea. That was about twice as long as the trip to Germany. Determined this time not to get seasick, I took a generous supply of motion sickness pills.

Traveling in the hold of a troop transport ship has to rank

among the most miserable of experiences. Fold-out canvas hammocks stacked four high from floor to ceiling, anchored by a steel pole at each end, made for havoc. The two bottom occupants were in mortal danger of receiving nauseous contributions from the top two. In a matter of hours from sailing time the floors and stairways, hallways, and latrines were awash with human regurgitations. The odor itself was enough to cause the staunchest stomach to add to the contributions. Indeed, seasickness does begin to subside after several hours at sea. By that time, however, most victims are so sapped and drained by dehydration that they are unaware things are improving. I had been through it all before. Even so, my familiarity with it didn't make it much easier to bear the environment.

I kept my word not to get seasick, but I did not escape having to go to the ship's infirmary. During those worst days, I made my way up the stairwell to get some fresh air on deck. Sailing does offer an abundance of fresh air if one can get topside. As I reached the top of the stairs, I turned to go to the exit. Just then the ship lurched, causing me to stagger backwards, slipping and sliding until my back slammed against the guardrail.

I have never felt such grinding pain. My stay on deck was only for a minute or two before I had to return to my hammock. For the rest of the day I was in acute pain. Medics finally came, gave me some painkillers, and told me to rest for the night. They promised to check on me the next morning to see if I felt better. Who could possibly rest in such unpleasant sounds and surroundings?

I couldn't get up for supper or for breakfast the following morning. I could only moan with all the others who were suffering misery from a different affliction. The medics were true to their word. They arrived the next morning in their fresh, snappy white uniforms and found me in the throes of what I considered "near death." They must have agreed. They helped me out of my hammock and literally toted me to the infirmary. It was spic and span, quiet, and smelled of cleanliness. Immediately they brought me breakfast, the first meal I had in more than 30 hours. Then they gave me several sorts of pills, massaged my back, put a heat lamp on it and told me they would see me when I woke up. They did. When I awoke, I gained hope that I would recover from the ordeal. I was in the infirmary for three days.

We arrived in Inchon, Korea, in early January 1960. The troops debarked, and I boarded a train for Pusan, the southernmost port city of the country. I was based at Hialeah Compound near downtown. After a few days of orientation, we were assigned to our duties. The following Sunday I attended worship services at the chapel and met Chaplain (Major) Albus. He was Presbyterian and served as chief chaplain for the Pusan Area Command.

A day or so later I was called to the chaplain's office. Unbeknownst to me, the chaplain had reviewed my record and discovered I was a licensed local pastor in the Methodist Church. He wanted to know if I would be interested in becoming his chief chaplain's assistant for the Pusan Area Command. I was astonished and simply overwhelmed.

He said I would supervise two other assistants and a Korean driver. I would relate to all the Protestant Men of the Chapel (PMOC) groups throughout the command. And I would work with all missionaries in the area, assisting any way I could in their ministries. I accepted his offer with much excitement and gratitude.

The chaplain seemed pleased that I accepted. Since my military occupational classification was food service, I had to change my field of service to chaplain's assistant. My request for such a change was granted on the recommendation of Chaplain Albus. Before I left his office, the chaplain put forth one stipulation. I was to be the "chaplain's assistant," not the "assistant chaplain." It was a distinction and clarification I employed as I moved onward and upward in leadership of the church. Ever since, I have been grateful for the clarity of what he implied. All of that was yet one more striking sign that God was at work in my life.

That afternoon I moved my belongings from my Quonset hut into the chief chaplain's assistant's quarters in the office area. It was definitely an upgrade in accommodations.

Within days I became involved in the Protestant Men of the Chapel. Two weeks later I was elected president of the group.

It was a job I would come to enjoy thoroughly. By train, jeep, helicopter, and bus I traveled around the southern half of South Korea, coordinating programs, networking with groups, and starting new chapters. It was a marvelous opportunity to watch veteran soldiers live out their faith and commitment to Christ daily. I preached in many chapels and civilian churches in addition to my responsibilities of preaching and teaching Sunday evenings at the base chapel in Pusan.

My responsibilities of working with missionaries were especially enlightening and enriching. Right away I met Helen Rosser, a Methodist nurse from Georgia. She had been serving in Korea a long time. When the Korean War broke out, she was captured and made a prisoner of war. She was not released until the end of the conflict. The story of her years as a prisoner is inspiring.

Helen was past retirement age but refused to go home. While I was visiting in her home with other guests, she related her story as a missionary and prisoner of war. I was deeply moved. More about Helen later.

I also met Lucy Wright, a Baptist who had been serving long before the war came. Lucy and Helen were a lot alike. Their theological persuasions were different but invisible, making it impossible to tell which was Methodist and which was Baptist. They were foremost missionaries who were out to serve the spiritual needs of a desperate nation and to make as many disciples as possible.

Then there were the Hunts, who were Presbyterian. They had been in Korea longer than any other Protestant missionaries I met. I visited in their home and was deeply touched by their humble and sacrificial spirit. At dinner in their home, we were served several indigenous dishes I had never tasted before. We were also served several incredible stories of their hardships, faithfulness, and leadership for their Lord. In so many ways these missionaries informed, enlarged, and inspired my budding ministry. Every time I preached at the monthly missionary gathering, they would eat first, then critique my sermon. Not only were they merciful and supportive, they were sincerely encouraging.

The Protestant Men of the Chapel group was growing rapidly—especially in our home chapel at Pusan. We met once a week for supper. Then we would pray together, study a section of the Bible, discuss our needs, encourage one another, and discuss probable projects like orphanage support.

Soon the word got out. Or was it God's doing? A request came to my desk that we come to a certain orphanage near Pusan in hopes we could help the desperate children. Three members of our PMOC group and I responded with a visit. The four of us found children in critical need of food, clothing, and medical attention.

I was undone at the plight of children in threadbare rags. The stand-in caretaker broke down and cried because she was unable to help the children. Her predecessor had abandoned the children when the money ran out for her salary. For more than a week all the children had to eat was rice gruel, something like cornmeal mush watered down so thinly the children could drink it. What little rice the orphanage had left was critically low.

The children clung to us with silent eyes, pleading for our help. We gave each child a piece of candy we had brought. We stayed for quite a while trying to figure out where to begin with help. We held hands with the children and promised God we would do everything we could to help. To begin with, the PMOC group would return in two days (Saturday) to give the children a picnic of hot dogs, chips, cookies, powdered milk, cheese, candy, and fruit. We would also bring as much rice as we could accumulate.

Without realizing it, we returned to the base almost totally in silence. Each of us was engrossed in heavy thought of what we could do beyond Saturday. The PMOC gathered to hear what we had found and what we promised the children. It was some sight to see husky, tough men with tears in their eyes. To a man, we heard it said, "Let's do it!" We collected a sizable donation from the men. The same four of us were to go buy as much as we could, including picnic items.

At that same meeting the group agreed that each one would write to his home church to ask that used children's clothing, blankets, gloves, and shoes be sent as soon as possible. To a man, again, each promised to write the letter that very evening before going to bed so the items would arrive before winter. Already it was the last of July. In all my life I had never seen men so stirred to do something good for the benefit of others.

Most members of the PMOC group went with us to the orphanage for the picnic Saturday. Upon our arrival some 60 children rushed out and surrounded us. Some hugged our legs. Others took hold of our fingers. All smiled with their desperate innocence. By the time we had unloaded everything and built a fire, the men's eyes were glazed over with emotion. We handed out hot dogs fitted onto coat hangers for roasting. We had brought enough for two hot dogs apiece with all the trimmings. The children let loose with squeals of delight. They had never seen such a sandwich but had no problem with how to eat it. After a marshmallow roast, the men taught the children several games played by American children.

By midafternoon we prepared to leave by passing out individually wrapped cookies and candy bars. We also left two 50-pound bags of rice. With tears in her eyes, the caretaker thanked us profusely with bows and gestures of gratitude. We then informed her of our wish to adopt the orphanage as one of our ongoing projects. We would be continuing our support, including our confidence that our home churches would be sending warm clothing for the children before winter arrived. Here came the caretaker's tears again. We returned regularly to bring treats, supplies, and food for the children—nearly all of which was made possible by donations from the men and with money we raised through projects. Our churches responded with lots of clothes and toys.

I preached often, on and off base, going into Korean churches and preaching through interpreters. Willie Sanders, a hunk of a soldier, invited me one Saturday to go with him where he had been preaching. I went, thinking we would be going to a church. We arrived at the traffic circle in downtown Pusan, right in front of the police station.

Willie began to preach. Quickly a crowd of some 50 people moved into the circle. They acted as if they had come there before, and indeed they had. I learned Willie had been preaching there through an interpreter regularly Saturday afternoons. Not wanting to be left out, I joined in the singing and service. I am sure that by the time Willie had finished at least 100 people had joined in. Willie then prayed and asked the people to pray for him as he would be preaching the next day at a Korean prison compound.

(*Note:* Some months later, the chaplain, our driver and I found ourselves at this very traffic circle, this time trapped and completely surrounded by thousands of students who were protesting Sigman Rhee's government and demanding his immediate resignation. Debris filled the streets. The police station was in shambles. Police cars were upside down and burning. Acrid black smoke hovered over the area as throngs of students screamed their demands. Completely engulfed by the mob, we became quite alarmed and absolutely helpless. It all had happened so quickly. Strangely, the students made no move against us, perhaps because the staff car we were in was marked with a cross as a chaplain's car. The students laid their hands gently on all sides of the car and walked us slowly to the open street up ahead a few blocks away. It was as if they were escorting us out of danger. What an experience!)

Willie was not an educated man. At times in his preaching, he would violate the English language with erroneous grammar. Yet his heart for God and love for people were as big as the world.

A few weeks later Willie asked me to go with him to the prison where he was to preach Sunday afternoon. I went mostly to see what he would do and say to the prisoners. He dangled participles as usual and split infinitives rather eloquently. The interpreter seemingly was not bothered by it all, or maybe he didn't know about participles or infinitives. Or maybe he preached his own sermon at times. At the end of the service, Willie gave a simple invitation to those wishing to "become a disciple of Jesus." A dozen or so came forward to pray and give their lives to Christ. Willie worked with each person. At the end he gave a closing prayer and made an announcement.

"Next Sunday afternoon," he said, "Brother Ray Owen will be bringing God's word to you. He is a licensed Methodist preacher, so you will want to be here to hear his message!" Just like that. I was incensed and certainly disconcerted. On our way toward the prison gate I assured Willie I would not be there the next Sunday and that he had no right whatsoever to commit me. For a minute or so he endured my blathering objections. "No way," I concluded.

Willie stopped us in our tracks and said, "Well I declare! Here you are, a man called to preach! You are even a licensed Methodist preacher! Where is your holy boldness? Where is your faith that God will overcome all your excuses?"

I surrendered. The following Sunday when I had finished preaching and given an invitation to become Christ's disciple, dozens came forward to confess their faith in Jesus as their Lord. Several men from the PMOC group came with me and assisted Willie and me to help those who had come forward to understand more fully the meaning of their actions.

At the next meeting of the PMOC, it was suggested we do something about the foul language that was so prevalent on base. Needless to say, some kind of action was greatly needed. The group asked Willie to head up a "clean speech" campaign and to bring some idea to our next meeting. Willie did something better than that. At the next meeting he brought a shoebox full of small cards. On one side of the card were the words "Clean Speech in Hialeah Compound." On the flip side were "10 Reasons Why I Use Foul Language." Number one read, "I curse because it pleases my mother so much." Number 10 read, "I curse because it shows how smart I am." Numbers two through nine were equally pointed.

Each of us received a hefty portion of cards with instructions to hand one out every time someone mouthed some foul words. We did so. The "user" would look at the card and read the words. It was a risky business. We never knew if the recipient would hit us or hug us. But it worked! I know one man who collected quite a bundle of cards. He thought it was a good idea, which improved his own ability to communicate with less vulgarity and profanity. Willie had taken on a hard task and made it easy, effective, and in many ways a lot of fun. *(Note: these two particular accounts of my relationship and learning with Willie are told in my earlier book, Each One Disciple One, John Wesley Press, 1999.)*

A few weeks later I preached at the monthly get-together of the missionaries in and around Pusan. After the meeting Helen

Rosser invited me to spend a day with her visiting several of the prenatal and postnatal clinics she had started and was overseeing. I gladly accepted, since part of my responsibilities as chief chaplain's assistant was to accommodate the work of missionaries and to coordinate any assistance the command chaplain's office might render.

The following week I made the rounds with Helen to three of the eight clinics she supervised. Pregnant women and new mothers were being treated for minor illnesses in addition to receiving powdered milk. As I entered the first clinic, an assistant was dipping powdered whole milk from a barrel into a bag for a baby's and mother's consumption. It was evident all mothers and babies were malnourished. At that door I saw something for which I will always be grateful and could support vigorously for the rest of my ministry.

As the assistant removed the bag of powdered milk, I saw the words "Church World Service" on the barrel. I had seen those words before, as a part of Highland Park's apportionments. From that moment I saw the good that Church World Service was doing for people in great need. Later I would tell this story to budget committees in churches I served. Acceptance of all apportionments rode on the coattails of my firsthand knowledge of the good Church World Service was doing. Not only did the churches accept their full share; they paid them in full.

Helen and her assistants weighed the babies and expectant mothers to monitor their progress. Helen asked all patients questions concerning their diet, including its adequacy. It was moving to watch the tender care and counseling extended to each one. She dispensed whatever her scanty supplies of medication would allow, such as aspirin, ointments, and over-the-counter medicines.

Even my uninformed eyes could see that Helen was operating on scanty resources because of an equally scanty budget. She was mostly distributing the love of Jesus to receptive persons and encouragement borne of sincere concern.

On the way back to her home, I asked, "Helen, what is the greatest need in your clinics?"

She paused as if gauging the depth of so many needs. "Ray,"

she answered, "one of my heartaches is watching so many children afflicted with rickets—a disease that is so easily prevented by simply taking vitamins. We have so few vitamins up against so many in need. I wish somehow we had enough vitamins of all kinds. They would go so far in helping mothers and children of all ages to stay more healthy."

I felt the inner sobs of Helen's heart.

Well, I had asked the question! Now I had to ask another question, this time to myself. "What can I do?," I asked silently. All night long I wrestled with the question. Rest and sleep evaded me as if insisting I answer before dozing off. I flipped and flopped, sat up in bed, and talked to myself. Again and again I heard myself reply, "There's nothing I can do!" My emotions moved from pity to frustration to anger to helplessness. I will never forget that night.

The next morning I wearily paid a visit to the hospital pharmacy where one of our group worked. His name was Drew. I shared with him my conversation with Helen and asked him if the hospital pharmacy ever received sample vitamins—or were there any vitamins to be discarded because the usage date had run out. He replied that a week or so earlier the hospital had destroyed its annual supply of dated drugs, including vitamins. He also informed me the pharmacy seldom ever received significant supplies of sample vitamins unless they were new on the market.

I was crestfallen at the thought of having a second night of wrestling without sleep. Just then an idea erupted in my mind. Call it foolishness, desperation, or whatever. I called it divine intervention. I asked Drew, "Could you give me the names and addresses of a few pharmaceutical companies back home?"

He looked puzzled and said humorously, "I suppose so. I don't know of any Army regulation that would prohibit my giving the chief chaplain's assistant the names of a few drug companies. It will take me a little while to dig out the information. I'll bring the list to you at our PMOC meeting tonight."

He did! After the meeting that evening I wrote to three companies on the list. I simply shared with them who I was, with whom I was working, and what I had seen for myself. I asked if the companies could help the mothers and children. I explained the enormity of the need and that a small carton simply would not help. I slept soundly through the night.

The next morning my letters were on their way. Though military mail is priority, it took a long time to get a response. After weeks of anticipating mail that never came, I pretty much gave up hope. The PMOC meetings, my travels, and our projects kept me alive but also concerned as time grew closer and closer for my return home.

As I sat at my desk one day looking over my schedule, one of my assistants came in and whispered excitedly, "Ray, there's a colonel on the phone from Seoul. He wants to talk to you, and he sounds upset."

Well, I didn't know any colonel in Seoul. Gingerly I took the phone and said hello.

"Are you Sergeant Raymond H. Owen?" the voice demanded.

"Yes sir," I said.

Gruffly he said, "What are you going to do with a truck-load of vitamins valued wholesale at more than $10,000?"

For the next several minutes I explained the entire story about the clinics and the children's needs. I also said the shipment would be stored on base in the secured Quonset hut assigned to the area command chaplain until the vitamins could be distributed as needed. Finally, I told him the area command chaplain was fully aware of my requests and supported the entire project.

Having heard my account, the colonel was somewhat calmed and actually seemed civil. He then said, "If what you say is true, and after I have looked into the matter, the shipment will be sent to the area command chaplain's office. I'll check everything out!"

Suddenly I realized why the colonel had been so gruff with me. He probably thought I was going to sell the vitamins on the black market for a small fortune. Certainly I could understand his reason for calling me!

Late the next day I received a phone call from the colonel's office advising me the shipment of vitamins would be on the train three days later. I was to be at the depot to sign for the load and transport it to the secured storage area.

When I called Helen to tell her the good news, she was as

astonished as I was. I asked her to come to our office to see the shipment and to bring a plan for distribution over the next several months. A week later, she came and inventoried the various kinds of vitamins. To our amazement, we had every size container in every kind of dose. We all had a difficult time controlling our heartfelt emotions. The donor company was a major pharmaceutical producer. What a letter of gratitude and appreciation I wrote to the company.

Somehow the military newspaper *Stars and Stripes* picked up the story and published an extensive article. The PMOC, the missionaries, the chaplain's staff all celebrated what we literally thought to be a miracle, with God's hand in it all.

Shipments from the other two companies arrived later. Each was smaller by far than the first. Yet we considered each one an enormous contribution. By that time we had a supply of vitamins to help other missionaries in their projects for a long time. Helen became the supplier, since she knew the work being done by her missionary colleagues.

Helen asked me to accompany her on her next rounds at the clinic. She had already told the personnel about the shipment. She wanted me to go with her to hear her get promises from all her patients not to give away or sell any vitamins on the black market. Their pledges were firmly made through their tears. If ever I have seen spiritual gratitude, it was on those rounds.

As the membership of the PMOC grew in members, it also grew in its concern for one another's spiritual health and well-being.

At a later meeting of the PMOC, it was noticed that one of our regulars had been absent for several meetings. One of the group volunteered to check on him. We learned he had stopped coming because he had violated the morality covenant we all had made with each other. His was indeed a serious violation. Our friend was so besieged with guilt that he "could not face the group."

We prayed for our friend and agreed that we would stand with him and do all we could to help him find release from his guilt and peace in his soul. It took several weeks, even though he returned to the group's weekly meetings. On a later occasion he blurted out his confession and remorse and asked us to pray for him. We did. We had experienced what Wesley called class meetings, in that we were close enough to one another we could hear each other's burdens and be accountable to the group.

The PMOC was very active in the service club on the base. It furnished entertainment, snacks, a library, fun events, movies, and all sorts of activities for those who wished to participate. The club was staffed by two professionally trained hostesses and several Korean assistants—all of whom worked so diligently to make our time in Korea enjoyable and productive. They went beyond the call of duty to bring us the best programming of any service club in South Korea.

One of the men got the bright idea of putting on a party for the two hostesses. Everyone agreed. A script was developed and amended at every secret rehearsal. Premier night was to be on Bingo Night. When the day arrived, a huge crowd showed up. The two hostesses were amazed and wondered why the big crowd. They proceeded with the bingo game through the first winner. Then those appointed proceeded to the stage, removed the bingo equipment, escorted the two absolutely befuddled women down to the floor, and seated them in special chairs brought in and decorated. Then it was announced this was "Georgie and Earline" night. All the planned activities and spontaneous antics were dedicated to them. I was elected to play the role of Georgie, the director. The same man who had given me the names of the drug companies supplied me with a nurse's uniform (with padding in some strange places). Someone else played the role of Earline. The script was soon discarded. The musicians lost their way. Cues got mixed up. Makeup washed off from sweat. It wound up being hilarious and disorganized pandemonium, with bumblings, ad-libs, jokes that went sour, and craziness. Our two honored guests loved it as they watched our antics on stage. At last the end brought on booming applause and a standing ovation for the honorees. They couldn't believe we had pulled the whole thing off without them having the slightest hint of its development.

Later, at the 8th Army awards night for the best service club in South Korea, our Hialeah Club took first place. The attractive award plaque was mounted in a prominent place, naming the two hostesses.

Just a few days before I was to depart for home, I was working hard in my room on my final sermon for the chapel service the following Sunday evening. A hard knock sounded on my door. To say the least, it startled me and disrupted my concentration. I opened the door to find a giant of a man standing there. I had come to know him aboard ship on our way to Korea. He held in his hand a rolled-up sheet of paper.

Perplexed, I asked him to come in. As he sat down I could tell he was deeply troubled. When I asked why he was there, he swallowed hard and began to cry. I waited for him to regain his composure.

"Ray," he said, "for 12 months now I have hated every day I have been in this stinking place. Here in my hand are my orders to return home."

By then I was really puzzled. "Then why are you so distraught?" I asked. "You have your ticket home in your hand."

With words broken by sobs he said, "I can't go home and face my wife and family because I have lived such a hell of a life ever since I arrived!"

We talked and talked for a long time. He finally asked me to pray for him, which I did. We talked some more and prayed some more before he left, still much distraught.

I tried to turn again to my sermon, but it was no use. I couldn't concentrate on anything but the man who had visited me, burdened by the weight of sin upon his soul. I found myself praying for him throughout the wakeful night. I prayed for myself and my apparent inadequacy to help him find peace. I could only trust he somehow would experience the tender grace of God applied to his wrongdoing.

A week or so later I sailed for home. Bishop Robert E. Fannin and I discovered 38 years later that we were on the same ship home. Neither of us could have ever believed we would someday be members of the Council of Bishops. Little wonder, then, we so enjoy the genuine friendship we have developed since 1983, when first we met on our trip to Kenya. Our lives have traveled parallel tracks ever since, even to our election to the episcopacy within hours of each other.

Our ship arrived in San Francisco December 19, 1960. I was processed out and honorably discharged. With genuine gratitude for nearly 12 years in the military, I never looked back. Nor have I regretted it. I boarded a plane for Tennessee and my family. We spent the Christmas holidays with both sets of parents. Then we packed our belongings in a U-Haul trailer and left Tennessee the last days of December. We arrived in Lawton, Oklahoma, before the first day of the New Year.

5

Journey in Same but Different Church

Effective January 1, 1961, I was appointed pastor to Highland Park Church a second time. An interim pastor had been appointed to serve until I returned from South Korea. In future years I would become convinced that being appointed again after leaving a church was rarely a good idea. The church I had left some 13 months earlier simply was not the same.

Immediately after moving into the parsonage again, I enrolled in Cameron College in Lawton for the spring semester. Nearing my 29th birthday, I needed to get on quickly with my education. A few weeks later, I resigned my commission as an officer in the United States Army.

Our family was excited about greeting the friends, leaders, and members of the congregation. I was eager to pick up where we had left off with the vision we had formulated before I went to Korea. Within two short weeks I realized the church was drastically different.

The vision we had so carefully crafted had been set aside. The Building Fund was at a standstill. Finances were in a crisis. Attendance at worship was in steady decline. Sunday school participation was barely breathing. Quibbling and carping flowed freely through the membership. No one seemed to have any dreams anymore. Or even to care.

The congregation was fractured and dysfunctional. It all

centered around three persons at odds with one another. All three of them had held key leadership positions when I left for Korea.

"What has happened here in just 13 months?" I kept asking myself.

To put it bluntly, I was devastated, hurt, and thoroughly discouraged. Moving back had been like moving into a terribly troubled congregation whose members wrangled with each other on the very edges of self-destruction. Much of my influence on leading the church had eroded, although no one seemed displeased with me personally. Quite the contrary. Every member seemed overjoyed with our return. Still, the infighting continued to quench the very spirit of God.

On any given week it would be rumored that I was catering to one of the three leaders, which caused the other two to be vocally unhappy. The next week it would be a second faction leader, causing the other two to be unhappy. On and on it went. It was awful.

"What had happened to this happy, courageous, and visionary little church?" I kept asking myself.

Once, in the grip of extreme frustration, I was tempted to call the congregation together to say to them what Moses said to the unruly Israelites at Mount Sinai: "All who are on the Lord's side, come over!" But I thought better of it for fear all three sides would question whether even I was on the Lord's side.

In spite of the churchwide grumblings, some good things were quietly taking place. New faces were showing up for worship and Sunday school. By the end of our first month back, two couples had united with the church. One couple especially proved to be a godsend—both to the congregation and to our family and me.

Jack and Bobbie Lyons, with their two sons, Tom and Mike, had recently returned from a tour of duty in Germany. They were to become a tremendous blessing to the congregation. They were also to become our closest friends. For more than 40 years now, we have cherished every opportunity to spend time with Bobbie and Jackie and to recount some of our special experiences. Like, for instance, the day Bobbie and I conspired to take their incorrigible, cyclone-fence-climbing mutt to the dog pound. I don't know for sure even now if Jack has forgiven me. I think there is some evidence he has, in that he is still married to the coconspirator.

Bobbie and Jack lost no time getting fully involved in the troubled life of the congregation. Jack and I had similar military backgrounds in food service. Our two families hit it off in just about everything. Their two boys and our two boys treated one another more like brothers than friends. It seemed as though our families had known each other all our lives. We still feel that way.

A few months after Jack and Bobbie arrived, we came to a severe personal crisis. We had left a salary in the military of some $6,000 a year to take a church with a salary of $1,900 a year. We simply had run out of financial reserves. Lavelle and I both felt the weight of our situation.

In the midst of our financial exigency, Jack and Bobbie dropped by for a visit. As they departed, they left the tithe of an unexpected income they had received. We were humbled by their act of love, but that's the sort of people we have found them to be throughout our years together. Their gift, along with Lavelle's finding a part-time job later, helped tide us over.

In the spring of 1961 a quarterly conference was called for the purpose of recommending Jack for a license to preach. He later confessed he had been "running from the Lord's call to ministry." He had not wanted to start going to church with Bobbie and their boys, lest he would be compelled to answer that call. Well, he started anyway. Sure enough, that call weighed so profoundly upon his life that he said "yes" to a life of ministry. He too would give up a considerable number of years in the active military service and never look back.

On April 23, 1961, the quarterly conference of Highland Park Church unanimously recommended Jack be granted a license to preach. At the upcoming Oklahoma Annual Conference session a few weeks later, Jack was appointed pastor of Wesley Chapel, a small, loving, and courageous rural congregation not far from Lawton.

Though Jack and Bobbie would never agree, their joining Highland Park probably served as the catalyst that turned the congregation's eyes back upon what was our overall mission. What a blessing Bobbie and Jack have been ever since—not only to us but also to all the people in all the churches they loved and served faithfully in the name of Jesus Christ.

Somewhere in the mix of our growing friendship, Bobbie was heard to say, "One day Ray will be a bishop of the church." On July 16, 1992, I decided it was time for me to believe everything Bobbie Lyons ever said. On that day I was elected to the episcopacy at the South Central Jurisdictional Conference of the United Methodist Church at Fort Worth, Texas. Bobbie and Jack were there to celebrate. They have been there for us all along. How thankful and privileged we still feel with just being their friends.

At that same annual conference session of 1961, I was reappointed to Highland Park Church. Though in five months the church had made significant strides forward, it still faced tremendous challenges and struggles. Despite membership and attendance growth the following year, there lingered still a defeated, "we can't do it" attitude. Administrative board meetings became an endurance rather than an inspiration. Perhaps unknowingly, the chairperson of the board contributed to the "we can't do it" spirit by calling consistently upon the treasurer to make the opening report.

The treasurer was a charter member of the church. She and her husband were faithful, loyal, and supportive members. She had been treasurer far too many years. She also possessed a rather pessimistic spirit. Invariably, she would preface the treasurer's report with how the money was not coming in and that she couldn't take any more threatening duns, letters, and phone calls from creditors. The longer her report, the more despondent and dispirited the board members became. They would sit slumped shouldered, staring at their feet. With the end of the report, she would shove the ledger, bills, and notes of the treasurer's office to the center of the table, a signal that she had had enough of the job. Following that, she would lean back heavily in contagious despair.

Any other report forthcoming or new idea worth birthing was already dead before it got to the table. Then, at the end of every discouraging meeting, the treasurer would retrieve the ledger and materials and in her whiney voice say, "I will continue as treasurer for one more month, until someone else is found to take the job."

I had to do something before the last two remaining "saints" declined to accept the responsibilities of treasurer. I don't know if it was the Holy Spirit prodding me or my own frustration, but I said to God, "Lord, the next time she shoves that ledger to the middle of the table, I am going to grab it and find someone else to take the job. If this is not in accordance with your will, you stay my hand. Else I am bound to do it!"

Well, at the very next meeting it was the same routine. She had "put up with it too long already." With that, she shoved the ledger and materials to the center of the large table around which we were sitting. She had done that so many times from the same chair that a rut must have been worn into the tabletop. Else, how could the book stop precisely at the same spot?

As the ledger came to rest, I reached over and took the books quickly. She was surprised, if not altogether stunned. And I was in God's will because my hand had not been stayed. Other reports were given, and I was asked to give the benediction. Quickly following the "amen," the former treasurer said aloud, "Brother Ray, I'll take the job for one more month until you can find a replacement."

I thanked her and said, "No, we've caused you enough suffering and stress. We all thank you for your service." I wanted to advise her I had already enlisted another person to take on the job of treasurer, but I didn't. The next day the new treasurer was in place, and the church had crossed a Rubicon.

In a very short time the entire church witnessed a transformation. The former treasurer became a bubbly, more positive person. All the board members noticed the transformation, as did most of the congregation. From that experience, and for the rest of my ministry, I made certain the treasurer would be a positive influence, not only for the sake of the board but for the benefit of the entire congregation. God never stayed my determination to that end, either.

Because the Building Fund had had no increase in value in some time, the board decided to abandon the hope of relocating and building a new church. The fund was to be used to remodel a small separate building into Sunday school rooms and a tiny fellowship hall. It seemed a reasonable action. With that decision, however, the congregation pretty much decided what its future would be. It could not sustain a future of growth and vitality without relocating and providing adequate facilities and parking. Indeed, the church couldn't survive, but it seemingly wouldn't die.

In late spring of 1961 a rather remarkable thing began taking place—not so much in the incident itself but in its results over the following year. It all began one Saturday morning as I was finishing up my sermon for the next day.

Our oldest son, Dana, came in to ask me to help get his kite up on the school ground across the street. He was having a hard time with it. Reluctantly, I muttered my way out to the school ground. It took only a few minutes to get the kite up and flying. Watching nearby was the girl from next door, who had her kite. She, too, needed help. We got it flying also. As I was about to return to my sermon, her father came out and began a conversation with me. I became a bit fidgety to finish up my sermon. The man's name was Cecil Cox. He and his family lived right across the street in front of the church. The four children were the only ones in the family to attend church. Everyone in the neighborhood knew him. Already I had heard he was a confirmed alcoholic of long standing.

Anxious to get back to my sermon wrapup, I was about to excuse myself when he said to me, "Could I talk to you privately for a few minutes?"

Already thoroughly interrupted, I said "Why not? Come on, and we'll talk in my study."

What a different story it might have been had I excused myself from conversation with him that day.

Cecil was a tall man with a big frame. To shake his hand was somewhat like taking hold of a small ham. The small parsonage trembled a bit at his walking. Entering the study, I invited him to sit in an old overstuffed chair someone had probably donated to the parsonage after buying a new one. Cecil sat down heavily and mortally wounded that chair. Dust of the decades squirted out from all directions. He didn't notice, and I tried to ignore it.

Before I could ask him what he wanted to talk to me about, he said bluntly, "You probably know I am an alcoholic. I've been through all kinds of treatments that dried me out but didn't last. I've gone to Alcoholics Anonymous for months at a time. I've tried everything to quit drinking, but I just can't. Do you think God can help me?"

I guess I must have had more faith than knowledge about his plaguing malady, so I boldly declared, "Cecil, I believe God can do for you just about anything you can trust him to do."

"Where do I start?" he asked.

Well, I was not altogether sure, so I said what most pastors in a quandary would say, "Why don't you pray about your need?"

Still pushing me, he said, "What do I say to God?"

A bit desperate myself by then, I answered, "Tell God just what you told me, and ask Him for help."

Before I could say more, he got up, turned around, fell to his knees, and rammed his head and huge shoulders into the back of that ugly green chair. It groaned as if it had died on the spot.

"Lord," he prayed, "this is Cecil. You know my problem. I want to quit drinking and get my life straightened out. I can't do it alone. I'm asking you to help me."

That was it. He stood up, turned to face me, looked straight into my eyes and said, "This time, Brother Ray, I mean it! Now what?"

It all sounded so simple and easy. It wasn't. His urges at first were oh so frequent. He would come over, and we would pray and talk and go get coffee or root beer until he felt he could resist until the next siege. His visits were so frequent and regular that the family knew he had arrived by how the house trembled. He no longer needed to knock on the door. The visits gradually became less frequent.

In the meantime Cecil and his family got involved in the life of the church. He didn't try to hide his struggle. Everyone knew about it anyway. He was a good carpenter, concrete finisher, fish fryer, and doer of just about every thing else human hands could. Soon he was supervising the Methodist Men's project of building a roof over the front entrance doors. Then he took charge of building and installing a beautiful lighted cross on the roof. All the men loved him, supported him, encouraged him, and prayed for him. He was making much progress.

I said to him one time jokingly, "Cecil, you seem to be making good progress over your addiction, but it has come at heavy cost to me."

A bit concerned, he asked, "What do you mean?"

"Now I'm getting addicted to root beer," I replied.

We both laughed, then came another bear hug, which I barely survived. We laughed again and thanked God for the evident change occurring in Cecil's life.

All these developments were taking place in the summer and fall of 1961. Every area of the church's ministry seemed to be growing but not dramatically so. Cecil's struggle seemed to have pulled people together. Laughter and cooperation grew as time passed.

In midwinter Cecil came unannounced into my study. He plopped down in that crippled green chair.

"Brother Ray," he said, "I've got something to tell you."

Wondering if he had fallen off the wagon, I asked, "What is it?"

"I believe I have beaten this thing!" he declared.

Quickly I responded, "Now, Cecil, don't go overboard with this thing. You are not out of the woods yet. You know it takes a long time even to get control of it."

Then I asked, "What makes you so sure you have beaten it?"

"For years, during quail season, I've escorted high ranking military officers on a hunt at Fort Sill," he replied. "They're always good to me, especially when we have a good hunt. Liquor of all sorts is available. They always include me in the drinks. Yesterday a colonel noticed I wasn't having my usual drink. He knew my past, so he said to me, 'Sergeant, help yourself to the liquor.' Then and there I said, 'No, thank you, sir. I don't use it any more!'"

In a critical test Cecil had taken on the monster and held it at bay. No wonder he was so elated. He had never been able to resist before. No wonder, too, that we prayed and thanked God for Cecil's progress.

Several weeks later he made his way again to my study.

Sitting down, he said, "Brother Ray, I've got something I must tell you!"

I thought, "Oh, no! He has had a drink!"

Before I could respond, he stated, "I believe God is calling me to preach, and I can't even read!"

The double surprise caused me to drop both my pen and my jaw. Cecil went on to say, "All I can do is sign my name on the payroll at Fort Sill."

I knew Cecil was not an educated man, but I had no idea he couldn't even read.

"Well, Brother Ray," he went on, "what am I going to do? How can I say no to God?"

It was time to pray some again, which we did. I told him I would see what I could do and get back to him later. I knew he must have been disappointed at my response.

After Cecil left, I sat alone in my study and asked myself, "What am I going to do?" Finally I had an idea. "I'll call the district superintendent," I said to myself. "Superintendents know everything."

Later that day I tried to explain the problem to Dr. Howard Davis. I was in a mild dither. Smiling, Dr. Davis said, "Ray, he feels the Lord has called him. We've all watched him battle his cravings!"

"But Dr. Davis," I interrupted, "he can't even read!"

Ignoring my seeming panic, he said to me calmly, "Let's give Cecil a chance. I have a church where he will fit in. Let's put him through the licensing process, and if he makes it, we'll chance it. A layman can read the scripture for his sermon while he learns to read."

Well, I was right. District superintendents did know everything. I reconfirmed my belief—almost—when I became a superintendent years later.

When I informed Cecil of my conversation, his huge body shook with tears of gratitude. I readily admit to contributing a few tears myself.

I informed the congregation about Cecil's call and the district superintendent's response. The whole church celebrated and pledged support, even though they had seen Cecil fail many times before.

In the fall of 1961 Robert Young and his family had come into the membership of Highland Park Church. Immediately he got involved with the Methodist Men and came to know Cecil.

Robert was a somewhat reserved person. I thought of him as an individual who measured his words before he spoke or acted. He and I shared a special kind of relationship. We could talk with ease about most anything. He told me that for some time he had given thought to going into the ministry. Being one who measured his every decision and action, he needed a "definitive sign." I suggested he keep praying about it and said I would join him in prayer.

Sometime later he became rather frustrated.

"Ray," he said, "I've prayed a lot. I've told God I was willing to enter the ministry, but I wanted to be sure that's what God wants. I just want to be certain this is the right thing to do."

I didn't know what to tell Robert to help him. I had not the wisdom of years or experience that would help me counsel him. I had only the experience of my own call, and it was obviously different from his. So I just said to him, "Robert, why don't you act in faith that it *is* God's call to ministry and proceed in the process toward a license to preach? It may be you are unsettled about it because you want God to act first. It could be that God has already acted."

It made sense to me. I suggested he make the move and keep on praying. Finally I said to him, "Let me know how I can be of help."

I had no idea that clarity for him would come so quickly. The next morning he called to tell me he had done what I had suggested and was now at peace about the call.

On March 6, 1962, the quarterly conference recommended both Cecil Cox and Robert Young for licenses to preach. Shortly thereafter, the district committee on ordained ministry approved the recommendations. But Robert was not appointed to a church because he was transferred a few weeks before the annual conference session convened. He departed with much excitement and hope of serving a church at his next destination.

The 1962 Oklahoma Annual Conference session proved to be a doozy. I was appointed to start a new church in south

Oklahoma City. That would afford me the opportunity to finish my undergraduate degree at Oklahoma City University. It was a dream come true.

At the same time, Cecil was appointed to pastor two small rural churches in the western part of the district. Upon learning of Cecil's desire to read, the school administration arranged for Cecil to attend classes with his sixth grade son. He learned rapidly to read and a lot more. The community rallied around him in support. In a short time Cecil earned a General Educational Development certificate.

A year later I saw Cecil again. I greeted him and asked how his churches had done over the past year. He responded by saying he had received 17 persons into membership, most of them by profession of faith. I was astounded. Those two churches had not had that kind of growth in decades.

"What in the world have you been doing to get such response?" I asked.

As if surprised, he looked at me and said, "I've been telling them what you told me to tell them!"

I became a bit uneasy, so I asked, "What did you tell them I told you to tell them?"

Seemingly surprised again, he replied, "You told me in your study just to tell them what God had done in my life. That's what I've done in a lot of different ways!"

I was relieved. And thrilled.

Jack Lyons succeeded me as pastor of Highland Park Church. He served one year and then took another appointment to continue his education. In June 1963 Jack was succeeded by W.W. Stephens, a retired pastor. He served only seven months. On December 31 the church was officially closed. Some months later, the property was deeded to the Oklahoma Indian Missionary Conference. Later still, the building was condemned and declared unsafe for worship services.

Following my last worship service at Highland Park, Reverend Snodgrass lingered to greet me in private. When everyone had gone, he took my hand, looked me in the face, and said, "Ray, God has much in store for you in Oklahoma City and beyond. You are my son in ministry. As long as you live, I will go on preaching through you!"

What a compliment! What an endowment he had bequeathed to me! Years later I would have cause to remember his words and to understand more fully the depth of their meaning. That was my last time to see Herman Snodgrass. He died June 4, 1962. I did not hear of his death until after the funeral.

Highland Park Church had lasted only 12 years. So brief a life might seem to some to have been a failure. Not so! It probably achieved a marvelous, if not matchless, distinction. In the course of its 12 years, Highland Park Church sent eight pastors into the ministry.

Only five are named. Page 3 of the *History of Highland Park Church*, dated February 25, 1962, says Dean Wynn, who became pastor in 1955, was the first. In 1956, "Three men made decisions to become ministers." These unnamed ministers became the second, third and fourth. I was the fifth. Jack Lyons was the sixth. Cecil Cox was the seventh. Robert Young was the eighth.

Only God has an inkling as to the magnitude of Highland Park's contribution to the kingdom through the lives of those eight pastors. Indeed, it had been for me a journey "in the same but different church" at Highland Park, and I, myself, was the same but different pastor.

6

Journey through Johnson Grass and Trash

With a bit of sadness at leaving many dear friends in Lawton, Lavelle, our two sons, and I departed the last days of May 1962. We felt we had done a credible job of ministry at Highland Park Church. Now it was time for us to move on to the challenge of founding a new church while I finished my bachelor's degree at Oklahoma City University.

Since there was no parsonage waiting for us, my district superintendent, Dr. Leland Clegg, had arranged for us to move into a four-room furnished apartment. Though it was small, it would serve as our housing needs temporarily.

Right across the street was the thriving Asbury Methodist Church, pastored by the Reverend Guy C. Ames Jr. What a blessing that arrangement proved to be for us. From the outset we felt connected. Guy and his wife, Jean, extended to us genuine support, welcome, and friendship. Years later in our careers, we and the Ameses would share a common blessing in that we would both have two sons (their Guy C. III and Cooper) in the ministry of the United Methodist Church.

The congenial spirit of the Asbury congregation quickly enlarged our feeling of being supported. Every member we met seemed excited to greet us, as though they had been prepared for our arrival. Looking back, I now know Guy Ames encouraged the members to reach out to us and to assist us at every opportunity.

The Reverend Ames also assured us that Asbury Church was eager to uphold us in the challenge looming before us. With gracious discretion he even furnished me the names of several inactive member families who had bought new homes in the area where the new church was to be built. "These families," he said, "should and probably would help start the new congregation." His gesture simply certified his magnanimous spirit. In time, several of those families would indeed play key leadership roles in the birthing of the new church.

With a mixture of excitement and anxiety, I plunged headlong into the work that had to be done. Soon, however, my excitement about the magnificent possibilities ahead was thoroughly tempered by anxiety about just where and how I was to start bringing the dream of a new church into reality. Seemingly there were dozens of things urgently needing to be done—all at one time.

A few days following my arrival, Dr. Clegg asked me to meet him at the site of the future church. The property had already been bought and paid for by the district board of missions. The site consisted of five acres on South Pennsylvania Avenue. New homes were popping up all over the west side of the street. Our five acres were on the east side, with a splendid crop of Johnson grass and a repository of dumped trash. Our side of the street had not been paved or curbed along the frontage. The city was pleased to inform us the street would be finished soon after the new church paid the costs.

For several minutes Dr. Clegg and I stood in the street, looking over the situation. Reaching up, he took a coat lapel in each hand, rocked back and forth on his feet, and said to me, "Brother Ray, there on the west side are the people you are to bring over here to the east side as members of your church. That is what we have brought you here to do!"

Well now, that was plain enough. It was also sufficiently scary. I have to say, though, that every time I called him for help or guidance, Dr. Clegg was there for me. I am sure, however, he had not expected a call from me so soon, when his wife handed him the phone upon his return home and said to him,

"Leland, Brother Owen is on the phone and needing to talk to you!"

Inexperienced as I was, I had not much idea where or how to begin. For the first few weeks I operated mostly on raw instinct, common sense, and personal initiative. Everybody seemed eager to help me, if only I could tell them what first needed to be done. I spent a lot of energy. I also made a lot of mistakes, from which I learned what *not* to do.

As the results of my mistakes compounded, my energy depleted, and fatigue besieged my body. Two overriding conclusions became clear to me:

1. The new church would not rise out of the inertia of my running helter-skelter in all directions at the same time and at breakneck speed.

2. The new church would not rise out of pastoral leadership devoid of spiritual reserves that derived only from deliberate prayer, Bible study, and time set apart each day seeking God's guidance for every agenda item at hand.

These two conclusions put me on the right track and likely saved me from failure.

With my spiritual center now reestablished, I was able much more effectively to carry the weight of my responsibility. Now more keenly focused on one priority at a time, I put together a community-wide, door-to-door census.

St. Luke's Church was the official sponsor of the new church. Dr. McFerrin Stowe (elected a bishop two years later) was pastor of the 7,000-plus member congregation. Through his help and that of Reverend Ames of Asbury, I was able to assemble a large group of senior high students to do the survey. I had never seen such serious and dedicated young people. They worked all day with a marvelous spirit and attitude.

Their work made visible to the community the dreams of a new Methodist Church. The census cards identified 83 families who were eager to become members of the new church. More than 150 cards identified families "definitely interested" in the church once it was organized and under way. A third group of cards identified 79 families who were pleased that the church would be built and would give serious consideration to becoming a part of the congregation at a later time.

Following the census, a large, attractive sign was posted on the site indicating the "Future Home of a New Methodist Church." My name and phone number were also displayed for "Further Information." As pastor, I took it upon myself to visit each of the 83 families on the first list.

Never will I forget the very first call I made. It was Saturday afternoon. The information on the card stated the family's strong interest in becoming a part of the new church. I wanted my first call to be fruitful, so I placed that card on top of the stack.

With an upbeat, confident spirit, I stepped onto the stoop and rang the doorbell. I heard a bit of ruckus and yelling going on inside but thought it was probably the television. After a second ring of the doorbell, the door was jerked wide open so forcefully it crashed against the doorstop. Standing there disheveled and glaring at me, the woman asked, "Who are you, and what do you want?" Stunned and definitely intimidated, I told her who I was and that I was following up on information that the family was interested in helping the new church get started. Growling at me, she yelled a few expletives and said, "I don't care who you are or what you are trying to do!" With that, she slammed the door with such rapid force it jarred my teeth, mussed up my hair and seemed to suck the air out of my lungs.

Totally shocked and dispirited, I sauntered slump-shouldered back to my car, mumbling to myself, "If that is the 'strongest interest' and 'top of the stack' prospect, what can I expect from here on?" I checked to see if I had come to the right address. The house number was correct. So was the name on the mailbox. Mystified, I said to myself, "I must have interrupted a royal family fight, which caused the ruckus I had heard."

Still hurting from my very first reception, I was sorely tempted to get quickly back to my apartment and quit the cause on the basis of uncivil residents. For several minutes I just sat in my car, telling God I was not the man for the job. After a siege of self pity and with faith frazzled by failure, I proceeded to the second-best family in the stack. Cautiously, I approached the doorbell and pushed it. I didn't know just what to expect this time, but it was not what I suspected.

Both husband and wife came to the door and greeted me

most pleasantly. When I told them who I was, they looked at each other, smiled, and invited me to come in. As I sat down on the couch, they said, "You won't believe this, but we were just talking about the new church and when would it be getting under way! We were excited when the two youths came by to get information from us. We are so glad you came to see us. We want to be a part of the new church from the beginning!"

Relief! Renewal! And gratitude!

I visited three other families that afternoon. At the end of the day, four of the five families were eager to be at the meeting to help launch the church later that summer. On my way back home, I asked myself, "What if I had gone home after that first visit? I probably would have harbored such woundedness as to stymie the dream that had been placed into my hands." I certainly realized the value of the old adage "Failure often comes on the heels of quitting one try too soon."

My prayers that evening included repentance and asking forgiveness for having almost quit one try too soon. It was a timely adage that would return again and again as the reality of the church became an increasing fact.

My initial visitations were followed with enough positive commitments to convince us the church would come to birth. The first week of July 1962, we sent notices to all the families on all lists. We announced that the new church would hold its organizational meeting at 2:30 p.m. July 22 in the Hillcrest Heights Presbyterian Church, located in an adjoining area.

As the time drew near, we began to question the wisdom of organizing so soon. "Would enough people come?" we asked ourselves. "It's the middle of summer. Families will be on vacation and away from home." We were doing a pretty good job of downsizing success. Finally it was said, "Why don't we just start with however many God brings to us?" It was appropriate counsel.

When the day arrived, more than 50 people showed up for the first service. We worshipped together around the text of Judges 7:1-17. We opened the doors of membership and invited all who would join to come forward and so indicate. Ten adults, representing six families, placed their membership in Oklahoma City's newest Methodist Church. We then organized ourselves as a church. We elected a beginning slate of officers; we named the church Southern Hills. The following Sunday, 11 more adults presented themselves for membership. At the end of our third service, 10 more adults joined the congregation. That represented 14 families on the roll.

In only three weeks our attendance and space needs were putting pressure on the host church. We needed additional space for Sunday school classes and a nursery. Also, it was apparent that we needed to be meeting on our building site— even if it meant using temporary structures.

In mid-August I called Dr. Clegg. He agreed that we needed to be visible on site for the community to take note of our growing presence. A few days later I went with him to see several types of military buildings at Tinker Air Force Base. They were for sale to make room for more modern and efficient facilities. The wooden building we selected was sturdy and could be moved without any problem. With some remodeling, it would accommodate nearly 100 worshippers, three Sunday school classes, a small nursery, and restrooms. We could easily turn the worship area into a fellowship hall by putting up folding tables and rearranging the folding chairs.

In a pouring rain September 9, 1962, our first worship service on our property drew a full house. We called the building the Mobile Chapel. It would remain with us only until our first permanent building was completed. Then it would be moved to the site of another new church.

Membership that day stood at 41. Many had come into membership by profession of faith and baptism. One baptism was of particular delight. Carvell Stallings, who came to be one of my closest friends, wanted to be baptized by immersion. A large clear pond was located in the area. As he and I waded out into the water with a goodly number of members looking on, I stepped into a deep hole that stripped the loafer off my right foot. I instantly recalled the shoe I had lost in the watermelon ordeal years earlier and decided I had a knack for losing a shoe in strange places. By the time I regained my balance in the pond I had no idea where the shoe might be. Besides, the water was too deep to retrieve it without diving. We went on with the baptism as joy was added to the occasion by "the preacher losing his shoe." Carvell and I had many laughs about the day of his baptism. Being with him has always been an occasion of fun and fellowship. He became an outstanding leader in the church.

Phone calls and inquiries about the church came regularly. As my identity in the community increased, another major undertaking was needed. I felt it critical for my family and me to live in the community where the church was located. I was being looked upon as the "visible preacher" available to the area simply because Southern Hills was the first and only church present in the new development.

Dr. Clegg agreed my reasoning was sound and said, "Ray, you are absolutely right. I'll call the district missions committee together for a meeting of approval. In the meantime, you and Lavelle pick out a new house in the area. The district will make the down payment and pay the closing cost and the monthly installments until the church is able to take it over!"

I thought it interesting that Dr. Clegg had already authorized buying a new parsonage before he had even called the committee together. Years later, a retired elder said in reference to the matter, "That's the way things got done in the good ol' days when the bishop *bished* and the district superintendent *superintended*." I don't know if what my older elder said was true or not. I do know that by the time I became a district superintendent and later a bishop, such "good ol' days" had long since seen their sunset.

Having been told to go pick out a house as the parsonage, I pressed a bit further by asking, "Dr. Clegg, where are we to get the money for furnishings?"

Hurriedly he said, "Tell the church to buy the furniture and make the payments. They need to take on some of the responsibilities for themselves."

The conversation ended. So did the church's notion of "free ride" any longer. Even so, it was a hefty challenge for a church not yet six weeks old.

I called the officers of the church together and advised them the district missions committee would pay for the closing costs, down payment, and monthly installments on a new parsonage in the area until we were able to assume the debt. A howl of joy erupted, accompanied by happy applause. I then told them the church would have to buy the furnishings. A pall of silence fell upon the group. I informed them Lavelle and I would be looking for a house. I asked the trustees to appoint a committee to go with us to select the furnishings when we had found the right house.

In less than 30 minutes the entire membership was abuzz with the news of getting a parsonage and that the church would have to bear the costs of furnishings. The next day Lavelle got an offer from one of the leading women of the church, suggesting that she had a "perfectly good breakfast room set" in her garage that she would like to give to the parsonage.

"It would save the church some money," she said.

When Lavelle asked why the table and chairs were in the garage, the woman replied, "Oh, we bought a new set when we moved into our new home."

Then and there Lavelle set a timely precedent for the church regarding parsonage furnishings. Graciously but firmly Lavelle replied, "If the table and chairs are not suitable for your new home, I'm sure they would not be suitable for our new parsonage."

Lavelle's precedent-making comment might have come from our experience with that perfectly good but ugly stuffed green chair someone had donated to the parsonage at Highland Park Church, which Cecil Cox had so thoroughly mangled and finally killed. The word got around. No more offers of "almost" generosity were made concerning parsonage furnishings.

We moved into our lovely parsonage with all new furniture and a fenced-in back yard for the kids. We really did feel good about the adequate space for our family.

On November 11, 1962, we closed the charter membership list at 84. We were moving forward at a healthy growth rate and with plans for the future. That same evening a quarterly church conference reviewed the architect's plans for the first of a five-phase dream. We voted on a $77,000 bond sale to fund the building construction, furnishings, paving of the street, and curbing.

When finished, the building would have three Sunday school classrooms with folding partitions that could open up for a fellowship hall, a chapel that would seat 150, two class-rooms for small children, two restrooms, and a small office for me. It was a well-planned building that would accommodate our needs for a few years until time for the next phase.

Dr. Clegg presided over the quarterly conference session pertaining to the bond sale. Everyone seemed happy when the vote to approve was unanimous. Dr. Clegg then closed the conference and left me to preside over the review of plans and their approval. It didn't take long for me to wish he hadn't left me alone to deal with what happened. As the discussion proceeded, the same woman who had offered the chairs and table became upset. It all amounted to her desire to have the chancel area in the east end rather than in the west as the architect had placed it to accommodate the succeeding phases. Such a major change at this point would have increased the cost significantly. Also, such changes would delay by several months our moving into the new facilities. We were growing, and time was of the essence.

Even so, the woman began to grumble about several other things that displeased her. She, her husband, and four other couples were all huddled in the back corner of the room. It was obvious something was going on among them. As the discussion continued, more grumbles and negative comments came out of the corner group. An otherwise joyous occasion was rapidly being squelched.

The lay leader happened to be sitting right in front of the group. He was highly regarded among the members for his graciousness and his wisdom. Seeing what was happening to the meeting, he turned around, called the woman's name and said, "For God's sake and the sake of our meeting, be considerate of those who have questions and deserve answers!" Though kindly spoken, his words served to ignite her exploding anger.

"You go to hell!" she barked back.

Stark silence rippled rapidly across the stunned congregation. Mouths flew open in sadness. Heads sagged with embarrassment. Other heads were bowed in silent prayer. I was so undone that I just stood there not believing what I had heard. Only a few seconds had passed, but it felt like minutes. Amid the silence, the lay leader turned around again, looked the woman in the eye and said kindly to her, "I'll not do that!"

What a classic response! There was more silence. Then the whole congregation burst out laughing and applauding. His response had simply dissipated the fire of anger.

Immediately the woman, her husband, their two sons, and the other couples stalked out in a huff, vowing never to return. My heart broke. Only an hour earlier we had announced 84 members and approved a $77,000 bond sale for our first building construction. Now we had 70 members and what felt like a broken church.

There was nothing we could do about those who had departed, so we proceeded with the discussions until someone moved we approve the plans as presented. The motion also was approved unanimously. Groundbreaking was set for early spring. Handshakes of mutual congratulations were exchanged. Backs were slapped, and hugs were given to one another. Joy returned as quickly as it had dissipated a few minutes earlier.

Never did I hear anyone mention that sad moment in the life of our infant church. Nor was a disparaging word ever uttered about those who left that night. Not only were we growing up rapidly, we were also growing in spiritual maturity.

But my heart all night long was filled with sadness. I did not sleep much at all. I moped around in the wee hours of the morning as if I had myself lost the vision and as if somehow I had failed the group of 14.

Shortly after noon the following Sunday, I was informed that the entire group of 14 had joined another church *en masse* that very morning. It was time for me to call Dr. Clegg and to give him a precise account of what had happened. He had just heard the news himself. Naturally, I was anxious about the whole ordeal. He put me at ease as he said, "Ray, this is not your doing. New churches always have to go through a pruning or two to produce prime fruit. Get on with the work before you."

Our groundbreaking was delayed until March 1963. Construction began immediately. The architect and contractor assured us the new church building would be ready for occupancy by our first anniversary in July. For the rest of my tenure, there was never any disagreement about where the church was going nor what we had to do to get there. Genuine love for one another, peace, and unanimity prevailed in every decision we made.

The 1963 annual conference year came to a close the last days of May. Southern Hills reported a membership of 110, with 41 families. Average worship attendance stood at 97 and Sunday school at 67. Our Methodist Men, Women's Society of Christian Service, and the Methodist Youth Fellowship were all organized and functioning well.

It had been a remarkable year of achievements. My third year toward my degree was finished. The church had raised my salary to $4,400, an increase of $400. Lavelle was expecting our third child. We had room in the parsonage for an additional resident. I had much for which to be thankful. I was content.

We took a vacation to Tennessee in June, which we all needed. Upon our return, plans were in full swing for occupying the new building the following month. On July 21, 1963—exactly on our first anniversary—we consecrated the building to the glory of God. Then we blessed its use for the people of God who would compose its membership in the future. I preached a "second edition" sermon from the same text I had preached the day Southern Hills was born. The emphasis of the message was different. Apparently no one seemed even to remember. Since then I have been relieved when no one ever seemed to remember my poor sermon by the end of the week. God is merciful to sermonizers as well as receivers, I suppose.

When the consecration service inside was over, the congregation proceeded outside to unveil the bronze plaque at the entrance. I was asked to come to the front and stand with the trustees. As the heavy paper was removed, I saw they had named the building in my honor by designating it the Ray Owen Chapel. Rumor had it earlier that the trustees might name the building as such, but I thought it was idle teasing. I know it was an honor I felt unworthy to receive. I still feel that way. I vowed to myself that never again would I allow such a thing to happen. It turned out to be a wasted vow. In the nearly 40 years following that day, no other church was ever inclined to honor me by naming any new building after me. Sometimes I guess it is somewhat noble to make a promise to yourself that's not likely to come about anyway.

Following consecration of the building, the church organized all standing committees and made plans for further growth. For the first half of my second year, I spent energy and time developing lay leadership, visiting in the community, and working on my undergraduate degree. At Oklahoma City University I served as president of the Methodist student movement. We sponsored a Campus Crusade for Christ and brought Don Moomaw in to lead it. It turned out to be a significant event, although I missed the last days of it. I was under quarantine after being exposed to spinal meningitis from a church member.

November 23, 1963, Dyton was born in the midst of the turmoil following President Kennedy's assassination. Also that fall I had to make up my mind about which seminary I would be attending. From the outset of my ministry, I had expected to attend a one seminary where I would feel comfortable in my theology. Several of us seniors visited another seminary, which I felt was not for me.

But by late fall I really felt led away from my original seminary choice to attend Perkins School of Theology at Southern Methodist University in Dallas. It was among the schools I had ruled out earlier. Now I felt a lingering pull in that direction. I decided to pray about it until the first of the year. By that time I would have to decide.

Everything was going well in the church, although we were not growing as rapidly as I thought we should. My work at the university became more and more demanding and time consuming, which kept me from visiting in the community.

My spring semester was even more demanding. In January 1964 I came to the conclusion that Perkins was the school of theology I needed to attend. I made inquiry and received an invitation to visit the campus to discuss financing my studies. Upon my return I was fully convinced I would be going to Perkins and that God was in my decision.

On April 24, 1964, Eddie Kidd, a successful young businessman, asked the quarterly conference to approve his desire to preach. Eddie not only had become my highly regarded friend;

he also had demonstrated abilities and gifts related to the pastoral ministry. It is little wonder, then, that he was enthusiastically recommended to the district board of ordained ministry for a license to preach. He received his license in time to be appointed to the Aline Church, from which he could commute to Phillips Theological Seminary in Enid for his graduate work.

During this time I talked to my new district superintendent, Dr. Don Schooler, about going to Perkins. He was delighted and said, "Ray, this is the place you must go at all costs. You will benefit immensely from the education you get there. I will put it out at the cabinet meeting that you are going to Perkins. But don't be surprised if at least two superintendents want you in their district so you can go to Phillips Seminary in Enid." He said further, "I will call some superintendents in the Dallas/Fort Worth Area to see if they will have an appointment open for you so you can attend Perkins."

I felt so good about the decision I had made, especially since Dr. Schooler had so eagerly supported it. All of April I waited to hear something from him. I needed to know whether I would be going to Perkins or would have to go to Phillips. I didn't want to go to the latter. Phillips was a fine school, with many able and effective graduates serving leadership positions in Oklahoma. Still, I was convinced my schooling must come at Perkins while I served a student appointment.

Finally I called Dr. Schooler, only to hear disappointing news. There was no church in southern Oklahoma or in the Dallas/Fort Worth Areas for me. It looked like I would have to take an appointment near Phillips Seminary. I really was low and disheartened. I had been so sure Perkins was where God and I both wanted me to go.

A few days later Dr. Rufus Walker, superintendent of the Enid District, called and asked me to come to his office to discuss a possible appointment. I had come to know Dr. Walker when I was at Highland Park Church in Lawton and he was pastor of the prominent Centenary Church downtown. The next day I drove to Enid to talk with him. He began as if to raise my spirits by saying, "Ray, it doesn't make any difference for a man like you where he goes to seminary. You have already demonstrated what you can do."

I thanked him for trying to make me feel better, but it hadn't helped.

Dr. Walker then drove us out to the student appointment. One of my friends had served the church but would be moving at the end of the upcoming annual conference session to a new appointment. I knew too that the church had a reputation for being good to student pastors, so I tried to feel better. Dr. Walker then drove us back to Enid as we talked some more. Upon my departure he said to me, "Ray, I want you in my district."

All the way back home I felt weary. It was already May, and I had little hope of going to Perkins. I kept myself distracted from the thought of Phillips by keeping busy trying to focus on the church's meetings and my community visitations. The congregation's spirits were as down as mine because of my leaving.

The middle of May arrived, so I concluded I would be appointed to the student charge and attend Philips Seminary. Then on the Thursday before our annual conference session convened on Sunday, Dr. Brown Lloyd, superintendent of the Waxahachie District in the Central Texas Conference, called me. He said, "I understand you are looking for a student appointment that will allow you to go to Perkins."

"I sure am," I answered.

"Well," he responded, "I have the best student appointment in the conference. It has just come open. It is in Sardis, about 35 miles from SMU. It's yours if you want it."

Thrilled, I answered, "I'll take it, and I can't tell you how much I appreciate your help."

We hung up, and I praised the Lord out loud. It was indeed the answer to my prayers—though delayed long enough to teach me more about trusting God.

For several minutes I just basked fully in the glow of my fulfilled hope. Then, all of a sudden, I said to myself, "Good grief! I have accepted an appointment without my district superintendent's knowledge of it, or the bishop's! I am in big trouble." My dream come true was fast fading into a nightmare. What would Dr. Walker do in light of his expectations of my going to Phillips? Every way I looked at my blundering situation I saw only bad news.

There was nothing I could do but accept full responsibility and face whatever the consequences were. I called Dr. Schooler and told him in detail what I had done. He laughed. Then let out a "Praise the Lord!" I asked his pardon, but his mind was already on making my decision work. I then reminded him of the conversation I had with Dr. Walker and his expectation of my coming to his district.

"Don't you worry about that," Dr. Schooler replied. "I'll take care of telling him, so don't call him."

I was glad I didn't have to talk with him. Dr. Walker could be unpleasant when he was riled up

Dr. Schooler said, "I'll call Bishop (Angie) Smith to let him know you have an offer in Central Texas for an appointment."

I was almost ecstatic, but not for long. Almost immediately Bishop Smith's secretary called and said, "Wait on the line for Bishop Smith!"

I could just imagine being chewed out, for everybody knew Bishop Smith did not look lightly upon anyone making decisions about appointments unless they were appointments from him. Nervously, I held the phone.

"Brother Owen," said the bishop. Before I could respond he asked, "How long will it take to get from your church to my office?"

"About 25 minutes," I answered.

"Be here in 30 minutes," he replied. "I have cleared my calendar for a talk with you!"

I felt like a volleyball being bounced from dejection to joy to fear and now to uncertainty—all in the course of less than an hour.

I left the church hurriedly and fretted every block of the way to the bishop's office downtown in the Cravens Building. Upon my arrival the secretary told me to have a seat and that the bishop would be with me shortly. I was a bit early, from stretching the speed limit. The secretary's phone buzzed, and I was told to go in. Just as I reached for the doorknob the door opened. There stood Bishop Smith. I stepped through the door and took his outstretched hand. He greeted me and thanked me for being on time. He then asked me to sit down across from the desk.

"Brother Owen," he said, "your district superintendent called to tell me you have an appointment in Sardis."

Expecting the worst, I was about to reply "Yes, sir."

He went on to say, "Good! I know exactly where that church is. You will have a fine ministry there. It is a strong student appointment."

Joy was flowing again.

Most of my hearsay conceptions of Bishop Smith were grossly overstated. I had never met a more gracious, understanding, and encouraging man in my life. None of his supposed gruffness came across his desk. We must have spent half an hour talking. Our conversation ended abruptly with a warning:

"Brother Owen, don't let those Texans get any idea of your staying in Texas. I will not transfer you. Understand?"

I gladly understood, thanked him for taking time to talk with me, and departed a rejuvenated pastor. I would have opportunity again to visit with Bishop Smith before graduating from Perkins.

The next evening Bishop Gerald Kennedy was to preach at St. Luke's Methodist Church downtown. Dr. Mack Stowe invited all the pastors to have dinner with Bishop Kennedy before the worship service. He would bring a greeting and speak to us for a few minutes. As I made my way into the buffet line, I happened to come up right behind Dr. Rufus Walker. When he saw me, he gave me a blistering lecture.

"Young man," he said, "you are making a mistake! Your ministry at Carmen would have put a feather in your hat. I am just sorry you didn't recognize or appreciate all the efforts I made on your behalf."

I felt horrible, thoroughly abused, and embarrassed, as all eyes seemed riveted on the two of us.

I looked up to see Dr. Schooler coming toward us. He had heard and seen everything. He walked up, put his hand on my shoulder, looked Dr. Walker in the face, and said, "Rufus, Ray feels strongly that he should go to Perkins. I'm the one who wanted him to take the appointment you offered. The bishop has visited with Ray and fully agrees that he should go to Perkins. If you have anything else to say about it, talk to the bishop!"

Apparently nothing else was to be said.

The Oklahoma Annual Conference session met a week before the Central Texas Conference session convened. That meant we had to vacate the parsonage at Southern Hills for my successor to move in. That left us without an available parsonage in Texas for more than a week.

Arrangements were made for us to move into a vacant, fully furnished home in Sardis owned by Roscoe and Ima Allen, members of Sardis Church. We were welcome to live there until the present pastor could vacate the parsonage. Their gesture was typical of Sardis hospitality, for which we were most grateful.

Leaving Southern Hills was really difficult for us. In just two years we had seen a church rise out of a field of Johnson grass into a thriving and promising congregation of 208 members. Apportionments were paid in full with worship and Sunday school steadily climbing.

As with Highland Park Church, we left with a few regrets and with strong convictions that we had given a good account of our ministry to the annual conference, to the congregation, and to ourselves. I had finished my bachelor's degree at Oklahoma City University, except for one course. That course I would take during the summer at Southern Methodist University so I could graduate before classes started at Perkins in September.

Our only concern was that Southern Hills Church was land-locked with only five acres of space. That fact alone would inhibit it from ever becoming a large church. Even so, the church has steadily grown into a stable congregation of nearly 1,000 members. Its outreach to the community is significant, as the area has now been fully developed.

7

Journey through Struggle and Seminary

As an expression of his appreciation for our deep and abiding friendship, Eddie Kidd took charge of moving us from Oklahoma City to Sardis Church near Waxahachie, Texas. That was the caliber of generosity Eddie and his wife, Nita, extended to us from the time they became part of Southern Hills Church. His final act on our behalf was a gift we have remembered and been most grateful for.

A few days after his return home, he accepted his first pastoral appointment to Aline Methodist Church in the Enid District. From there he could commute daily to classes at Phillips Seminary. He immediately sold his lucrative and growing business and never looked back.

My years in seminary would come in the middle 1960s, in the milieu of numerous national struggles. The Cuban Missile Crisis had left the country in an intensified state of Cold War. The bomb shelter market was doing a robust business. The race to conquer space would move all efforts ahead with full throttle. The civil-rights movement, along with its strategy of protest marches and sit-ins, would awaken the moral consciences of the nation. Military technicians dispatched to Vietnam would be replaced with trained armies of combat troops to do their duty in a full-scale war. College campuses would become the battlefields for protesting our being in Southeast

Asia, while the nation divided itself. The "God is dead" theology would pay a visit to every seminary in the country to raise critical questions about the value of our faith. The assassinations of Martin Luther King Jr. and Robert Kennedy would so dishearten the nation that it would cry out, "What next?"

Indeed, the mid 1960s would challenge seminary students and demand that they formulate, define, and refine their theological footing for the living of their lives in their ministry years ahead.

Upon our arrival in the Sardis community, we had no trouble locating the church. It was a tall, stately, white-framed building at a prominent crossroads. The long-standing congregation came from open farm country. The parsonage we would be moving into was just across the road from the church.

We first moved into a vacant, furnished home that Ima and Roscoe Allen had made available to us. Everything indeed was furnished, including dishes, silverware, pots, pans, even a television. The Allens and several other members of the church dropped by to greet us. They brought many dishes of prepared food as signs of their welcome. Then they left us to get on with getting temporarily settled. We unpacked only what we would need for a week or so. The rest we left in boxes for moving as soon as the outgoing pastor vacated the parsonage.

It had been a good day of moving. Everything was working out as planned. After dinner we sat down to rest and watch television. As the evening came on, three troubling surprises were waiting for us.

The first surprise arrived as a parade of scorpions moved in for an all-night visit. We were not much informed about such critters. What little we knew about scorpion temperament and behavior came by way of frightful hearsay. In the course of the evening we managed to dispatch several of the uninvited guests. That caused us to stay up half the night, besieged by our fearsome imaginations. The other half of the night we spent checking on our three boys, especially Dyton, who was barely seven months old.

Very early the next morning I called Roscoe about our parade of unwelcome intruders. He chuckled a bit and said, "I hate scorpions, and I'll be out right away to put the fixin' to them." By then I was chuckling at his graphic description for taking care of scorpions. He arrived in a very short time.

He sprinkled generous amounts of powdered poison all around the house foundation and along the wall ends of the front and back porches.

"This will put the fixin' to them in a hurry," he said.

When he had finished, we sat on the back porch and had a delightful conversation about scorpions. I wanted to know more about them to protect my family and me.

Roscoe grinned and said, "We live in Waxahachie now that we are retired. This house is vacant most of the time, but we use it pretty regularly for special occasions and get-togethers. When a house is left empty around these parts, scorpions get to thinking they own it and try to take over. You shouldn't have any more of them showing up."

I was heartened by his confident promise.

I quickly learned Roscoe was quite a storyteller. He could spin a tale with coined terminology and wrap it in hilarity. There on the back porch he told me the story of how he had come to hate scorpions. He and Ima lived on the farm in their early years of marriage. I assumed their home was the farmhouse where we were sitting

As a farmer, Roscoe had to get up early to see after livestock so he could get to the fields for plowing, planting, or harvesting. Every evening Ima made him remove his plow shoes and socks on the back porch so as not to track up her kitchen floor. One morning "everything happened" to make him hate scorpions. In a hurry, he sat down on the cane-bottomed chair on the porch and rammed his bare foot into his shoe. Instantly, he let out a squall because of the thundering pain on top of his foot. His yell so aroused the hound dog that he began barking viciously at what he didn't see, and every dog in the neighborhood joined in. Roscoe jerked off the shoe to see a huge red bump at the base of his big toe.

"It felt like someone was holding a coal of fire to my foot," he said, with such graphic gestures that my own toe felt the pain. At the same time, I was so amused that I was laughing tears.

"Holding my foot," he continued, "I glanced down to see that scorpion sitting there pleased and proud on the tongue of my shoe as if to mock me. About that time, Ima came out the back door and asked, 'Roscoe, what in the world is the matter with you? Your screeching and hollering will wake up the dead and bring neighbors over here to see what's wrong!'"

Roscoe answered her, "See that scorpion strutting his stuff on the tongue of my shoe? That's what's the matter!"

"Well, for heaven's sake," Ima said, "kill it, and stop all this racket!"

As Ima turned to go into the house, Roscoe said to her, "I'm going to kill it, all right! Get me my shotgun!"

By that time I was laughing so hard I was almost glad those scorpions had dropped in on us. Catching my breath, I asked, "Roscoe, you really didn't shoot that scorpion with a shotgun, did you?"

Quickly, he replied, "I most certainly did! I got my 12-gauge shotgun, sat down in the chair again, aimed the gun right between his bugged eyes and fired!"

Hurting from laughter, I asked him teasingly, "Did you kill the scorpion?"

With a deadpan face he said, "I couldn't prove it, but a thousand pieces of my shoe scattered all over the back yard. If buckshot didn't kill him, any piece of my shoe he was riding meant 'death on arrival' for him when it hit the ground!"

I was reluctant to ask what Ima did when she heard the shotgun blast.

There on the back porch of our temporary quarters, I knew our time at Sardis Church would be an interesting and wonderful experience. Since Lavelle grew up in a farm family and I was familiar with farm work, we both felt at home with this small congregation with a heart as big as some of the tall tales told to us.

Our second surprise came the next day when we learned that our parsonage water supply would have to be hauled in 1,000 gallons at a time and emptied into a concrete cistern. From there it would be pumped into the house. Not only that, each load of water would cost us $7. With a seven-month-old baby, two small sons, and the two of us, we knew the cost of our water supply would be prohibitive. Indeed, our second surprise gave us grave concern.

It didn't help when we learned that a new rural water system was already being constructed for every home in Sardis and the outlying areas. What flimsy optimism we could muster was quickly squelched when we heard that the system would not be up and running for several months.

Even in light of all that, we didn't regret coming to Sardis. In so many instances before we got there, we had come through seemingly insurmountable obstacles. We believed, therefore, that somehow we would get through this one as well.

A few days later I checked in with Dr. Brown Lloyd, my district superintendent. He welcomed us and said he was pleased we were in his district. He asked whether we needed anything. Reluctantly I mentioned the water situation. Immediately I felt his rising displeasure.

"What?" he asked. "You mean the church is expecting you to pay for water to be hauled in a thousand gallons at a time and at $7 a load? You can't afford that, and you shouldn't have to pay for it! Besides, they were supposed to have dug a deep well for the parsonage!"

Suddenly I felt myself betwixt two emotions. One was my appreciation for his expressed care for us. The other was my regret for not having first talked to the leaders of the church about our predicament.

Dr. Lloyd instructed me to arrange a meeting for the following Sunday evening and said that he would be there to preside.

"You don't need to carry the ball in this matter," he said. "Just tell them I want to meet with them about your coming and to deal with a few matters."

I was most grateful that he had taken the burden from my shoulders regarding the water problem.

The meeting was held in a fine manner. The leaders realized what a burden the water bill would be for five occupants moving in, one of whom was a baby in diapers, compared to the two adult occupants moving out. They said the church would pay the bill without regard to cost. We were greatly pleased and grateful for their full support. Their spirit made us want to use only as much water as was needed.

The first two surprises were dealt with and resolved very

quickly. The third surprise, however, would not be so easily addressed. At the end of our first two weeks, the treasurer handed me my first salary check. He was a wonderful and dedicated gentleman, precise and meticulous. He explained that I would be paid twice a month. I thanked him for his explanation and put the check in my pocket. Later I was stunned to discover that the Sardis salary was more than 20 percent less than what we were receiving at Southern Hills. When Dr. Lloyd called me to offer the Sardis Church, neither of us thought to bring up the matter of salary. The decrease, plus the added expense of travel to and from Dallas four days a week, was bound to put us in an enormous financial strain once seminary classes got under way. Since no mention of salary had been raised in the conversation with Dr. Lloyd, the church had assumed that all of us were in agreement.

In my mind, it would have been unfair to bring up the matter for the official board's consideration. The budget had already been set for the conference year. We would take the salary as set and never mention it to anyone. Besides, I didn't believe the salary reduction of Sardis Church would have dulled my eagerness and desire to come. I never doubted that Sardis Church was indeed where God wanted us to be.

If expenses became critical in the fall, Lavelle would look for a job to keep us afloat, if only barely. Neither of us liked the idea of her working, since the boys needed their mother at home—especially Dyton. If all the spouses of Methodist student pastors were ever recognized for self sacrifice, most surely Lavelle would stand among those at the head of the line.

The 80-mile round trip to Perkins became easier as I learned new shortcuts. The semester went by quickly. I made respectable grades and enjoyed the work on campus. At the same time, the church was progressing, with an increase in membership and attendance in worship and Sunday school. A good spirit in the congregation prevailed as we began to talk about our need to expand the facilities of Sardis Church.

Our personal financial prospects for spring of 1965, however, looked tentative to say the least. Lavelle and I both spent regular time in prayer about our plaguing financial circumstances. The struggle seemed endless. Somehow we would always have enough, but not a dollar too much or a day too soon. Many times on my way to seminary I would remind myself that "enough" is all God ever promised to furnish us. It was good theology but not so good for encouraging me for better days.

With sporadic tidbits of income from unexpected sources and an agreement with a major oil company to pay my gasoline bill on the installment plan, we were barely able to keep our heads above water—but never in sight of a life preserver.

In the spring of 1965, my class work was more enjoyable. I joined the Perkins Choir. The director placed me between two excellent tenor voices to offset my unworthiness. The church, too, was on the upswing. Then a glorious announcement was sent to all Sardis residents—the new rural water system would open its valves within a week! What a blessing to see clean, clear water from the deep Trinity Sands flowing through every spigot in the house. The parched flowers raised their wilted heads in praise. Especially was it good to have a normal supply of water for a bath. It was an event fully celebrated by the entire community

In May 1965 a member of the Sardis congregation, Grady Lynn "Corky" Wadsworth, was recommended and approved for a license to preach. He was to receive his license later. Since he was still in college, he was in no hurry to take an appointment. We moved back to Oklahoma the following year. Corky's family moved close to Fort Worth at about the same time. Later we would receive word that Corky had died suddenly from a heart-related ailment. We were shocked and saddened to hear the news.

The conference year came to a close in June 1965. We had much for which to be thankful. My grades were still respectable. The church was still growing. Participation was also up, including for our "Lord's Acre Day"! It was designed to raise additional funds for the church's outreach and ministry. The church raised my salary $300 a year. It was a big help but would not stave off future financial exigency.

Early that summer the leaders of the church realized the time was overdue for a much-needed expansion of the facilities. We needed space for a kitchen, fellowship hall, a second entry with a foyer, two restrooms, a pastor's study, and some sanctuary renovations. All of the church's dinners had to take place in the old schoolhouse that had been given to the Sardis area as the community center.

It was usually difficult to reserve time at the schoolhouse because other groups needed it, too. We especially wanted the two restrooms because the outdoor facility had long since passed acceptable serviceability. Our parsonage bathroom served for emergency use, and that became increasingly inconvenient, to say the least. A pastor's study also was urgently needed.

A few miles east of Sardis Church was a similar community named Boyce. The Boyce Methodist Church and the Sardis Church were identical, designed by the same architect and built about the same time. The Boyce Church, which had closed several years earlier, had beautiful stained glass windows. There was enough lumber in the structure for the needed space at Sardis. The stained glass windows could be installed into Sardis' frames with very few adjustments.

I went to see Dr. Lloyd to inquire if we might have the building for our expansion. I explained what we wanted to do at Sardis and that we would disassemble the Boyce building, move the lumber to Sardis, and clean up the site.

"Ray, that's a splendid idea," Dr. Lloyd responded. "I'm sure the district trustees will agree. The property would be easier to sell with no building on it."

I went back and reported what the superintendent had said. Everyone in Sardis seemed excited. We got the building.

In honor of the Boyce Church's life and faithfulness in the past, we decided to name the new fellowship hall "Boyce Hall." We would remove the rectangular plates memorializing Boyce "saints" from the stained-glass windows in the old church building and install brass plates on the sill of each window in the new fellowship hall showing the Boyce member's name. Sardis families wishing to memorialize former members of Sardis would install new stained glass plates. Proceeds would help pay for the expansion project. The Boyce community was thrilled by our decision and very appreciative.

The entire congregation joined in disassembling the Boyce

structure. Men high on the roof worked downward. Piece by piece, women pulled nails out of boards and sawed off rough ends. Youths placed the cleaned lumber into assorted stacks according to length and size. Others gathered up debris into small piles and burned them. At last, the Boyce building became several stacks of lumber ready to be hauled to Sardis Church.

Because of the significant savings from using the Boyce lumber, the entire project came to a bit more than $12,000, including remodeling and the foyer entrance. The service of consecration was set for several months later.

A few days before our family went on a well-deserved vacation with our folks in Tennessee, a church cleanup day was declared in preparation for the construction to begin. As we were working in the yard, one of the men of the church—a joker who'd gotten the best of me before—sidled up to me and asked a question.

"Preacher, what are we to do with the outhouse behind the church now that we will have restrooms?" he asked. "It's been here since the early '30s."

Thinking he was setting me up for another joke, I replied with a straight face, "Since it has served for so many years, you might want to restore it and put a plaque on it so that when the bishop and district superintendent come to consecrate the new building, we will include it as a part of the consecration ritual."

He looked at me rather puzzled, scratched his head, and sauntered away saying, "OK, if you say so."

I grinned and thought, "For once I got him before he got me!"

When we returned from vacation the outhouse was gone. The ground around its location was well groomed with a fine crop of grass growing in its place. I never heard how it had disappeared, nor did anyone ever explain to me what happened. I guess we all felt no further comments were necessary.

Early the following year Bishop Kenneth Pope and Dr. Lloyd led our service of consecration and congratulated the congregation for its "visionary and innovative achievement." Several former members of Boyce Methodist Church attended the celebration. One of them said to me, "Our beloved Boyce Church lives on, even if it's a few miles west at Sardis." Many were moved deeply by her words.

In late summer of 1965, I was invited to be a part of an evangelistic effort in Boston and the New England area. The invitation had come from the General Board of Evangelism. It was quite an honor for me to be among those participating and to preach at several churches in the area. Especially was I grateful to sit under the tutelage of Harry Denman for two weeks. Later, in 1984, I thought of him when I received the Harry Denman Award for Evangelism at the Oklahoma Annual Conference session.

By the time the fall semester of 1965 got under way, the family was again stretched to the limit financially. Without Lavelle knowing it, I wrote to my brother P.J. He was a businessman. I simply shared with him our situation and asked him to help me out with a small loan. I advised him I would not be able to pay interest and that I didn't know exactly when I would be able to repay him. Any loan he ventured to make certainly would not qualify as a class AAA risk category.

I really hadn't wanted to ask such a favor from him. P.J. was an honest but shrewd businessman. As such, he was very careful about risking his resources. That was entirely sensible. I was not sure I would have made myself a loan under such circumstances. At the end of the letter, I asked him to send his response to the church's post office box number rather than to our home address.

About two weeks later I went to the post office on my way home from errands. P.J. had responded with a small loan. It came at a critical time. A strange thing followed. As I arrived home, Lavelle asked if I had gone by the post office to check for mail. She went on to say, "Last night I dreamed P.J. had sent us some money." I handed her the letter.

Could it have been a coincidence that the letter arrived the day following her dream? As far as we were concerned, it had not been happenstance. We both had been praying, so we gave thanks to God for providential care of us, once again in a critical time of need. By this time we were learning to live by the passage in Matthew 6:25-34—the text from which I preached my very first sermon. No wonder that text became a favorite upon which I have stood through many later difficulties.

The fall semester of my second year got under way. I was on my way to seminary and feeling much better after receiving P.J.'s letter. Then, just a few miles up the road, came a crisis from which I feared we would not recover. My faithful 1950 Chevrolet coupe's motor threw a rod and blew apart. I coasted to a stop at the side of the highway and broke down in despair.

"I'll just have to drop out of seminary," I said to myself. "We can't go any further."

Never in my entire life had I been so despondent and discouraged.

I got the car towed to a garage in Waxahachie and was informed that it was permanently dead. All day long I fretted, and all night I worried about what I could do the next day. All I could think of was seeing if our bank would make a loan to me for another car. I had no collateral and no one I wanted to ask to go on my note. I had to find a used car in good shape for little money—"not much to ask," I said to myself.

How it happened, I do not know. But I got a phone call from an elderly woman the next day. Her husband had died a few years before. They had bought a new Pontiac that had been in little use since her husband's death. She had heard about a young preacher in seminary whose car was beyond repair. She wanted to know if I might want to buy the Pontiac, which had only 40,000 miles on it. I told her my story and said that I would like very much to have it, but I doubted I could get a loan for what it was worth.

"Do you think you could give me $350 for it?" she then asked. "I would like to help you get through school."

I was astonished, and so very grateful for her kindness. I went to the bank as fast as I could get there and explained my need to borrow the money so I could continue in seminary.

To my surprise, the loan officer said, "Brother Owen, you are one of our pastors in the area. I think this bank can lend you the $350 without a second signature."

I deposited the money and bought the car. As I suspected, it was in excellent shape. I was convinced anew that God's providential care had to be involved in the whole experience for it to come out so well.

I registered the car in my name and went by my service station for gasoline. I would be able to get to school in time for my two afternoon classes. I bought a soft drink and peanuts, then went out to fill the tank. I drove to the traffic light at the end of the block. While waiting for the light to change, I realized I had not paid for the gasoline. I drove around the block to find the owner grinning.

"I knew you would think of it somewhere between here and Dallas," he said. "So I decided not to send the cops after you."

We had a good laugh at my oversight.

Back at the traffic light, I held my right foot firmly on the brake. I took a few peanuts in one hand and lifted the soft drink toward my mouth with the other. Suddenly, the front seat was literally knocked out from under me—the car had been rear-ended. Soda cascaded onto my head and dripped off my face. I was sure it was blood. My feet and legs were pinned under the dashboard.

Finally I got the door opened and got out of the car, splotched with cola. I walked back to find an elderly man in his car, bleeding a bit and mumbling incoherently. Help arrived from all directions. An ambulance rushed the other driver to a Dallas hospital. We learned that he had had a stroke and had driven across a viaduct and through a traffic light on the way to hitting my car at the end of the block.

When I had recovered a bit, I told the police officer what had happened, and witnesses confirmed my statement. My newly purchased (with borrowed money) Pontiac was "totaled." The police advised me later that the driver of the other car had no insurance. I had collision insurance and liability insurance but none on an "uninsured motorist."

There I stood, soaked with soda pop, $350 in debt for a car I had owned for an hour, now made carless by a driver who carried no insurance. I was now worse off than when my Chevrolet had self-destructed. I almost wished I had not gone back for honesty's sake to pay for the gasoline. This time I had reached the end of the rope. There was no option left.

The next day I hitched a ride to seminary with a classmate who drove out of his way to pick me up. I went that day simply to inform the seminary I would have to drop out of school indefinitely. I thought that when the Chevrolet had died, I was at the bottom of the pit. This time I felt as if I was miring in the muck below the bottom.

I went to see Dr. Lamar Cooper, who was in charge of student affairs. I told him my story and my double-whammy predicament. The only thing I could do was to drop out.

"You will do no such thing," he responded. "You go on to your classes. We are not going to let you drop out. You can start looking for another used car when you get home. We'll find the money for it."

It seemed every time I was at my rope's end and losing my grip that someone somehow was there to lift my spirits. Even if I had not been a person of faith in God by then, I would have been compelled to believe.

I returned home. Late that afternoon, before I had time to look for a car, I received word from the owner of a private auto shop that the Pontiac could be repaired. An entire rear end section of a same model Pontiac had been located in a nearby junkyard. The man had heard of my accident from a Sardis Church member.

It was uncanny when the man said to me, "Preacher, I have looked at your car. It's been hurt, but its injury is not fatal. I can fix it for $350."

At that moment, I felt as if the whole community had been summoned to come to my assistance. Dr. Cooper was delighted to hear the news.

The next day at school I received a check for more than enough for the costs of repairs. The balance I used to pay down the bank note. We had many reasons to give thanks to many people, the seminary, Sardis Church, and most of all God.

Several days later I visited the other driver in a Dallas hospital. He was improving but was unable to speak. His wife spoke for him. Weeping, she told me how sorry she and her husband were for all the trouble he had caused me. She said they would try to find the money somewhere to pay for the damages to my car, since they had no insurance. It was obvious they were a couple advanced in years and of very little means.

The police had notified them that her husband's license

would be suspended unless I signed a waiver relieving them of damages. She held no license because of a disability. At that moment I was reminded of the parable of the master who forgave a man's huge debt when the man could not pay it immediately. That same man in turn went out and had a man who owed a small debt thrown into jail until the money was paid. Upon hearing of the first man's action, the master demanded full payment of the original debt because of the man's hardness of heart.

That parable came so clearly to my mind at that moment. How could I not dismiss the older couple's cost of damages to my car when I had just received more than enough for my car's damages? I took the waiver from the woman's trembling hand and signed it. Those two people were overcome emotionally. I have never regretted it, even though a classmate said I had not been responsible.

"You freed the man to go out and hit someone else's car, which might cause serious injury," he said.

The next time I visited, the woman told me her husband would recover somewhat, but he would never be able to drive again. Our prayer this final time together was a mixture of joy and sadness over the continuing struggle for the two of them.

That same fall of 1965 I was invited to preach two revivals for student pastors. It was a good feeling to be accepted sufficiently by classmates to have me preach for them. Both revivals produced new disciples and a few reclaimed souls. Their invitation to me was only indicative of the way an "outsider" was treated by the Central Texas Conference. Though "on loan," as Bishop Smith had put it, I was accorded the same courtesy and assistance as any Central Texas student—including a $50 a semester book allowance. I felt fortunate to serve in that conference.

The fall semester ended. Despite all my unforeseen hardships, it had been a fruitful and enjoyable time. Christmas came, and the church gave us an old fashioned "pounding" of food of all sorts. It was a huge help with our grocery bill.

The spring semester of 1966 got off to a good start. I had a dependable car, and our financial situation stabilized. Lavelle thought it the right thing to do to accept a job in a variety store in Waxahachie. The owner was a fine churchgoing gentleman.

The only drawback was finding someone to take care of Dyton, who was at the time more than 2 years old.

Lavelle asked Margaret Lou Ralston if she could keep Dyton during working hours. Margaret Lou jumped at the chance. She and Bill were both retired and would be glad to keep Dyton—"without charge." Lavelle wouldn't have it, so they settled on an amount barely above nothing.

My second year in seminary would prove to be the most challenging of the three. It was the "year of systematic theology" for both semesters. Obviously, it was the most crucial course for all of us students. Its purpose was to see that all students developed their individual theological understandings into a credo as they were exposed to the minds of numerous theologians and theological premises. The class met twice each week and was taught by three prominent theologians—Albert Outler, John Deschner, and Schubert Ogden. In addition, we were required to read and absorb the premises of world-known theologians. Like most students, I considered it the most demanding and sometimes frustrating course. Still, it was basic to our future ministry.

Because of my military background I was older than most of my classmates. Consequently, I had established a few pivotal "immutable convictions." I did not want anyone to challenge me. On a given day of class, Ogden would lecture with such compelling intellect that I would declare my allegiance to his position. At the next class session John Deschner would unravel Ogden's point of view with his own viewpoint. Outler would affirm both and then proceed to establish the real truth according to *his* position. Each followed again on the heels of the other two until I wasn't sure what I believed or which one was on the true course. To say I was frustrated is an understatement, especially when Bart, Brunner, the Niebuhr brothers, and many other giants of theology entered the fray with additional viewpoints. The more I attended the classes and lectures, the more defensive I became about my own wispy, if not warped, theological concepts and convictions.

I felt as if all those theological minds were in a conspiracy to tear down all my well-established theological "understandings." It took only about half of the fall semester for my tiny brain to be overloaded and my emotions to need some relief before I became an agnostic or a cynic—or both. I had to talk to somebody about the way I was feeling. Too many refined theological minds were pouring forth upon us students for me to appreciate what was taking place in my own mind. Early on, as I considered which seminary I would attend, a friend had said, "Perkins will tear up everything you believe if you go there!" I came anyway, and now I was measuring the value of his words.

Since I felt John Deschner the most approachable, I asked if I could visit with him about a problem I was having.

"Sure, Ray," he replied, "why don't you come by after class, and we will talk."

In time I learned that Ogden and Outler would have been equally available and eager to meet with me.

After class I went to Dr. Deschner's office. He was there waiting for me. I unloaded all my frustrations and discomfort. Deschner responded with occasional nods of seeming understanding.

Finally I said, "Dr. Deschner, I have come to the place that I'm not going to bother myself with what all these theologians think. Their theology is theirs. I have to find where I am in my beliefs. I guess I would say I don't care what all the theological minds are saying about their views of truth. It's what I have to go to bed with at night that I am concerned about."

I had said everything I had wanted to say—and more to boot.

He smiled, got out of his chair, came around the desk, took my hand and said so approvingly, "Now, Ray, you are on your way. It is not my theology you will hammer out or that of any other theologian. You are now free to hear our positions and to glean from all the minds to which you are exposed. In the end, however, it is what you have to live with and apply that matters in your ministry."

What a sensible revelation he helped me to see. My basic problem had been my own fear to claim my own theology, refine it, and apply it for as long as I lived.

At the beginning of my seminary work, I had been told, "Every theological student will eventually come face to face with the value of his theological premises. After that, everything will fall into place." I had come face to face with mine. I was liberated to hear counter theological positions and to appreciate all of them in the total swim of theology. From the halfway point in my studies, seminary became an exciting adventure in faith development and growth. I came to know not only *what* I believed but also *why* I believed it. In short, I learned what the real purpose of seminary training was all about for a life in ministry.

During the spring semester of 1966, Bishop Angie Smith scheduled meetings at Perkins with each student from Oklahoma. He set aside about half an hour for each of us. My time with him was near the end of the list. He greeted me and took my hand.

"Brother Owen, I'm glad to see you!" he said.

I felt the same warmth from him that I had in his office talking about the Sardis appointment two years earlier.

We talked about several of his agenda items. The end of the half hour was drawing near when he asked, "How is everything going for you?" I shared truthfully about our financial struggle, made worse by the unexpected decrease in salary upon my arrival. I also relayed to him some of our achievements at Sardis Church. He was already aware of some of them.

In closing he said to me rather gruffly, "Well, if these Texans don't know how to take care of a good pastor, I'll just bring you back to Oklahoma. You can complete your senior year's work commuting back and forth!"

On the one hand, I was deeply grateful. On the other hand, I was a bit anxious that the people would hear I left because of low salary support. They still did not know the difficulties we had wrestled with because of the shortfall. Had they known, I am sure they would have raised my salary more for our second year.

The spring of 1966 was especially enjoyable for the family. Lavelle's salary was supplementing our income, bringing financial survival. The bank note for the car had been paid off. I was enjoying seminary work at Perkins. Dana and Darryl especially were enjoying country life.

A shallow creek bed down the hill from our house furnished them many hours of boyish fun and adventures. There was just enough water in the creek for them to splash and play. The banks of the creek provided treasure troves of oddly shaped rocks, insects, and animal life. They dug out cold, slow moving snakes of different sorts in the winter, none of which was poisonous. One day they were delighted to bring a few to the side porch of the parsonage. From there they called their mother to come and see their display. Only once did they show off their findings from the creek banks. Lavelle had no desire to see the different specimens and gave them strict orders not to dig out any more snakes because "where nonpoisonous snakes were to be found would be poisonous ones as well."

Our boys' rural living was fully exploited and enjoyed for the two years we were in Sardis. Spring was fast moving toward May, and the completion of my second year at both the church and seminary. We had come to appreciate more and more the people of Sardis Church. We had not heard anything else about our possible return to Oklahoma, so we assumed we would be staying for a third year. That would have been fine with us.

A few days before the Oklahoma Annual Conference session convened, Dr. Lloyd Peters, superintendent of the McAllister District, called me.

"Ray," he said, "Bishop Smith wants you back in Oklahoma. I am the lucky one to have an appointment for you so you can commute to Perkins for your senior year."

I told him I would be happy to go back a year early.

"Your appointment is the Antlers Church in southeastern Oklahoma," he said. "I'm really glad you will be in this district. I'll fill in Bishop Smith about our conversation!"

I had not known Dr. Peters or his wife, Maxine. Soon, however, our whole family would come to love them for their genuine care toward us. Especially would I come to appreciate Lloyd for his integrity, strong leadership, and strong interest in my ministry.

At the end of May, we packed our belongings in yet another U-Haul trailer and headed for Antlers—wherever that was. The same joy and sense of having given a good account of our ministry accompanied us. We looked back upon our appointment at Sardis as among "rural royalty." The members had been truly loving toward us and loved by us.

Another page in our ministry was turning. We were filled with gratitude to God. We were thankful for the people at Sardis whom we had just served and for the people of Antlers whom we were about to serve.

8

Journey among Deer and Dear People

Before we departed Sardis Church, we received word from the outgoing pastor at Antlers that the parsonage would be clean and ready for our occupancy. It was welcome news.

We headed out early the next morning for our new appointment. The trip was uneventful. Our midafternoon arrival at the Antlers parsonage and subsequent move-in was not. Apparently, the former pastor held a vastly different understanding from us about the meaning of "clean."

We were more than a bit aggravated at the parsonage's state of cleanliness—especially after having been assured it would indeed be ready for us to move into immediately. We certainly had left the Sardis parsonage spotless. Now we had another one to clean. The situation heaped upon us a great deal of stress. For one thing, the U-Haul vehicle had to be turned in before 5 p.m. at Hugo, some 20 miles away, to avoid a sizable penalty that I certainly could not afford. At the same time, we could not unload the U-Haul until the house was thoroughly cleaned. Lavelle and I and our three small boys couldn't do it without some help.

I called the pastor-parish relations committee chairman, explained our circumstances, and asked if he could enlist some members to help us clean the parsonage. He was upset and embarrassed at the state of the parsonage. Within a few minutes, two people were there to help with the cleaning.

We unloaded the U-Haul onto the front lawn, and I rushed off to turn it in, barely before the deadline. Hurriedly I returned to the parsonage. We got it cleaned and our belongings into the house before nightfall. By the evening of our first day, we surmised that our ministry at Antlers was bound to be challenging, interesting, fruitful, and frequently humorous.

Located in southeastern Oklahoma, Antlers is the county seat and largest town in Pushmataha County. At the time of our arrival, Antlers' population was about 2,000. Nineteen churches were within the city limits. The Methodist, Baptist, and Presbyterian were the three largest.

Our first worship service the following Sunday morning went well. We were introduced and welcomed "with joy" by Lee Clymer, the lay leader. Very few seats were vacant in the sanctuary. Even the front pews were well occupied. The large crowd was enough to inspire any pastor. Yet I was experienced enough to downsize the significance of the attendance. It was not unusual for a larger-than-average crowd to show up on the first Sunday with a new pastor. Even so, the faces of so many helped me preach with freedom and forcefulness from Psalm 51.

Following the worship service, we were received warmly by individual members and visitors. Near the end of the line came one of the church leaders. Stuart and his family were all long-time members of First Church. His father had owned a drugstore that was passed on to Stuart after his father retired. Stuart was as frank in his speaking as he was loyal to the church. As he greeted me, he said bluntly, "Well, preacher, you won't last long around here if you keep preaching sermons like that one today!"

I was mystified. In those brief seconds of silence, I said to myself, "Good grief! I've been here only one Sunday, and already he is warning me I will be gone in a little while! What in the world did I say in my sermon to evoke such a comment?"

Stuart must have read my quizzical look, but without smiling he went on to say, "You are too good a preacher for our little church!"

I felt as if I had just received a backhanded compliment.

That evening at our first official board meeting, Stuart rose to his feet and moved that the church raise my salary $600 to help with my upcoming travel expenses during my senior year at seminary. The motion was approved unanimously and without debate. I was utterly surprised and most grateful for the church's expression and care for my family and me. Only then did I conclude Stuart's words to me that morning had indeed been a high compliment.

That fall I conducted the funeral of Stuart's wife, who had lost her battle with cancer. Shortly before I left for my next appointment, I had the pleasure of uniting Stuart and his new wife in marriage.

Our family has always managed to get settled quickly in new parsonages. Monday morning I made my way to the church to unpack my books and put my small study in order. Later that morning I walked to the post office to pick up the mail. The Oklahoma Indian Missionary Conference session was to convene in Antlers that afternoon, so I was in somewhat of a hurry. I planned on going to the conference session to bring greetings from First Church. As I neared the post office, a fellow pastor in the Oklahoma Conference turned his car sharply to the curb just in front of me. I was glad to see him, although I didn't know him very well. He too had just been appointed to another church a few miles away.

Abruptly, he asked me, "What's so great about you, Ray, that you get to come to Antlers and I get appointed to a smaller church with less salary?"

I thought he was teasing, so I chuckled a bit.

"I've been an elder in full connection for five years," he continued, "and you won't be ordained elder in full connection until next year!"

It must have been as terrible a moment for him as it had become for me. It was my turn to say something, so I mumbled to him that I did not know why he had been appointed to his position any more than I knew why I was appointed to mine. With that he drove off, and I sauntered sadly into the post office. My first workday at the church certainly was not getting off to a sterling start. To this day I do not know whether he was kidding. Neither of us ever again mentioned that incident to one another.

Some 11 years later I would be appointed superintendent of the district where he was serving. His work in the district was excellent. He had a brilliant mind along with many talents and skills for an effective ministry. Many times I have mentioned his name as one of the most creative and gifted pastors I had ever known when it came to bringing a message to the children in children's church.

I threw myself into sorting out priorities for the fall, in addition to attending seminary two days a week. I also spent a lot of time visiting in the community and meeting the members of the church. In those few weeks I learned a lot about Antlers and its history.

Legend had it that Antlers was so named because deer would come inside the city limits as if they knew crack-shot hunters would come to the area in droves when the deer season opened. I don't know to what degree such a legend was accurate, but it was relayed to every visitor and newcomer.

I never saw large numbers of deer in town. I did notice increased numbers of deer scattered about the vicinity when gunshots echoed during hunting season. Later that fall I accepted the invitation of two members of the church to go with them on my first deer hunt.

One of the men warned me to dress warmly because we would be going through snow to get to our hunting area. I was somewhat puzzled. I had already heard Pushmataha County had some high hills in its northeast sector, but I hadn't thought the hills were so high as to harbor snow. But I said OK. The next morning I dragged myself out of bed long before dawn so we could be in our different "stands" by daybreak. A few miles before reaching our destination, we drove through the tiny community of Snow. I was shown the sign as my two hosts laughed and enjoyed initiating another greenhorn newcomer.

Each day for three days I perched among the leaves of different trees, shivering with creeping cold in the thick woods of Pushmataha County. Patiently and silently I waited to take my quarry. I never saw even one deer. Neither did my two hosts. Good naturedly, they spread it all over town that I had brought them bad luck.

The day following the close of deer season, I was driving to a meeting and came abruptly upon a fine buck standing in state across the middle line of the road. It was just outside the city limits. I had to come to a complete stop and honk the horn before the buck sidled off casually into the roadside bushes. He seemed to be mocking me now that the season was over. I took the encounter as an omen of my fortunes in future hunting trips. I never went hunting again and never desired to do so.

Antlers had many qualities for which it could be proud. The people were friendly, open to a point, and, for the most part, easily laughed at themselves. Those traits alone had a way of endearing themselves to newcomers. Like every community, the citizens possessed a few quirks. On the whole, they seemed to know who they were and to feel good about themselves.

Two restaurants on opposite ends of the same street downtown served as centers for daily fellowship, sharing of common concerns, and gossiping. The week following my arrival I stopped by one of them at midmorning for a cup of coffee. It was the regular time for gathering. Sitting on counter stools and around tables were several church members. It was a typical coffee klatch with talking, teasing, and befogging cigarette smoke.

I was introduced as the new Methodist pastor. I joined the clatter by ordering a cup of coffee. On the wall across from the counter a sign read, "All the coffee you can drink for 10 cents." In the course of conversation, I ordered another cup of coffee.

Having poured it, the waiter said, "That will be another dime."

A hush fell over the room, and all eyes fell upon me.

I feigned an objection, saying, "The sign says 'all the coffee you can drink for 10 cents.'"

Without budging or blinking, the waiter said, "Now, you see, that's the way it is with newcomers. They don't understand our language around here. The sign is perfectly clear; one cup of coffee is all you can drink for 10 cents."

Everybody enjoyed the laugh on me. I had been approved for induction into the group.

As I handed the waiter a dime, someone called out to me, "Preacher, Ol' Joe (not his real name) owns this place and is one of your 'part-time' members of the Methodist Church. He is even less than that as a contributor, so don't expect him to be buying you a second cup of coffee!"

This time the roar of laughter was on Ol' Joe, not me.

In time I would find the information about Ol' Joe to be true on all counts. As I walked back to the church, I grinned and mused to myself that our journey in Antlers was bound to be interesting, fruitful, and frequently a lot of fun.

I really came to appreciate how the folks in Antlers could "whomp up" reasons to laugh at themselves. While having a midmorning cup of coffee at the other restaurant a few days later, I asked what I thought was a serious and pertinent question: "What are the major natural resources in the surrounding area?"

Instantly, one of the men answered, "Pine trees, ticks, and chiggers!"

I would soon learn he too had told the truth on all counts.

There were many more resources, however, in "Push" County than those three. Tourists came each year in large numbers to view the fall foliage. Besides hunting, there was good fishing. Indian lore also brought many to the area. Cattle ranged over the hills and valleys. There were several large ranches. Trees other than pine were plentiful and fed the needs of a large paper mill a few miles east. In the end, however, the people were the most valuable resource of all.

Antlers residents were known for their ability to endure, make the most of hardship, and extend compassion to those in the community needing help. One example imprinted permanently upon Antlers memories came the day President Franklin Roosevelt died in April 1945. On that day, Antlers was the target of a horrible tornado that struck downtown. In the aftermath, 87 people were dead. Many more were seriously injured or maimed for life.

The Methodist Church stacked its pews and turned its sanctuary into a temporary aid station and its rooms into a morgue. My arrival as pastor came some 21 years later. Even after two decades, the Methodist congregation was much appreciated for providing ministry and care in a time of great grief for the entire community.

Like many small towns, Antlers had its share of interesting personalities, whose foibles served to entertain as well as enrich the entire community. Two such persons were in our church. Curtis was one. For many years he had operated a barbershop downtown. All the merchants and most of the citizens knew him. Curtis took pleasure in occasional mischief. Next door to his shop was a grocery store. Come break time, he frequently would go next door to get a soft drink and a snack. Occasionally, something would compel him to stir things up a bit. While some shopper was reading information on a package or can or was distracted by conversation, Curtis would amble by and put a can of snuff or some other item he had taken off a shelf into the shopper's food cart. At the checkout counter the victim would be baffled, first wondering if he or she had someone else's basket. Next the shopper would wonder where all those strange items had come from. The cashiers could generally straighten things out.

On one such occasion, a customer got pretty upset when the cashier came up with a bottle of lamp oil. The shopper calmed down when the cashier figured out that Curtis had just been in the store.

On my first visit to Curtis' shop for a haircut, we began a conversation about how long he had been barbering and about some of the town's history.

As his pastor, I asked. "Where do you live, Curtis?"

There was no answer. I thought he had not heard me, so I asked again.

"I'm trying to think!" he replied. "I've lived in the same house for most of my life. I've always picked up my mail at the post office. Everybody but you knows where I live, but I don't know what street it's on or what number is on the house."

I thought it quite amusing that a businessman could occupy a home for decades and know where he lived but not its location. Curtis and I enjoyed many delightful conversations. Assuredly, he was one of the many gems among Antlers' treasury of peerless personalities.

Cecil was another jewel. He lived two doors down from the

parsonage. Unlike Curtis the barber, who didn't know where he lived, Cecil not only knew where his home was but also its full address. He knew the precise location of most people in the entire county. He was a peddler (now known as "distributor") of Raleigh Products—consisting of hundreds of small but useful household items.

Cecil's wife was the accomplished pianist for the church. Their daughter was a linguist who was pursuing a career with the government's diplomatic corps as an interpreter.

Cecil was a homegrown philosopher. He possessed amazing insights and perceptions about life. He seemed always to be upbeat regarding the general affairs of daily living. Every week or so he would drop by the office at the church for a chat. On most every visit I would ask him, "Well, Cecil, have you sold a million dollars worth of Raleigh Products so far this week?"

"Not yet," he would always reply, "but I'm working on it!" Then he would say, "Statistics show us that I will make at least one sale out of three tries. Every time I get a turndown, I know I am no more than one more try away from a sale!"

Using that logic he would add, "Yesterday I had three turndowns in a row. That means today I can expect to make two sales on my next three tries. So I'm excited about today's prospects. Life is good!"

Life seemed so daily for Cecil.

Cecil's positive spirit not only made him a good living. It also endeared him to countless people. I heard one person say, "He not only sells good products; he peddles goodwill and sunshine to everyone he meets. His attitude is worth emulation by every household in Antlers."

Both Cecil and Curtis were always present to every passing moment of life. They took each day as it came with the calm belief that each day could be a good day if we would work at it. In the course of my ministry in Antlers, I gained so much from these two special personalities. I was immensely enriched by the friendship we shared.

Our first six months in Antlers— summer and fall of 1966— were filled with activity and hard work. Every new day seemed to unwrap a new challenge. Trailing behind every new challenge would be a new promise of exciting ministry ahead. I worked hard on my preaching. I also spent long hours getting acquainted with most of the merchants and leaders of the town.

As I visited the members of the church, I met a dozen or so shut-in members. I determined to find a way to help these faithful shut-ins to be more aware of and involved in the life of the congregation. Eventually we established a "tape ministry," bringing audio tapes of worship services to these home-bound members.

In my visitations I asked each family to give me names of and information about people not affiliated with a church, folks they would like to see become a part of the Methodist family. Such names would include family members, relatives, friends, coworkers, youths, etc.

Before summer's end I had accumulated quite a lot of names and information. Consequently, it was necessary to activate the committee on evangelization for immediate training in relational evangelism. Such training would include cultivation of personal friendships, faith sharing, witnessing, invitation to Christian discipleship, and shepherding of any new members who came into membership. My list of names called for a workable and promising plan for the committee's work.

I drafted a basic strategy for making disciples. Later this strategy would be perfected, published, and implemented in 1983 as an Oklahoma Conference manual for use in every local church. I titled it *Ingathering* and used it in every succeeding church I pastored for the rest of my ministry.

Realizing evangelism was only a part of the church's total ministry, I set about designing a comprehensive vision for the church. It consisted of six distinct but inseparable facets. The first facet, of course, was evangelism. The other five pieces of the vision were leadership development, stewardship and tithing, aggressive Christian education, missions visible and viable, and outreach to needs of the local community. Each of these six foundation stones would be critical for inclusion in the 1967 budget.

Those six factors would not be ranked in order of importance. Every piece had to receive enthusiastic and concurrent support for the entire church to move ahead in effective minis-

A Twice-Taken Journey

try for Christ. With each piece of the vision contributing to the other five, the whole ministry of Christ would be enhanced and strengthened.

Almost immediately, in the middle of what commonly is known as "summer slump," we found new faces and families in worship and Sunday school. We noticed new spiritual vitality evolving among the members.

By summer's end five pieces of our vision were building, bubbling, and gearing up for launching January 1, 1967. Evangelism was already working toward ingathering. We set December 18 for our first Ingathering Day. Each member of the committee on evangelization was already praying for those assigned to develop friendships, share faith, and invite to membership.

As pastor of the church, I wrote a letter to each person and visited with as many on the list as I could. I encouraged them to take seriously our invitation to become another disciple of Christ.

Word got around about our Ingathering Day. Calls for information began to come in. Increased interest became evident. Results began to show as nine people came into membership before the date of the Ingathering. Four of these were by profession of faith.

Ingathering Day on December 18 was simply astonishing. We had to put up folding chairs to accommodate the record crowd. I preached on John 1:1-14. When the invitation to Christian discipleship was given, 35 persons of all ages came into membership. Twenty-seven of these came by profession of faith. By year's end we had received 46 new members. Thirty-two had come by profession of faith.

Truly we had reached the state of revival. Suddenly our facilities were strained, as participation increased in every area of the church's life. Excitement soared not only in the church but in the community.

In the midst of the Ingathering's preparations and fulfillment, I managed to complete the first half of my last year's work at Perkins. All my courses were seminars, which allowed me to drive early to school one morning, attend classes, study that night, attend more classes the next morning and be back home by midafternoon. That meant I had only two days at seminary and five days at home to prepare sermons, preach, go to meetings, work on term papers, make hospital and shut-in calls, and be a husband, father, and community leader. In addition, I had preached two revivals in the fall. To say the least, the fall semester had been demanding and at times extremely stressful.

The congregation supported my need to finish seminary. Never once did I hear anyone complain about my seminary requirements. So I had one more reason to be grateful and appreciative of the church's understanding.

Christmas 1966 was truly a time of jubilation. The joy of celebrating the Christ child's birth with many new members made it for many the most memorable Christmas they had ever known.

Shortly after the first of the year, I had an experience with what I thought was just another transient person looking for a handout. He apparently had been told to see me by someone he had approached on the street downtown. He asked me if I could help him out. Though his clothes were rumpled and ill fitting, they were not soiled. Nor did his person indicate an urgent need of a shave or bath.

At first I was a bit cautious, but I asked him to sit down and tell me about himself. Surprisingly, he was quite frank about his situation and his need for help. After serving his full sentence for a felony he had committed, he had been released from prison. All the funds he had been given upon departure from prison had run out.

"I have paid my debt to society in full for what I did wrong," he said. "I am not mad at the world. I should have been punished for what I did. I am sorry for what I did. When I left prison, they gave me a few dollars. I have used it to buy food and to find a job—any kind of job. I'd like to find work in these parts since I grew up not far from here. No one wants to hire me around here. I need money to buy food and a bus ticket to somewhere else. I have to find someone who will give me a job. I am desperate, but I am not about to break the law again!"

I must admit his openness and frankness moved me. We

talked for a long while. I asked if we could find work for him in the vicinity. He shook his head, frowned, lowered his head, and said, "No, I've already tried. A few people still remember me, and the word will get around."

I had only a $5 bill on me. I asked if that would help.

"Yes sir," he replied, "it would be a big help."

I handed him the money, and he thanked me through watery eyes.

"Pastor," he said, "I will pay you back once I get on my feet. You can count on it."

Well, I had heard that so many times before that his promise soon faded from my memory. Somehow, my encounter with this ex-convict was different from that of any panhandler I had ever met before.

Almost to the day, one year later, I was at my church study on a Saturday morning. A loud rap came upon the outside door, startling me. I called out, "Come in, the door is unlocked!" In walked a clean-shaven, neatly dressed man in work clothes, wearing a light topcoat. I had not immediately recognized him.

He stepped forward, reached out to shake hands and said, "Pastor, do you remember me?"

Instantly I did. Then I asked him to sit down.

Before I could say anything else, he said, "I am here to pay back the money you gave me about a year ago. I told you I would pay you back, so here it is."

"Tell me about yourself, and what you have been doing," I said. He told me he had found a job just a few days after our meeting, not too far from Antlers.

"The man who hired me is a good man who believed my story and took a chance on me," he said. "I hope to stay with him for a long time."

When he reached over to hand me the $5 bill, I had an idea.

"Why don't you keep that $5 tucked away in you billfold," I said. "When you have opportunity, give it to someone in the situation you were in when I gave it to you. Give it with the same challenge, for him to pass it on to still another person in need." Then I said to him, "Let's see how much good we can do with a single $5 bill."

He smiled and said, "It's a deal."

We prayed together again, and he left to get on with the rest of his life.

Of course I never saw him again. Yet I have often wondered if that same $5 bill might still be floating around, applying its benefits to yet another person in need.

The year 1967 roared in with several agenda items with which I had to deal. Foremost was enrolling at Perkins for my final semester. My schedule of class work and travel remained essentially the same.

In February I finally implemented our "tape ministry" to a dozen or so shut-in members of the church. The entire worship service, including prayer requests, hospital patient names, and shut-in news, was on tape. Since I had no Perkins class Mondays, I shuttled my tape recorder round-robin for most of the day. All the shut-ins were so pleased to participate in worship, even though it was via a recording. Soon some of them asked if they could do a few things for the church, like addressing, stamping, and stuffing envelopes. That was a blessing to the whole church. Eventually a few laypersons took over the round-robin tape ministry, releasing me for other matters of the church and community.

During the spring I preached two revivals with good results. I also conducted three funerals in a row for nonmembers of First Church. I mention them because those services served as "teaching moments" for the rest of my ministry.

The first was that of an elderly man who lived with his two sisters on remote acreage passed on to them by their parents. The youngest of the three was 78. None of them had ever married nor had they ever joined a church. They did claim to be "Methodist, for the most part."

The funeral home owner asked me to conduct the brother's funeral. He seemed frequently to call on me when the deceased was not affiliated with a church. He said it was because he liked me. I wondered.

Of course I agreed to conduct the "short graveside service" at the home place on a plot where the parents had been buried. Upon arrival, I found only five people there beside the funeral director, me, and the two sisters. The graveside tent had been set up. We placed the casket on the bier with the efforts of all present. The two sisters, each quite heavy, arrived. They were highly emotional. They took their seats, sinking the chair legs into the soft earth. As I began to speak, wails of sizable proportions began to echo across the valley. The more I spoke, the louder and more frequently the wails came. I ended the service and stepped to the head of the bier to await the viewing of the body of "Brother."

With some effort by others, the two sisters were raised to their feet and led toward the casket. The volume of their wails of woe increased to the point of being unbearable. As the first sister approached the bier, the second sister fainted into a sitting up position. The first sister hadn't noticed. As she took hold of the casket, she bent over the side to kiss "Brother" goodbye. Had I not been holding the bier with my left hand, it surely would have turned over. She kept trying until I was losing my grip. All the other attendees were gathered around the collapsed sister. Something had to give from my side of the emergency.

I grabbed the woman's shoulder with my free hand, jerked her back from the casket on the downside of her wail, and said, "Stop it! You almost overturned the casket! Go back to your seat and be quiet!"

She ceased her wailing in a second, glared at me for another second, then went to her chair, and sat down in utter silence.

In the meantime the funeral director and the others were working with the sitting sister, still in her faint.

Someone asked, "Is she breathing?"

"We'll know in a minute when she gets a whiff of this ammonia ampule under her nose," the director said.

She came very much alive. They got her to her feet and helped her toward the bier and me. I braced myself. She walked by, took a glance at "Brother" and went back to her seat. The short benediction came quickly.

On our way back to Antlers, I asked the funeral director not to "like me" so much, since the other pastors in town needed equal opportunity for such life-enlarging experiences. The teaching moment of that funeral, which I applied in my future ministry, was: Anything, even the bizarre, can happen at a funeral—and probably will.

The second funeral was for the mother of a career military man. The mother apparently had lived with her son and family after her husband's death. The funeral director still liked me so much that he asked me to conduct the service. The woman long since had bought a gravesite in the Antlers cemetery. The service was held in our church with only a few people other than family members.

After the interment, the son and his family came by to express his family's thanks. He told me he would be retiring in Antlers in a few more years. Much to my chagrin, he said someone had told him that his name and his mother's had been removed from the church's membership roll some years earlier. He expressed his hurt. He stated he and his family had always been active in the military chapel ministry wherever they had been assigned. He had supported the chapel because he had been taught to "give the tithe where I worshipped."

I tried to apologize for the removal of their names and said that I would reinstate them immediately. He thanked me, but I could sense he still felt wounded by the church's action.

My teaching moment on that occasion was that I would not allow any person to be removed from the church's roll until status could be definitely determined. I fought a few battles over that issue in years to come, but I never backed down. I felt membership in a local church was a sacred trust given to a church. I still feel the same way.

The teaching moment of the third funeral came when I was asked by a former member of Tuskahoma Church to conduct a service for her friend. Tuskahoma was some distance from Antlers. The church there had been closed for some time. I conducted the funeral and was about to head back to Antlers when the same woman asked for a few minutes of my time. She was "doubly sad"— first because her best friend had just died and second because her church had closed down. She asked me if I would come back to Tuskahoma the following Sunday afternoon to meet with her and a few more people about what they could do to bring a Methodist presence back to Tuskahoma.

"We will pay your expenses if you will come at 3 p.m.," she said.

I agreed to meet with them and said that there would be no expense.

On the way home I thought about four men who were trained lay speakers. Because Tuskahoma was so far from Antlers, I knew I couldn't preach at two services so far apart. I asked Lee Clymer, J.B. Denny, Harry Alexander, and Norman Bridwell to take responsibility to preach at Tuskahoma once a month. I would arrange to go every fifth Sunday afternoon to preach, baptize, serve Holy Communion, and receive any new members.

The four men jumped eagerly at the opportunity. I called the district superintendent, Dr. Lloyd Peters, to get his permission. It was not only granted, but we had his full support. In October I received into membership 10 persons—three by profession of faith, three by transfer, three by vows from churches other than Methodist, and one preparatory member. That was 34 years ago. A local pastor now serves the church, which has 31 members and an average attendance of 22.

This teaching moment taught me that smallness is no reason for closing a church—not when dedicated lay speakers can grow the church in partnership with a pastor. Such a Methodist presence can be permanent.

Because Antlers First Church continued to grow in size as well as excitement, the time had come to consider a long-needed additional building for children and youth classrooms, an adequate fellowship hall, restrooms, and an enlarged pastor's study. More than a dozen infants and toddlers were being cramped into a 9-by-12-foot room. Young couples were complaining about too many children in too small a space—and rightfully so!

A meeting of the official board was called to discuss the matter. It did not go well. One longtime resident and bachelor objected, saying that in his day "babies and small children didn't need all that space." A few "Amens" followed, and the matter was squelched. In my closing remarks I reminded the board that if the church did not move forward with an expansion of facilities, it could expect to see a decline in attendance and in new members within a year because of lack of space.

May arrived. I received my master of theology degree from Perkins. A few weeks later I was ordained an elder and received into full connection in the Oklahoma Conference. Now I was a full-fledged, qualified Methodist clergyman with all the rights, privileges, and responsibilities thereto appertaining.

I was elected president of the Antlers Ministerial Association. At my first meeting as president, the subject of a "beer joint" just outside the city limits came up. Pushmataha County was a dry county. The beer joint was indeed a nuisance, with weekend brawls, injuries, arrests, and disturbances in the surrounding area. Every pastor at the meeting rose in righteous indignation, saying the "disgrace to the community had to stop!" No one, however, offered much of anything but spluttering outrage. An air of anger filled the room in the absence of definitive strategy.

Half in jest, I said, "I know how we can shut down that joint if you really want to do so."

Quiet descended. Twenty-four ears perked up, followed by 24 eyes focusing on me.

Without pause for thought, one eager pastor said, "Let's do it."

I suggested we form teams of two and take turns spending two hours each in the joint Friday and Saturday nights! Our drinks would be *soft*.

"What?" one pastor shouted. "I'm not about to be seen at that hellhole of sin on any night!"

Another yelled at me, "Besides, how would such a fool stunt like that help?"

"I suspect some of our sheep are customers," I replied. "I don't know about your members, but I'm sure none of my members would be in a hurry to go out there if they knew I was inside."

I thought the group was about to attack me. We hurriedly adjourned, with consensus we would continue the beer joint question at our next meeting.

During the interim, the beer joint mysteriously burned to the ground. I was ready to deny having anything to do with it. I was also relieved of my fear that the group might have a change of heart at the next meeting and take my solution seriously.

As fall approached, the national political campaigns were getting as much air time on the sidewalks as on television. J.B. Denny was a staunch Methodist and an equally strong Republican. He filed to run for the seat occupied by Carl Albert—the speaker of the House of Representatives. While in J.B.'s business one day, I asked if what I had heard was true.

"It is!" he replied. "No politician should ever get to run unopposed—not even the speaker of the House." He went on to declare, "There are maybe a half dozen registered Republicans in Pushmataha County. I should at least get their votes!"

When the polls closed J.B. received results of four supporters and two turncoats. He had made his point!

The church was still growing, but the facilities had reached their capacity. The subject of a new addition came up again. This time we called a church conference. The district superintendent would preside. No opposition was visible except for the same bachelor and one woman. Hopes, therefore, were quite high. Thirty-one people showed up for the meeting—not a good signal for a church of some 500 members. Discussion was lively. The vote was taken, with 17 against and 14 for the expansion. The superintendent was deeply disappointed. So was I. We had worked so hard to strengthen the church in membership, stewardship, and discipleship, only to see defeat of a critical part of our vision.

The next day I learned why the question had failed. Most of those in favor of the project didn't attend the conference because they didn't want to add to the controversy. Talk about the negative prevailing because the positive failed to take a stand!

I was really down. That afternoon I dropped by J.B.'s business, looking I suppose for a little pity. Showing my glum spirit, I commented, "J.B., I don't think I fit in here at Antlers."

"You don't!" he replied. "You are a newcomer!"

"But I've been here almost two years!" I objected.

"I've been here 11 years," he replied, "and I'm still seen as a newcomer! Besides that, a few people in this church and this town have enough influence to hold suspect anybody or any-thing from outside the city limits!"

Of course he was exaggerating a bit. But at that moment I wanted to agree with his assessments.

Twenty-five years later I was invited back to Antlers to help dedicate the new building we had failed twice to approve. Funds for the entire building and remodeling of the existing structure came from the estate left to the church by the bachelor who had spearheaded the two defeats. Ironic? Perhaps! In any case, the new facilities now serve the needs of the church and the community—but a diminished congregation.

The only building project done while I was there was a much-needed carport at the parsonage. The whole family was quite grateful for the convenience it afforded us.

Christmas 1967 was celebrated with all the usual festivi-ties. In the spring of 1968, I managed to preach two revivals. I did a lot of discipleship training for new members.

In the late spring meeting of all the pastors in the district, everyone was talking about who might be moving after the upcoming annual conference session. No one knew anything for certain. Still, the conversations were entertaining.

While returning to Antlers that afternoon, Lavelle said to me, "Well, we'll be moving after conference."

"Oh," I replied, "how do you know? I am the one to be notified!"

"The district superintendent told me as we were leaving the restaurant after lunch," she responded. "He said to me quietly. 'You had better be collecting a lot of boxes!'"

Lloyd Peters, the superintendent, and Lavelle were always teasing each other. It would be like him for mischief's sake to inform her first, just for the fun of it. We arrived home realizing our remaining time was a matter of only a few weeks. Later that day Dr. Peters called to confirm what he had told Lavelle.

At the end of May 1968, we were appointed to First Church in Hugo—just 20 miles southeast of Antlers. Certainly it was considered by us to be a promotion.

Our journey with Antlers First Church was for only two years. Yet in that brief time the church thrived in every area of its ministry. The membership had increased by 16 percent.

Participation in the life of the church was increasing even more. Youth ministry had more than doubled. New young families increased significantly, as did per capita giving.

Our journey, though brief, had indeed been as challenging, interesting, fruitful, and frequently humorous as we had predicted the evening of our first night in town.

Assuredly, Antlers was deer country full of dear people. As Cecil might have put it, "We were blessed!" and "Life was good!"

9

Journey of Challenge and Change

While living in Antlers, we often had to drive through Hugo to shop at Paris, Texas, or to attend district meetings in other churches. The double-track railroad crossing in Hugo was the roughest one could imagine. There was no way to get over it without being bounced about, beaten, and bruised inside the car. Many times I thought the engine would fall out and the muffler would be torn off. Although regular attempts were made to fix the thing, the crossing seemed resistant to longtime repair. That meant half the time the crossing was breaking up cars and the other half being under repair.

On one trip through Hugo I decided that the crossing had attained its highest degree of roughness. By the time we got across, I was furious. "Good grief!" I muttered out loud. Then I said to Lavelle, "I've said silently so many bad words and harbored so many bad thoughts about this crossing that it would be just like God and the bishop to send us here!"

My reckless comment came from a frustrating and aggravating moment. In response, Lavelle said, "You had better be careful what you say. You just might be appointed here someday!"

Well, sometimes, "someday" comes quite quickly. Less than a year later we were on the road to our new appointment to First Methodist Church in Hugo. Whether or not my outburst had anything to do with possible prophecy, the fact was we would be arriving in a matter of minutes to take up my pastoral responsibilities.

The move of only 20 miles from Antlers to Hugo was the shortest and easiest we ever made. A major reason was that Gordon Frederick loaded our belongings onto his large truck and delivered them to our new parsonage. Gordon had become a member of Antlers Church during the 1966 Ingathering. His profession of faith and baptism had brought a noticeable change in his life. We had become good friends.

While we were still in Antlers, Gordon and his wife, Gretchen, suffered their greatest sorrow. Marilyn, their teenage daughter, died of head injuries received from falling off her horse. It was a horrible time for both of them. Yet Gordon and Gretchen looked to God for strength and their faith to sustain them. I conducted the funeral and watched our church family throw its arms of care and support around them. Their steady faith served to inspire and teach all of us about living through the grip of great sorrow.

While still en route to Hugo, we were feeling good about our two-year ministry in Antlers. We were also feeling a bit of excitement about our journey in a larger setting. Hugo was the seat of Choctaw County. The town's population was about three times that of Antlers. Likewise, the church membership was larger, and there were two full-time staff people and one part-time youth director. I had preached once to the Hugo congregation and had spoken several times at meetings and workshops at the church. Consequently, I was acquainted with many of the members and leaders.

Upon arrival in Hugo, we crossed that infernal double-tracked railroad into downtown. It was an especially jarring, jolting, and jostling experience. This time I held my tongue. I also held at bay any ugly thoughts, lest again I run the risk of self-inflicting prophecy.

We were met at the parsonage by a delegation from the church. They greeted us warmly and received us with much grace. We then set about moving in and putting everything into its proper place. Moving day for pastors was always on Thursday following the annual conference session. Having moved frequently all our married life, we never liked to be moving in for days on end. I was usually at my office desk my first Monday in town to respond to messages, meetings, and agendas. I made a long tour of the facilities.

The church was a beautiful edifice. It reflected the elegance of the early 20th century, when it was built. Four paris of large pillars graced the main entrance, 16 steps upward from the ground. The sanctuary had an impressive horseshoe-shaped balcony wrapped around three walls. Stained-glass windows underneath the balcony added warmth, color, and life. Pews semicircled around the chancel area and the center-stage pulpit. Elevated behind the platform and pulpit was the choir loft. The woodwork and painted wall in front of the loft formed the subtle shape of a baptismal font. All converged to create an elegant worship center. That sanctuary provided the finest atmosphere and environment for preaching of any church I served.

The back third of the building consisted of four floors for church offices and classrooms. The building had recently been renovated, leaving the top two floors to be finished when sufficient funds were raised. Those floors were unusable because of sagging plaster, water damage, and serious disrepair. If growth in membership and outreach ministries to the community were to be put into place, those two floors would have to be fixed.

I set to work immediately, visiting members' homes and businesses downtown. After several months of gathering information and insights, I would be able to formulate a number of objectives to be tackled in tandem when my leadership became more solidified and accepted.

Reigniting inactive members; growth in membership, worship, and Sunday school attendance; radio broadcast of the worship services; youth ministry; raising the giving level of members—all these priorities already needed immediate attention. In addition, an elevator with outside entrance to the sanctuary foyer was long overdue. First Church could not call itself inviting and user-friendly until it provided access to persons with impaired conditions. Of course, the task of finishing those two top floors must not get lost in addressing present needs. All these objectives in a larger, comprehensive vision were among the most urgent items to address.

Aside from our family's annual vacation in Tennessee, I was in ministry in Hugo the rest of the summer of 1968. Blessings of all blessings! The railroad crossing was at last fixed. I felt so good about it that I took back all the silent bad words I had spoken about the crossing and all the bad thoughts I had harbored.

I worked hard on my sermon preparation and my preaching. During the summer I also got acquainted with some of the other pastors in town. It would be September before I could meet the rest of them, when monthly meetings together would begin again.

By the time school started I was in the full swing of things and developing a vision to take to the administrative board in late fall. For the most part I felt the congregation was pleased with my leadership. I was told I was being talked about all over town as a "preacher worth hearing." I was not sure what that meant, but I took it as a compliment. Preachers need to hear good words about their sermons.

In fact, by mid-fall I was asked to preach a revival in the church. I was a bit reluctant, and the board and I discussed the matter. I agreed to conduct the revival if the members would set aside the whole week and would bring to the services friends they would like to see become part of the church. I was quite surprised when the leaders agreed with my suggestions.

The date was set for November 1968—barely six months after my arrival. Already we were receiving new members regularly. Already, too, many members were bringing friends, neighbors, and relatives to our worship services and Sunday school classes. The revival went from Sunday night to Friday night. The following Sunday morning we received into membership 15 people, more than half of whom came by profession of faith and baptism. The revival proved to be a catalyst that launched us on an exciting 31-month journey of ministry among the wonderful people of First Church, Hugo.

Like most long-standing congregations, First Church had a sizable number of members who were shut in or consigned to nursing-care facilities. Naturally, few of them could participate on site in the activities of the church. Our weekly newsletter kept them informed regarding church life. As frequently as I could I visited with them and brought them news of our progress.

These faithful and dear members especially hungered to come to worship services. There were too many of them for me to take taped worship services each week. I fretted about this need that we were not meeting.

I went to see the manager of our local radio station and shared my wanting somehow to get our worship services to our shut-ins. He saw what I was getting at, so he said, "Preacher, haven't you heard? That is the sort of thing a radio station does!"

I was about to acknowledge that very thing, but he beat me to the point. We could get the worship services on the air at 11 a.m. for a live broadcast. We made a verbal contract then and there to start the following Sunday, since another church had shown some interest in going on the air. I acted with no funds available to pay the costs.

I realized I had taken a big risk. But as a present-day company would put it, "The greatest risk is not taking one!" If that were true in the business affairs of the world, surely it must be no less true in the affairs of the spiritual realm. God expects us at times to be bold in our decisions and to take risks for the sake of being true to our faith and those in need.

In any event, I committed to the solution of a significant need. On my way back into town, I stopped to see one of our members. I told him what I had done and why I had acted so quickly. I asked him if he would pay for the broadcast for the next three months.

Without hesitance he said, "I think the ministry is a good idea, and I'd like to be a part of it. Of course I will be glad to pay for it, provided you will not mention who is doing it."

I agreed. I thanked him and prayed with him in his office. Then I left. I was to learn later that his response was typical of him.

As far as I know, no one else ever knew where financing for the ministry came from. I do know there was strong evidence of his continuing anonymous contributions to the radio ministry long after it had become an item in the budget. The ministry continued as long as I was at First Church, Hugo.

Indeed, by approaching the donor, I again had taken a big risk. At age 36, however, I was learning that unless a pastor is willing at times to take risks for the sake of ministry, that pastor is likely to live much of his or her ministry under intimidation, if not retreat.

I notified all the shut-in members of the broadcast time and asked them to listen and feed back to us their evaluation during the three-month test time. The following Sunday the radio ministry was in play, to the joy, praise, and gratitude of those unable to join us live in the worship service. In response, some of them became what they called "prayer warriors for the preacher." As information reached them about deaths, crises in the community, illness, families in stress, special church emphases, or any other concerns, these warriors prayed. They made a powerful impact upon the congregation and the community. Requests came to them from inside and outside the congregation.

The radio broadcast became a major outreach ministry to the entire area. Members would regularly ask for copies of the tapes to send to a friend or family shut-in someplace else.

Time seemed to pass so rapidly. Before we realized it, Thanksgiving and Christmas came and went in a flurry of activities. Dana and Darryl enjoyed their first term in school and made many friends. Dyton was attending his first term in kindergarten. The transition for all of us had been satisfying. The congregation was growing steadily in several areas. A positive spirit about our future was increasingly evident.

In early 1969 I preached a revival in a three-point circuit—Pleasant Hill, Redland, and Haworth churches—in southeastern Oklahoma. Redland was the host church, with the other two churches fully supporting it. The members in that remote circuit were among the finest and most dedicated United Methodists I ever met. I was never received with a more genuine welcome in my life. The meeting went well. One highlight took place when Luke Storey responded to his call to ministry.

Luke was from the Pleasant Hill Church but was well-known in all three communities for his "love for the Lord." In his mid 40s, he gave up ranching for the ministry. His wife, Chlora Dee, fully supported his decision. She, too, was a strongly committed follower of Christ.

Luke and I became close friends, though we never got to see each other much, since we were never in the same district together again. Our ministry did connect later. He was appointed to the Tuskahoma Church, which we had revitalized while I was in Antlers. In his 20 years pastoring churches, Luke served four different appointments. He retired the last day of December 1988. He died in October 1999. I was especially saddened to hear the news. I had looked forward to connecting with him again when I returned to Oklahoma to retire.

In early spring 1969 I asked the board to grant me time away from the church a few weeks each summer for three years. Scarritt College in Nashville was offering a master of arts degree in evangelism designed for the local church pastor. My request was granted. I folded my vacation time into the degree work so as not to be away from the church more than absolutely necessary. The family would stay with our folks during the course. That suited our three sons just fine, especially the time they spent with Lavelle's parents on their farm. The third summer I received my degree with honors. I have been grateful ever since to the church for granting me the time for the degree.

Later that spring I became acquainted with a retired pastor who drove some 60 miles each way each week to preach at two black Methodist congregations. St. Paul Church was near downtown Hugo. Waters Chapel was six miles south in the community of Grant. The retired pastor was a gentle and humble soul whom I quickly came to love and respect. It was evident, however, that he was advanced in years and not in good health. The weekly 120-mile round trip was really hard on him. We had many conversations, which we agreed were mutually a blessing to us.

On his way to Hugo one Sunday, he had a bad accident. Though he was not seriously injured, he sustained enough bruises and sprains to prevent his driving any more. Of course he was concerned about his two flocks and what would happen to them.

In my community activities I had come to know some of the members and leaders of St. Paul Church. Alvin Rogan was the owner of the neighborhood funeral home. He and his whole family were members. I also knew one of the leaders of the women in the church. I inquired if I might be able to help the two churches by preaching at early services at each church until a new pastor could be appointed. I was asked to meet with a few people that evening to discuss the matter.

I was jolted when they bluntly said they were surprised to learn I was willing to come. That response was a subtle indication of just how deep the racial divide was between the black and white communities. I was learning a critical lesson. I explained I could only conduct early hour services so I could be back at First Church for the 11 a.m. radio broadcast service. I mentioned to them again that I would be able to serve only until a new pastor could be found.

The two churches were a part of the Central Jurisdiction, which was established in 1939 as a means of keeping black Methodist segregated from whites. (That structure disappeared in 1972 when the black members of the Central Jurisdiction in Oklahoma were merged into the South Central Jurisdiction and Oklahoma Conference).

The two black churches were under the supervision of Bishop Paul Galloway, who lived in Little Rock. The district superintendent was the Reverend Amos Wamble, who lived in Oklahoma City.

The meeting with local leaders of St. Paul and Waters Chapel resulted in acceptance of my offer. We agreed to apprise both their bishops and superintendent and mine of our proposal. All four approved it, with instructions to get on with it and to keep them informed.

Suddenly I was working for two bishops and two superintendents in two different conferences. The following Sunday I preached at both black congregations. I was received with warmth and appreciation. Several weeks later I learned there likely would not be a replacement pastor because of a critical shortage in the Central Jurisdiction.

That's how I got involved in the black churches and their community life. For the remaining 19 months of my ministry in Hugo, I served as their pastor. It developed into an experience of far greater significance than anything I could have imagined.

Over the next few weeks I conferred with individual leaders of First Church, sharing ways the church's support would be critical for the two black congregations. One by one they supported the effort, although they were concerned about my overloading myself. No negative response rose up for several weeks. I felt heartened that First Church was feeling good about my conducting the services for the black churches.

Sunday mornings were indeed hectic and demanding. I scurried from one church to the other and then scrambled to get back to First Church in time to set up the tape recording for the radio ministry. While I was rushing back and forth from my study to get everything ready, one prominent member stopped me.

"Why are you so out of breath, Preacher?" she asked.

I explained I was a bit late getting back from St. Paul Church. Her response was the first indication that not all members were exactly pleased with my being involved with the black congregations.

"It seems to me," she said, "you have enough to do in this church that is paying your salary to be involved with black churches!"

I was stunned and a bit angry. My heart was already hammering, and my breath was labored from rushing about. I am sure that if I had responded to her statement, I would have regretted it.

Just at that instant the Sunday school superintendent walked up. Having heard her remarks, he wrapped his right arm around my shoulder, looked at the woman with a sweet spirit, and said, "You know, I think it is just wonderful that our pastor would give his time and leadership to those two black congregations! Only good can come of it, and I bet most of our congregation would agree with me!"

This superintendent was in his mid-70s.

For once in my life I said nothing. Instead, I slipped my shoulder from his arm, walked toward the study, and thanked him for such a beautiful response. His words had been far more gracious than anything I might have said in response to the woman's words. I literally had been delivered from a probably unpleasant confrontation.

I was still a bit shaky from the ordeal as the worship got under way. It colored my spirit as I began my sermon, which ironically was on the subject of including "outsiders" in the congregation. The more I preached, the more my personal feelings came to the surface. I blurted out something like, "We can head for hell on the Pullman coach of racial prejudice, but I will not be buying a ticket, thanks you very much." My words went by radio to the entire community.

The congregation looked as stunned and hurt as I had been stunned and hurt by words hurled at me in the hallway. Immediately I regretted my words, even though they reflected what I felt about racism. I kept telling myself later, "You stood your ground, so stop fretting about it." The problem was that no one in the audience had challenged me or even doubted my convictions on the matter. By penitent prayer, the grace of God, and the love of the congregation, I got away with my harsh words.

In the end, several members admitted to being annoyed by my outburst. They also said they respected me more highly for making it clear where I stood on the issue. For all the regret I felt for my unguarded blurting, I began to see more and more subtle expressions of racism popping up in all kinds of situations.

After several weeks of preaching in the two black churches, it became apparent that neither would be able to survive much longer. With the churches just six miles apart, the future would look much more promising if the membership were combined. I broached the subject at each church. At first both were resistant.

I shared with them what we could see down the road. Both church buildings were in critical disrepair. Waters Chapel was a tiny, one-room facility. Very few people could even get into it. Every part of its structure was in serious shape, from foundation to windows to rooftop.

St. Paul Church in Hugo was even worse. Though much larger, the wood frame building had been condemned by the fire marshal. The congregation had been allowed to continue meeting in it only until other arrangements could be made. The roof was precariously swaybacked and leaked all over the chancel area every time it rained. The congregation even joked about having had "rainy day baptisms."

The more we talked, the more sense it made to merge. Both churches agreed, though there was some opposition. We moved ahead after both superintendents and bishops approved the plan. The idea of merger had been based on the hope of raising enough funds to build a new facility on St. Paul property in Hugo. The new church would be named Paul's Chapel— taking part of each church's name.

A committee of people from both churches was formed to develop funding and architectural drawings. A new facility designed for the existing property would cost $40,000 for a sanctuary, three classrooms, a small kitchen, restrooms, and a fellowship hall. The building would be small but adequate for the present and designed for expansion. The church would raise $10,000 over five years. The district United Methodist Men would commit to raising $10,000 at $2,000 a year. I would try to raise the rest through grants and individual gifts from outside sources.

The following week I made application to the Oklahoma Conference Board of Missions for $10,000. Dr. Charles Wells, chairman of the board, was instrumental in getting the grant approved. I also requested $5,000 from the Conference Reconciliation Fund. Dr. Jack Featherston, chairman, was instrumental getting that grant approved in two annual payments of $2,500 each.

I brought the first check for $10,000 to the Sunday service, announced where it came from, and handed it to Arthur Manning, the treasurer. The congregation was thrilled. The following day Arthur called to ask me to go with him to deposit the $10,000 check at the bank. I was puzzled. When I asked why he needed me to go with him, he said there might be a lot of questions about where the check came from. He was a humble man, easily intimidated. I suggested he walk into the bank as treasurer of St. Paul Church and deposit the check. If any inquiry or discourtesy were shown to him, I would join him, and together we would make it clear how we felt about being humiliated. The bank asked no questions.

The following Sunday morning I brought the first of two $2,500 checks, announced where it came from and handed it to the treasurer. He grinned, winked at me, and took the check. I knew the reason for it and nodded back.

With $12,500 already in hand for the project, Alvin Rogan rose to his feet and said, "Reverend Owen, we now know this matter is not just a pipe dream. We now know you are dead serious about the new building. We want to thank you for helping us out."

Then, right there in the middle of everything, he called for a vote of $25 a month "travelling expense" for me in the future.

"And when he has spent that," he went on, "he's through!"

The actual vote was never taken but thoroughly approved by an outburst of applause. I had lost complete control of the worship service. I never expected or desired any travel expense, but I received it as an expression of love.

Each year the Methodist Men's dinner would take place in another part of the district. At the same time, Paul's Chapel set about raising its first $2,000 pledge by way of garage sales, chicken dinners, and other projects. Everybody was getting into the act, with a lot of accompanying joy. I was still working on raising the remaining $5,000 from individual gifts. The entire $40,000 was being underwritten. The plan was to accumulate at least $20,000 in cash and borrow the remaining amount over five years. The additional interest would be paid by the church if no other funds could be raised. The $20,000 in cash was raised, and then some.

The trustees put out feelers to both banks about a five-year loan when the project was ready to go. Neither bank expressed much excitement. Since the architect had not completed detailed drawings to give a more accurate estimate of the projected costs, we decided to let the matter of a loan rest for awhile.

The Oklahoma Annual Conference session met in late May 1969. When the appointments were read, I received responsibility as "counseling elder" to oversee an approved plan for the "Choctaw County Larger Parish." Four pastors serving seven churches had worked on a plan for those churches to join efforts in strengthening all. The parish would coordinate ministry, evangelism, missions, and training for all congregations. We organized work teams to repair and paint parsonages. We trained laypeople for witnessing and church growth. Classes on stewardship in the local church took place for all members of all churches to attend. The parish proved to be a good thing and lasted a while beyond my tenure at Hugo.

In our last meeting of the Hugo Ministerial Association before summer recess, the question came up as to why the local swimming pool was not available to the black community. Black children were being bused to a pool in Paris, Texas. I had not heard of this situation. A lively discussion ensued. The Roman Catholic priest and I were appointed as a delegation of two to learn the details of the matter and report as soon as possible.

It so happened that the president of the pool association worked two blocks from where we were meeting. We decided to go right then to make inquiry. By the time we walked into the president's work area, word had already reached her that we were coming to ask about the pool policy. She was ready for us. When we shared the reason for our coming, she bristled and said:

"I know why you are here! I'll save us all a lot of time by saying three things. The pool is privately owned! There are only two rules for admittance. One, you have to have a quarter! Two, you have to be white!"

She then turned and walked away. The conversation was over! The priest and I were astonished. We had come to get information, and we got it in a hurry!

The next afternoon the superintendent of schools dropped by my office. He was a trusted and respected member and leader in the community. He was also a close friend.

"Preacher," he asked, "are you aware of what is being said about you all over town?"

Puzzled, I replied, "No, I am not."

"The word is that you are about to lead a demonstration at the swimming pool," he said.

Once again I was shocked. I then explained that the Roman Catholic priest and I had made inquiry on behalf of the Ministerial Association about the pool policy.

"None of the other pastors is claiming knowledge of it," he interrupted.

It was a terrible and sinking feeling for me to think that members of our own fellowship were having no part of our inquiry.

I thanked the superintendent and explained further all that had transpired. He said he knew something of what I was going through because he had brought desegregation to the school system several years earlier. He left, encouraging me not to respond to what was being said and to get on with my work as pastor. At that moment I knew two things:

1. Racism was far from being licked.
2. I had not been done-in as pastor.

I visited with Alvin Rogan about how the black community was responding to the loose talk. He had already heard about it. He told me the black folks would not be demonstrating at the pool.

"They are not going to play into the hands of someone else's agenda," he said. "You put your mind at ease about it. We've got too much to do to let this slow us down!"

I now had two of the most respected leaders in Hugo telling me the same thing. So I went on about my work of pastoring the two churches. Nothing further was said about the matter.

At our next First Church board meeting, an item related to the new Fund for Reconciliation apportionment came up. Our share was only $267. One board member did not like apportionments in any amount.

"What is this new Fund for Reconciliation?" he asked. "Where does this $267 we pay go? Do you know, Preacher?"

Half in jest I replied, "I don't know where all of our $267 goes, but I do know $5,000 of that $267 has come back right here to Hugo for Paul's Chapel's new building."

He grinned and said sheepishly, "Oh!"

Full payment of all apportionments to our church got a big boost that day.

With the completion of the architect's designs for Paul's Chapel, it was time for us to get back to securing the five-year loan for $20,000. One day while making a deposit into my own bank account, I stepped over to the desk of a bank officer I knew. I shared with him what we were trying to do and that we wanted the bank to make the loan. I could tell he was a bit reluctant to consider it.

"Well, Preacher," he said finally, "we might be able to make the loan if you would sign the note." He went on talking about certain standards of liquidity and collateral, which he doubted the church could meet.

"The church has an account in this bank right now of more than $15,000 toward the $40,000 we need," I said. "The McAllister District of the United Methodist Church is behind the loan. That alone secures the loan pretty adequately, don't you think?"

He wanted to respond, but I kept talking.

"The church is to raise $10,000 over the next five years, along with $10,000 raised by the district Methodist Men," I said. "The church can handle the loan with the size of its membership."

He sat silently while I continued.

"I think this bank would want to make this loan for no reason other than to improve the looks of the street and community barely four blocks from here. We can get the loan outside of town, but it won't look good for this local bank to turn it down. As to your requirement for my signature, I cannot sign any note for any church, and I would not if I could."

I had said my piece.

"Preacher," the officer said, "would you call me in the morning and give me time to talk to some other people in the bank?"

By then I was a bit worked up and replied, "No, I won't call you. I would hope you would call me and tell me to have the trustees come and sign the note."

He grinned and said, "I'll call you in the morning!"

He did. The trustees could come by and sign the note when they were ready to receive the loan. Later those trustees said they were surprised at the ease of getting the loan.

In mid-1970 we were able to bring noted missionary-evangelist E. Stanley Jones to First Church. His coming proved to be a spiritual high point for the entire area. I had read a few of his books and was enamored with the simplicity of his words and the depth of their meaning. He was to be in Minneapolis, Minnesota, to lead a revival and a "Christian Ashram." I attended the in-depth study of Christian disciplines, and my whole Christian walk was illuminated and enlarged. The Ashram let participants experience what it means to be the kingdom of God on earth.

I sat with Borther Stanley at one meal and invited him to come for an Ashram and revival in Hugo. Since Hugo was a town of about 7,000 people, I did not hold much hope of his coming. After returning home I received his reply. He would like to come and be with us. I don't mind saying I was ecstatic. We set a date and started preparing for the event according to his standard instructions. We ordered his books on consignment, knowing once people heard him, they would want to read them.

Many in the community knew who Brother Stanley was. Some had heard him preach in other places. Banners stretched across downtown streets announced his coming. Members of other churches were eager to promote his visit with us. It could be said that his visit became a community-wide event.

No one was disappointed. His preaching reached into the depths of many hearts. The Ashram brought new commitments from those who attended. Brother Stanley preached on one radio station and was interviewed on another. Newspapers reported on his preaching. We sold out of his books. Our three sons were awed by him, yet felt the warmth of his life as he sat at our table for a meal. Stanley Jones lifted the awareness of God among us all to new heights. Even then in his mid-80s, he displayed boundless energy. Indeed, as one youth put it, "He is a mighty man of God."

Several months later I was asked to serve as the director of the Oklahoma Christian Ashram. By that time I had been elected chair of the Oklahoma conference Board of Evangelism. I accepted the job and folded the Christian Ashram into our Conference Program Booklet for local church evangelism. It was well received. I asked Brother Stanley to come and lead the conference-wide Ashram in Oklahoma City in 1971. That would launch a statewide awareness of the Ashram movement now growing in Oklahoma. More than 100 participants attended. All were deeply touched by his efforts.

On the last evening of the event, Brother Stanley said to the audience, "For some time now I have wanted to speak on the Holy Spirit, before I slip away." It was both a timely and prophetic statement. The Holy Spirit movement in Oklahoma was somewhat conflicted, centering around the "gifts of the Spirit." He spoke a long time and helped us in our own understanding of the work of the Holy Spirit as well. His talk was indeed the highlight of the Ashram.

The next morning he did not show up for breakfast. I went to his room and rapped on the door. He did not answer, although I could hear muffled talking. I went to the front desk and asked that his door be opened. I walked in to find him still in bed. With garbled words he told me he had had a stroke. We rushed him to Baptist Hospital, where he was treated. He remained there for several days, then was transported to his home in Baltimore, Maryland, to recover.

As I understand it, he made one last trip to the Satal Ashram in India, which he established during his half-century of labors as a Methodist missionary. Brother Stanley died shortly thereafter in 1973. He left not only a legacy of greatness but also a "great cloud of witnesses" who yet can attest to spiritual awakening because of his ministry. I know that to be true because Brother Stanley influenced my own spiritual walk with Christ more profoundly and lastingly than any other person.

Several times in late 1971 I put up a row of short, white painted posts along the curbless street on the south side of our parsonage. Their purpose was to keep cars from parking on our lawn and chewing deep ruts into our yard. The posts actually added beauty to the site. Yet each time I implanted them, they would soon be yanked up and distributed all over the neighborhood. I could not figure out who was doing such a thing or why. At first I thought it might be related to my involvement with the black church. Finally the police discovered that youths on the prowl late at night were responsible.

The idea came to me that such activity might stem from

their not having any place to go or anything to do better than pulling up curb posts and scattering them around town. I talked to a good friend and pastor of another church. Upon inquiry, we found the town had no place, aside from local churches, where youths could get together under supervision for recreation, fellowship, and activities. These teenagers apparently were not involved in any church.

My pastor friend and I decided to test whether any parents, business owners, and community leaders were interested in a citywide program for youth. A meeting was announced, inviting all interested persons to the fellowship hall at First Methodist Church to discuss the matter. More than 150 parents and other adults came. My pastor friend and I were dumbfounded that so many attended. We expected 50 at most.

We broke the crowd into several groups and asked each one to discuss different issues that we had listed on a sheet of paper. At our wrapup meeting we would assess the results and go from there. The last item on the sheet was a question about the need for a specific place for a community youth center. Overwhelming support was registered. One possible and perfect site was the closed railroad depot. Committees were formed and set into motion for financing, location, and programming. The committee was to report its findings shortly after the first of 1972.

I was moved to another church and never got to see the outcome of our efforts.

During my tenure in Hugo I met many "peerless personalities." These people not only enlarged my own life but gave personality to the city.

Miss Fannie

"Miss Fannie" was an independent-minded spinster and retired schoolteacher. Advanced in years, she walked everywhere. She often dropped by my study unannounced to talk about whatever was on her sharp mind. She held right-of-way crossing streets, no matter what the traffic lights indicated. Since she had taught half the town's population, very few doubted she was in charge, knowing "enough" on everybody to muzzle any objections.

She held title to the aisle seat on the back center pew of the sanctuary. Those who knew her dared not sit in her seat. Those who did not know her were ordered to move down. Even strangers obeyed her. On one occasion a new family of eight visited our church and took up the whole back pew. Miss Fannie came in and ordered the visitors to "scrunch up" since that was her seat. I just knew those visitors would never come back. They did and joined the church later. They all managed to scrunch up to make room for Miss Fannie.

On one unannounced visit in my study, she confessed that she just loved the taste of liquor.

"I easily could have been an alcoholic," she said, "but I refrained because I don't think it is a good advertisement for a Methodist to drink."

She went on to say she knew several Methodist imbibers the church didn't know about. Maybe that's another reason she had right-of-way in street crossing.

Shakespeare was her all-time favorite writer. She had read all his works many times and gave me a small but complete set of Shakespeare without bothering to ask if I wanted it. Underneath all her gruffness, however, was a heart beating for her Lord and the Methodist Church. She was faithful in her prayers, attendance, involvement, and generosity. I learned she quietly and quickly helped anyone she found in need. Especially was she helpful to children of poor families who needed assistance for education beyond high school. Truly, Miss Fannie was a community icon and a treasure of Hugo. She also was one of my all-time favorite heroes in First Church.

Bill

Another treasure of Hugo was a lifelong bachelor who was among the wealthiest people in Choctaw County. His parents had been devoted members of First Church. He had inherited their modest estate but apparently not their generosity. Bill did contribute the entire cost of that needed outside elevator into the sanctuary foyer. He gave it in memory of his parents.

Bill was known to be a morally upright and highly respected man. He lived in a large one-room apartment downtown over the corner drugstore. I was told he owned much of the property upon which businesses sat. The entrance to his upstairs apartment was off the sidewalk next door to the barber shop. He invited me to come on up for a visit anytime. "The door is always open," he said.

A few weeks later I was passing that door and decided to go up. I found him sitting in a cane-bottom chair reading the *Wall Street Journal* near the potbellied stove. Only one other chair was available. It looked like an expensive overstuffed seat, but one not often used. He acted pleased I had come.

"Sit down, Preacher," he said.

I did, and the dust of decades squirted in all directions. After a bit I said, "Bill, I've heard a lot about you. Tell me about yourself over the decades you have lived."

"Well," he said, "I've been broke several times, the first time during the Depression. I recovered and met a fine woman I thought a lot of. She felt the same about me. We wanted to get married, but I put her off until I could secure her future if anything happened to me. She kept wanting to get married, and I kept putting it off until she married another man. I kept making money until I made enough not to go broke anymore."

We talked some more. Bill was a fascinating person. Finally I asked, "Bill, you have had a long and prosperous life. If you could live life over, would you make any change?"

"Yes, I would," he said immediately. "The first thing I would change is to marry that woman, for you see, Preacher, everybody needs somebody to fill up life with!"

Bill had become a true treasure of the town, but he had missed out on the richness of "someone to fill up life with."

Doctor of Roses

Our family doctor was a fine physician, with a personality akin to that of Miss Fannie. He attended our worship services but was not much involved in the church's life and outreach.

On my first visit to his office with flu-like aches, pains, stuffiness, and multiple miseries, he began a general examination. I sought to explain what I thought was wrong with my whole body.

After about 30 seconds he said, "Preacher, I am the doctor!

I'll find out what's wrong. When I'm finished, you will pay me for what I know and can do for you!"

Well that was plain enough, but he was right. He told me what was wrong and wrote two prescriptions. I was shaken over the charges. I muttered that it was a hefty bill for 10 minutes of his time.

"It's not how much time I get paid for," he said. "It's what I alone can do for you."

We both chuckled, and I left.

This doctor was a widower of several years. Many people called him "Dr. Roses" because he grew and showed roses, winning many first-place awards. Several months after my visit, he began showing up for worship with one of the widows in the church. Soon afterwards they decided to get married. They asked me to perform the private wedding in the church sanctuary.

The ceremony over, he asked me, 'Preacher, how much do I owe you?"

Without pause I said, "$50."

He blinked, pulled out a $50 bill and handed it to me. Then he said, "That's pretty steep for five minutes of your time, isn't it?"

"It's not how long it takes me to get you married," I gleefully responded, "It's what I know and I alone can do for you!"

He grinned, shook his head and left with his new bride. He had remembered, and I had received the largest gift to that date for conducting a marriage ceremony. It did me little good, since custom was to give honorariums for weddings to the pastor's wife.

"Dr. Roses," despite his professional grumpiness, was another treasure of the community.

Alvin Rogan

Alvin was the owner of the funeral home in the black community. He, his wife, and children were all longtime members of St. Paul Church. His leadership and support were probably crucial to that church surviving as long as it had. Many times I found myself sitting in the glider on the front porch of his funeral home. People on foot and in cars waved or spoke to Alvin as they went by. It was apparent the entire black community considered him a trusted leader.

My frequent visits mostly were to consult with him on matters regarding our progress on Paul's Chapel. My labors as a white pastor trying to merge two black congregations were tedious, to say the least. I often felt the need to get Alvin's insights to avoid mistakes of judgment. The church members were confident he would give wise counsel. It is little wonder we became very good friends.

We joked a lot and enjoyed each other's company. The more I worked with him, the more I realized what a valuable role he played in the life of the entire area. He was a self-differentiated person. He knew exactly who he was, what he wanted to get done, and how he was to get it done. Because so many trusted him, they found him a source of common sense, wisdom, and practicality. The business community held him in high regard for his calm, thoughtful, and deliberate handling of potentially explosive situations. After I shared with him the matter of the swimming pool and heard his response, I concluded he was a community treasure the town could not do without.

Miss Tenny

From the outset of my involvement at St. Paul Church, Miss Tenny (nearly 80) was right there to support the effort with her prayers, voice, and sacrificial gifts toward the effort. All she had in the world was a tiny rundown house and her Social Security income. Yet when she sat on the back row and "revved up" the preacher with her "Amen," "All Right" and "Tell it, Preacher!" any visitor would have concluded she was in charge of the whole church.

She loved our entire family. On one occasion she called Lavelle to come right over. Lavelle went. On Miss Tenny's table were her monthly supplies of commodities from the county. Canned goods, staples, cereal, a small chunk of cheese, and a small ham were all a part of her cupboard for the month. Miss Tenny insisted Lavelle take part of the ham since, she said, she could not eat it all before it went bad. Lavelle declined at first but relented when sadness filled Miss Tenny's face. It was an amazing experience of Christian generosity.

Every time I talked with her, she would remind me that she was praying for my family, me, and especially for my endeavors for the black people in the town. At times she would reveal to me names of other folks she was lifting up to God for their change of heart and behavior.

After hearing later of my being appointed to a church in Oklahoma City, she tearfully said to me, "You have been God's man for all of us in Hugo, especially to us on our end of town. All of us are so grateful that you have walked with us while you were here in our midst."

Then she said, "We will never forget you. And God won't forget, either."

Our family has never forgotten Miss Tenny, either. She died shortly after our departure from Hugo. Long, long before, however, she had already qualified fully as one of the "little people" designated a community treasure.

James

For many years James had served as custodian of First Church. As a pastor I always made it a point to affirm and befriend the custodians I had known. James was special. He went about his schedule with precision and loyalty. He did more favors for members outside his job description than they had a right to ask of him.

Strange as it might sound, James became my resident confidant and friend. We went fishing when we both could find time. At break time, we ate watermelon out of the kitchen cooler, munchies, or whatever we could find—all of which one of us had put there. Before I would drive to an out-of-town meeting, he would go across the street to the parsonage to wash my car. When I tried to pay him, he refused to take the money. When I objected and ordered him not to wash my car without pay, he did it anyway. On every occasion he would say, "We don't want our pastor leaving town in a dirty car." I am sure I arrived at most of those meetings with the most spic-and-span car on the scene. I finally gave up trying to stop his efforts.

It was the same way with Lavelle. When I was away for a few days, James checked to see if all was well at the parsonage. If anything broke down or any other need arose, James would take care of it. He was the security guard, fixer-upper, and on-site assistant. Indeed, he was a trusted friend, coworker, and, at times, counselor. His gentle and kind spirit toward everyone endeared him to all colors and kinds of people. Always, he was doing something for a neighbor or running an errand for somebody else. Certainly he merited the title of "treasure of the community" for all the good he did for others.

Final days in Hugo

In early January 1971 I received a call from Bishop Paul Milhouse in Oklahoma City. It was just a few days before our scheduled groundbreaking for the new Paul's Chapel. Bishop Milhouse had an amazing memory for names, right down to the names of pastors' children. He had heard me state months earlier that our oldest son, Dana, wanted to go to Oklahoma City University when he graduated that coming spring. The bishop said he would like to move me to Epworth Church, just a few blocks from the university's campus.

"It is a fine opportunity for Dana to be at home while working on his degree," he said.

It would be a great financial help to us as well. Eagerly I accepted the appointment. When a bishop called to say he would like me to move, I knew I could not turn down his offer.

The following Sunday morning before the scheduled groundbreaking, I shared the news of my appointment to Epworth with both congregations. Paul's Chapel members reacted with sadness, and some with "put outness" with the bishop. I tried to calm down the situation by reminding then that Paul had planted and Apollos had watered, etc. My words helped but not much.

That afternoon's groundbreaking went well, with much-awaited anticipation and thanksgiving. The loan had been made. Gifts, grants, and five-year pledges underwrote the $40,000 goal and then some.

"The new church will happen," someone shouted as shovels turned the dirt.

The day of my departure from Hugo was near at hand. On my last day at the church study, one of the prominent women of Hugo dropped by. She was a member of another denomination. Her husband had died several months earlier. Her visit was short. She handed me a check for a sizable amount and designated it to the "Lord's work at Paul's Chapel." She offered several kind words on my behalf, then added how grateful she was personally to see the spirit of cooperation and appreciation for a better town. Her visit made special my last hours in my study. The gift was added to the amount beyond the $40,000 goal.

That night Miss Fannie called. She had heard someone had taken our family to dinner the night before.

"I want to be the last person in Hugo to eat with your family and to say goodbye," she said. "I'll meet you early in the morning at the restaurant on your way out of town."

She didn't ask; she told us. It was too late to object. Besides, the invitation was very thoughtful of her. We accepted and said we would be there at the early hour.

We left Hugo after a full breakfast. It had been a special time with Miss Fannie. Our hearts were full of joy. My journey at Hugo had challenged and changed me in so many fruitful ways. Certainly I had been privileged to serve as a pastor in Hugo. The Methodists there would live long in our memory.

Epworth Church in Oklahoma City was waiting for our arrival. We were eager to begin another leg in our journey of ministry.

It would be presumptuous for any pastor to rate his or her ministry according to the value of its particular parts. Only God's long view of one's ministry can accurately measure that impact. Even so, and at the risk of appearing presumptuous, I feel the most productive, pervasive, and long-lasting contribution of my 31 months in Hugo stemmed from my involvement with the black church community. It simply touched almost every other aspect of my ministry.

Several signs of that surfaced on the occasion of the dedication service five years later at Paul's Chapel, June 4, 1977. A large crowd from across the community over-filled the church. The bishop, superintendent, and dignitaries of several sorts were all there. I had been invited to return for the occasion. Sitting on the front pew was the woman who had scolded me years earlier for getting involved with the black churches. After the service she started toward me. She had been fully engaged in the energy of the service. As she approached me, I did not know what to expect.

"Preacher," she said without ado, "I was wrong about what I said in the hallway at First Church. I am sorry for what I said. This new Paul's Chapel has brought all of us closer together in this town. Bridges have been built between the black and white communities. We have come a long way in understanding one another better. We needed Paul's Chapel to show all of us how to find new beginnings and friendships and cooperation."

Hers was a beautiful statement. I was deeply touched.

Many other signs were more visible. New curbing along new pavement of the major street into the black community had been completed. Bank loans had upgraded and expanded several black businesses. Loans for home improvements made possible better living conditions. Paul's Chapel itself stood as a permanent sign that working together the entire community benefits. It was my understanding that the swimming pool was now open to everyone.

Dedication day, for me in particular, had been a great day.

Ray Owen's birth-
place, "the Dinkens
place," Weakley
County, Tennessee.

Charlie & Lula
Owen, 1918.

Lavelle Coburn
Owen's birth-
place, Frog Jump,
Tennessee.

Frog Jump, near Alamo, Tennessee, Lavelle's birthplace.

Ray Owen with a Korean baby at
Helen Rosser's clinic in Pusan, 1960.

Lavelle's parents, Lucille Archer
Coburn and William Isaac
Coburn, 1952.

The Owen family, 1963: Grandmother Venera Page (sitting), P.J, E.W., Virginia, Mayme, Mother Lula, Father Charlie, Ruby, Doyle, Ray.

Darryl, Ray, Dana, Dyton, Lavelle, and Crickett the poodle, 1968.

Lavelle and Dyton at the moment of Ray Owen's election as bishop, Fort Worth, Texas, July 1992.

Bishops Eugene Slater (left) and Ernest T. Dixon congratulate Ray as he is received as bishop of the San Antonio Area, September 1992.

Baptizing Pedro Torres with ice water during a mission project in Mexico, 1993.

Receiving land for the new United Methodist Center in San Antonio, Texas. From left, Dr. Steve Wende, David Sielheimer, Patsy Johnson, land donor Denny Hallmark, Bishop Owen, March 1993.

Briefing by Ambassador James Laney, Seoul, South Korea, 1995.

Bishop Roy Clark passing the president's gavel to Bishop Owen for the new General Commission on United Methodist Men, 1996, Nashville, Tennessee.

Bishop Owen presiding at the South Central Jurisdiction Conference, Kansas City, Mo., 1996.

Texas Govenor George Bush receiving a copy of the United Methodist *Book of Resolutions* from Bishop Owen and Dr. James Mayfield in Austin, May 1999.

Lavelle and Ray Owen,
United Methodist Center,
San Antonio, Texas, 1998.

Ray receiving the Texas United Methodist College Association Award from Bishop Ben Oliphant (left), director of TUMCA, and Dr. Joe McMillian, president of Huston-Tillotson College, February 1999.

United Methodist Center, San Antonio, Texas, November 1996.

Plaque in New Valley Methodist Church in Tennessee (right) commemorating where Ray gave his life to Christ.

10

Journey in Shadows of the Imminent

The date for our arrival at Epworth Church in Oklahoma City was January 15, 1971. I had already made a commitment to lead a seminar on evangelism for the United Methodist Congress on Evangelism to be held in New Orleans the first few days of January.

While there, I received a number of phone calls from members of Epworth. The board chairman was the first to welcome us. Several other leaders called to explain their roles and to add their welcome and greetings. Never before had we received so many calls from our next congregation.

A special call came from a woman who, I would learn, was another peerless personality, beloved by the congregation as "Miss Mary." She began by saying, "This is Mary E. McBrayer." With much dignity and grace, she went on to say, "I want to add my personal welcome at your coming to Epworth Church."

A retired schoolteacher, she asked the names and ages of our three sons. She ended our lopsided conversation by stating, "It will be my pleasure to greet you and your family on your first Sunday with us. You will know me when you see me."

When we arrived at the Epworth parsonage, a gracious and fun-loving delegation welcomed us and showed us through our spacious and well-furnished home. Every part of the house was spotless and made fully ready for our occupancy. Foodstuffs for initial meals were in the refrigerator. The garage and storage area above it were freshly cleaned. Even the lawn and shrubbery were immaculately manicured.

Such thorough and thoughtful preparation was an indication that we were already appreciated as the new pastoral family. Quickly we would discover such hospitality was not just that of the delegation but of the entire congregation. We felt confident our journey among such gracious people would be both fruitful and fulfilling. We looked forward to a long tenure, but that was not to be.

Attendance at the worship service the following Sunday morning essentially filled the sanctuary. I was impressed and encouraged. As the introit signaled the opening of the service, a stately woman with red hair, wearing gloves and a sizable, multi-colored hat, was formerly escorted by an usher down the left center aisle. She took her usual seat at the end of the pew on the second row. As she sat down, our eyes met briefly. She smiled and subtly nodded her head. I knew immediately she had to be Miss Mary. She warmly confirmed my conclusions as we greeted each other at our reception following the service.

Only one other person sat closer to the pulpit than Miss Mary. That was Brother Collier, an elderly, sainted, retired pastor of the United Pentecostal Church. He was very much a part of Epworth's life, since he lived very close to the church. Brother Collier sat on the front row at the opposite end of the pew and was generous with regular "amens" to the preaching.

My first sermon was based on the text from Proverbs: "Where there is no vision, the people perish." Later I would learn just how fitting that text had been. Epworth Church had been born out of a vision that simply would not die.

The Methodist Episcopal Church and the Methodist Episcopal Church, South, in 1901 undertook a joint venture to establish a Methodist university in Oklahoma City. With support of Methodist leaders, city officials, and the business community, land was secured northwest of downtown. Construction got under way in 1902 for a one-building facility to house the school.

By 1903 a four-story, rectangular brick edifice stood elegantly atop a hill in the middle of a 52-acre weed patch. The building provided 35 rooms for classes, faculty and staff offices, and a chapel. Articles of incorporation for Epworth University were filed with the state in 1903. In September 1904 the new university opened its doors to 116 students. That number increased to 210 by year's end. The joint venture of two Methodist bodies had become reality, but not for long.

When Epworth University opened its doors in 1904, a federated congregation of the two Methodist denominations was established. This congregation met in the Epworth University Chapel. Clovis Chappell served as the pastor.

For seven years the university and congregation struggled together for sufficient financial resources. In 1911 Epworth University went broke, closing its doors at the end of the spring semester. The federated congregation disbanded. Clovis Chappell went on to become a renowned preacher and prolific writer as he served premier Methodist churches in different states of the country.

By late summer that year a number of members of the former federated congregation decided they did not want to disappear as a Methodist church. They organized and to some degree mobilized the community. A modest structure was built for worship not far from the university. This new church became known affectionately as the "little brown church." On August 13, 1911, the congregation formally named itself "Epworth Methodist Church."

Ten years later, after long litigation, the Epworth University building and 11 acres of land went to the Methodist Episcopal Church, South. The new Epworth congregation then purchased the building and land for $40,000 and moved in. They didn't even have to change their church's name. (Apparently the "little brown church" property was sold.)

It would take several attempts by each Methodist body before a permanent Methodist university was finally founded. On June 4, 1924, Oklahoma City University was chartered and is still located at Northwest 23rd Street and Blackwelder—less than a mile from the old Epworth University property.

In 1927 the growing Epworth congregation spent another $40,000 constructing a sanctuary to seat 600 worshippers. The facade and massive pillars on the old front entrance of the university building were preserved and reinstalled as the impressive new front entrance of the still-standing Epworth Church. In 1952 the church added a splendid Children's Building, which even today is adequate for ministries for children.

Indeed, Epworth Church was born of a vision that simply would not die. By the time I arrived as pastor in 1971, numerous nationally known pastors, preachers, missionaries, and dignitaries had contributed to Epworth's remarkable history. Such persons as Clovis Chappel, Gaston Foote, Ira Williams, and E. Stanley Jones had left lasting marks on Epworth Church.

Early on in my time at Epworth, I realized how fortunate I was, even though I stood at the tail end in a line of distinguished and renowned spiritual giants of the 20th century. I knew whatever contributions I would add to the history of Epworth would be done in the shadows of the eminent.

What looked so bright and possible for Epworth's future at mid-century, however, had been greatly dimmed by 1971. The heart for dynamic ministry was still there but not the membership strength or the financial resources. Or the rousing vision of young families.

The once-prominent community of middle-class constituents had become the outer edges of the inner city. Property upkeep and value had followed the decline. Most of the first-generation homeowners had passed from the scene, leaving properties to nonresident heirs, who disposed of them at bargain prices. Many who managed to purchase at such bargains could not renovate and restore the homes. Potholes and broken curbing along the streets only amplified the community's deterioration.

Young families in the community were non-churchgoers. It was apparent the church was not attracting them. Not only that, more and more middle-aged members were moving to the suburbs. That meant the church's membership was increasingly "nonresident," leaving the community less identifiably related to Epworth.

On top of all that, the student body of the large senior high school across the street from the church was experiencing increasing drug use. That caused further deterioration in the community itself.

Still, the core participants in the Epworth congregation

were very much alive. I spent my first full week familiarizing myself with church facilities. Except for the Children's Building and the sanctuary level, every floor of the building critically needed updating and renovating to meet changing opportunities for ministries.

Time was of the essence for a new, bold, and creative vision to be developed, adopted, and implemented if Epworth Church were to engage and involve the racially and economically changing clientele of the surrounding community.

My early months at Epworth were the most demanding and draining I ever experienced. The pastoral workload alone was extremely heavy because of the aging of the largest segment of the congregation. I averaged two funerals a week. Every day we had several seriously ill members in the five hospitals scattered all over Oklahoma City. In addition, an increasing number of homebound members needed pastoral care and visitation. We managed to develop a team to distribute the Lord's Supper monthly to the shut-ins.

Though constantly on the move in pastoral care, I was much aware I was not meeting the needs. Yet I was somewhat energized and certainly blessed by the applied faith I found in these hospitalized and homebound members.

Spiritually, their faith was helping keep my own soul alive. Intellectually, I managed to finish writing my thesis for my master of arts degree in evangelism. It was accepted. I was notified I would graduate with honors the following spring. Emotionally and physically, however, it was glaringly apparent I could not maintain such a pace. I needed an associate pastor to take part of the pastoral care workload and to implement the developing visions.

As we moved into late summer of 1971, we implemented our tutoring ministry for the benefit of students in Classen High School. We were especially interested in reaching students from other countries who were en route to citizenship. The tutoring curriculum was rather basic: English language, writing, American history, math, etc. The faculty was composed mostly of retired persons. Those who taught and those who learned were both enriched.

In August our family endured a traumatic experience. The

church had hired Darryl, our middle son, to mow the church lawn. He was a good worker and enjoyed making a few dollars for himself. One morning he was having a hard time with a particular area overgrown with weeds and clover. The growth was damp from a recent rain and choked down the mower. I went out to see if I could help. I took the mower and pushed it into the tall weeds and clover. Darryl started to pick up a small limb just as I raised the front part of the mower a bit to get over the weeds. He slipped on the wet clover, and his foot went under the blade, severely injuring the top of his foot and great toe.

What a terrible accident. I rushed him to the nearest hospital. Darryl was so brave and calm, despite the immense pain he was enduring. He was taken immediately into surgery and spent several days in the hospital. A week later his school started.

He was laid up for two months, during which he spent four more days in the hospital undergoing a second round of skin grafting. A tutor from the school system kept Darryl abreast of his studies. A fine student, he made good grades and joined his eighth grade classmates in October. We were all so proud of the way he handled his ordeal.

Every year I received numerous invitations to preach revivals. I limited the number of invitations I accepted. I had agreed a year earlier to preach the revival at Kellyville, a small church not far from Tulsa. With all I was engaged in, I didn't much feel like going. I was tired and not up to giving the time and energy it would take for a week of revival preaching. But I had made the commitment, so I went.

Pastor Don Barefoot and the congregation had worked hard to prepare the entire community. To my utter astonishment, that small congregation received 24 new members. Eleven came by profession of faith and baptism. Every night the church was full. Every aspect of the worship service was uplifting and inspiring. The singing especially was inspirational. Again and again it was said, "God's spirit moved mightily among us tonight!" Instead of being even more exhausted, I came home refreshed, relaxed, and energized for the work piling up and waiting for my return.

I once heard an elderly preacher say, "The surest way to refresh your body, mind, and soul for the work at hand is to take in a revival!" Well, I had been to a revival and found that elder's words to be true!

By late fall of 1971, we had done a considerable study of the community's demographics. We had also made a preliminary survey of the specific needs Epworth Church should be addressing. A vision had slowly emerged, with more than a dozen major components. The church was to implement these components over the next five years. It was time for the committee's report and the administrative board's action.

The vision and its strategy were adopted with near unanimous support. The plan was to be set into motion according to priorities. The vision was a courageous challenge that would call for the commitment and dedication of every member family in the church.

The adopted vision brought renewed vitality to the congregation. Already we were seeing some increase in Sunday school and worship attendance. Some of our inactive members began to participate again in the life of the church. Growth in membership was noticeable but not dramatic. Deaths and members moving out of the community kept numbers static. Even so, a new sense of excitement was stirring us and spurring us onward into the vision.

When we implemented one component, it would spin off a new dimension of ministry needing to be addressed. For example, a new thrift shop furnished clothing for people of all ages in the community.

Members donated quality articles as they cleared their closets of seasonal clothing—from hats to shoes and everything in between. The shop never lacked ample merchandise. It was run by some of the kindest, most gracious, and most caring volunteers I ever met. They put customers at ease and treated them with genuine dignity and respect. The customers were made to feel they were persons of worth. They were invited to join in worship and Sunday school and to become a part of Epworth's vision. Some of them accepted the grace extended to them and joined.

Out of the thrift shop ministry emerged the need for a Community Cupboard, to which families could come for nonperishable foodstuffs. Like clothing, these foodstuffs were supplied regularly by members of the church.

The Community Cupboard soon revealed a need for funds to assist families in acute financial situations—an Alms Fund. Much of this fund helped transient persons in need of gasoline, a night's lodging, utility cutoffs, a meal, or perhaps a bus ticket to some reasonable destination. The Alms Fund was replenished regularly by anonymous gifts.

It seemed the more Epworth Church reached out, the more it discovered spinoff needs waiting to be addressed. Another spinoff vision component was spawned on a frigid day in the winter of 1971. An elderly and perturbed member called me for help. She had to see her doctor but could not raise the garage door to get her car. "Could you get someone to come over and help me?" she pleaded.

She lived only two blocks away, so I rushed right over. I couldn't raise the door at first, either. Then I noticed water had frozen along the seam at the bottom of the door. I kicked along the seam a few times and easily raised the door. She would make her doctor's appointment on time.

You would have thought I had rescued her from an inferno. She thanked me for several days. She must have told half the congregation how her pastor had saved her from a lot of problems. By the time the tale had made the rounds, it was a little bloated but still interesting.

Out of that incident we developed the Cadre of Concern. A few retired men volunteered to be on call for any odd job an elderly person needed done, whether or not the requestor was a member of Epworth Church. These men repaired leaky water faucets, changed light bulbs in ceiling fixtures, repaired pesky window blinds, oiled squeaky doors, and fixed window screens. They replaced burned-out receptacles and leveled concrete porch steps. Just about any minor job that needed doing mobilized the Cadre of Concern. The only pay these men received was an overabundance of praise and gratitude.

While the vitality of these ministries of outreach was adding strength to the church, I was becoming severely overworked and stressed. It was during this period of near exhaustion that

I had a profound experience of God's presence and renewing stability. I had been praying for some time for some affirmation that Epworth's efforts were indeed making a difference in persons outside the membership. I also had been praying for some sign of whether my pastoral leadership was having an effect as I moved about in the community.

That sign came in a strange way. As I made my way home late one afternoon after another hard day of doing one funeral and arranging for another, meetings in between, a wedding counseling session, and visiting several members in different hospitals, I was entirely ready to call it a day. Quite clearly I sensed a strange urge to visit a couple who had attended our worship service the past Sunday. I barely knew their names. I shrugged it off, reasoning that their home was too far out of the way and that I would drop by later when I was in the neighborhood. But the urge persisted, so I decided the notion was compelling and that I should be obedient.

I turned in to the driveway and found the husband tinkering with his car. He looked up, smiled broadly, and came toward me with hand outstretched.

"I can't believe this!" he said. "My wife and I were just talking about you a few minutes ago."

By that time she had joined us. Taking her hand, he went on to say, "The timing of your coming must be confirmation that we should belong to Epworth Church!"

They were baptized and received into membership the following Sunday and became devoted and supportive members.

The rest of my way home was invigorating. I shuddered, however, at the thought that I had almost gone home rather than obeying that strange urge. It was a learning experience that made me more aware of God's spirit leading, even in times of stress and fatigue.

While these components of the vision were getting fully into motion, the administrative board took on the priority component of renovating the Great Hall floor. The hall had a high ceiling, some 20 feet wide and more than 100 feet long, with a stairway entrance at each end. This area served as the main artery in the building. It was well-appointed with fine couches, stuffed chairs, lamps, tables, mirrors, and oil paintings with religious scenes and themes. No wonder it was the favorite area for visiting, fellowshipping, and receptions. Because of 30 years of constant use, every aspect of the Great Hall floor was critically in need of restoration. That included the parlor, one classroom, and pastor and staff offices.

What most board members thought would be a "done deal decision" at the called meeting turned out to be quite a scrappy and conflictive session. The cost of the renovation was not enormous. Still, a few members were not in favor of the project, its cost, nor its loan rate of interest. Patience among the board members was wearing thin.

Finally, an impatient retired businessman stood and said, "We can do this! We need to do this! So if you are hung up on the interest rate, I'll lend the church the entire amount at whatever rate is acceptable to the board. Let's get on with it!"

One faithful and influential member was particularly against the project. So in response he fired back, "This church is not interested in putting a feather in the preacher's hat by this project!"

Dead silence. Most of the members seemed shocked. Apparently he thought the "preacher" was pushing to get the job done. From my perspective, I was very much in favor of the renovation but not excessively so.

At first I thought he was kidding. Amused, I responded jokingly, "If I had been looking for a church to put a feather in my hat, this church would not have been on my short list."

Dead silence, again. Then came a spontaneous roar of laughter and applause. Even the objecting member joined in the laughter.

Still, it had been a foolish response from me as the pastor of the church. Even before the laughter subsided, I deeply regretted my unguarded remark. And said so.

The board went on to approve the project almost unanimously. The objecting member and I went on to become even better and more trusting friends. When the renovation was completed, the entire Great Hall floor was absolutely elegant and inviting. We scheduled an open house for the membership and community. My friend served as one of the hosts who, with pride and joy, showed off the facility to many visitors. Not only that, he had supported the project once the board had approved it. I regarded him even more highly for his loyalty and devotion to Epworth Church.

At no time in my pastoral leadership at Epworth Church had I seen the congregation so excited in spirit. It had already become evident that the adopted vision would require the hands-on leadership of an associate pastor. The board, therefore, gave the go-ahead to ask for an associate to be appointed. I was to work with Dr. J. Clifton Sprouls, our district superintendent, in facilitating the process. Bishop Paul Milhouse and his cabinet would make the appointment at the forthcoming annual conference session in May 1972. Dr. Sprouls asked me to nominate some of those I would like to have as Epworth's associate pastor.

The person I knew who could get aboard quickly and implement the vision components was Jack Lyons. He worked easily with people. He knew how to lead. He knew the value of setting objectives, developing strategies, and reaching established goals. He was the associate Epworth needed. Only one hurdle stood in the way. I was fully aware that Jack long before had emphatically stated he would never be an associate pastor for anyone. I hoped he would soften his vow and come to Epworth.

With permission from Dr. Sprouls, Lavelle and I met Jack and his wife, Bobbie, for dinner at a restaurant to discuss the possibility. I shared with Jack and Bobbie our vision of his coming to implement the remaining components. Each would be a major undertaking. As expected, Jack and Bobbie were gracious and seemed pleased to be asked. Still, they wanted to think about it and to seek God's guidance in prayer. Teasingly, I advised them I had already done my praying. We would talk further at their convenience.

In short, Jack agreed to the appointment, which would be finalized in May. It felt good to all of us that our two families would be together again in ministry, some 10 years after we were at Highland Park Church in Lawton.

How quickly my first year at Epworth had passed. Early in the new year a conflictive spirit emerged in a meeting that was called to make plans for the annual State Fair Project in September. For many years one of the Sunday school classes sponsored a project of cooking and serving three meals daily during the Oklahoma State Fair. The project raised a lot of money but required a huge work force. The entire congregation was solicited to help out.

Eventually, nonmembers of the class grumbled that it was the Sunday school class's project. Profits went to the class and were dispersed at the class's discretion. Even though the class did contribute some of the receipts to the church's budget or to some special need, the grumbling persisted.

I leaned toward the project becoming a churchwide endeavor, since most of the congregation gave time and labor to it. In return for my piece of logic, I was referred to as a "puffed up toad who wasn't good for the church." Not only that, I received word that a few couples had decided not to make any more home visitations or invitations to prospective members "due to the way things were at the church."

The image of my slender frame being that of a "puffed up toad" was rather comical. Some days being a pastor is just not much fun. For me, this was one of those days. I decided to let the conflictive spirit wear itself out while I got on with the church's vision.

When September came, Jack and I served as chefs in the kitchen, since we both were trained in food preparation. One day during the fair project, we were taken to task for eating some fried chicken and not paying for it. So we paid up, even though chefs are entitled to sample the products of their epicurean skills. The rest of that day wasn't much fun, either.

Shortly before Jack's arrival as my associate, we opened two parts of our three-part weekday Children's Ministry. The first was the pre-school. The second was the Mother's Day Out. The third part was a full-scale daycare ministry, which was to open after Jack's arrival in June. He would oversee the process of meeting state and city codes and regulations.

This component of our vision provided a convenient, clean, and safe environment for some 60 children whose parents held jobs outside the home. It would serve as the anchor for the weekday ministry for children. Everyone seemed delighted that a long-needed component was at last in play—especially Miss Mary.

With the school year ending in May, our youth ministry was growing stronger under the leadership of Mike Schlittler. He later became an ordained minister in the Oklahoma Conference. Later still, he became one of our associate pastors at First United Methodist Church in Bartlesville, Oklahoma.

As I was leaving the church late one afternoon, a junior high youth asked me to explain the meaning of the Lord's Supper. I gave him a brief overview of the sacrament. On my way home I felt I had done a poor job of responding to his request. Suddenly my mind was flooded with points I should have made. The notion gripped me to write out an explanation of Holy Communion, beamed especially to youth.

Arriving home, I rushed past my family to write down the outline in my home study. After supper I returned to the study and wrote in dialogue form the meaning of the Lord's Supper. At bedtime, the booklet *The Supper Experienced* was finished. Except for minor editing, it was ready for publication. I had become an author. The booklet was distributed to and studied by our own youth group. It was also used as a basic resource for youths in camp settings. So well was it received that a second printing was done in 1975.

During the annual conference session of 1972, I was elected chairman of the conference board of evangelism. I was grateful to receive conference-level leadership. Again I would be standing in the "shadows of the eminent," such as Dr. Finis Crutchfield and Dr. Leroy Sewell.

The Lyons family arrived at Epworth Church the first of June. Jack immediately undertook to put into play the remaining major parts of the vision. All of them would be ready when school began the following fall.

The front lawn of the church served as a gathering place for the two lunch breaks of students in Classen High. As could be expected, trash and debris they left behind cluttered the area. Not only that, the outdoor carpeting on the portico entrance into the worship center became the target for carved obscenities.

Our responding strategy was to place picnic tables and colorful, conspicuous trash receptacles on the lawn. The receptacles would subtly invite students to deposit their bag lunch remains, reducing the clutter.

As classes began, we saw marked improvement on the grounds. We found a few obscenities carved into the wooden tabletops. At least there were fewer of them, and they were less obvious to the public than the words on the carpet. In time, the Classen cheerleaders used the portico area to practice their routines with a live audience. Noontime was a bit noisy, but the neighborhood seemed not to mind. Most of the students behaved well and seemed to appreciate our front-lawn ministry. Yes, we had a few members who objected. Soon, however, everyone saw the benefits of carrying it on.

At the same time, Jack and his crew of volunteers were developing the Bus Ministry. It was designed to take children and others to and from Sunday school and worship services. Since many of the children left home without breakfast, Jack frequently furnished doughnuts and treats to the kids. He was known occasionally to do the same thing for those in the Weekday Children's Ministry.

Being a lifelong schoolteacher, Miss Mary objected. It is reported she once scolded Jack by saying, "I'm going to shoot you for giving those sweets to the children!"

Jack mischievously replied, "Shoot, Miss Mary! Shoot!"

She never did, nor did Jack cease and desist. Apparently such encounters between the two served only to endear them to one another.

The Bus Ministry brought 50 to 70 children to the church each Sunday. The children all sat in the front pews on the right side. When children's church was over, they were escorted back to the Children's Building for additional learning. The older members of the congregation gave strong support for the children riding the bus.

When school started that fall, the Youth Lunch Break Recreation opened in the church's Youth Center. High school students in both lunch breaks were invited to the fourth-floor center. It offered music, movies, board games, pool, ping pong, shuffleboard, and areas for conversation. Older adults served as doorkeepers and room roamers to assure no drugs, alcohol or profanity were used in the building.

The number of students participating daily ranged from 250 to 300. At first we were apprehensive. As it turned out, there were few incidents of misbehavior during the year.

Epworth Church indeed was reaching out as never before to all the constituents of the community on behalf of Jesus Christ. We were not growing in numbers despite all our efforts. Still, the church was much healthier and stronger. Certainly it was vitally alive in its availability to the entire community.

By February 1973, *Enabling Evangelism* was published. It became a widely used resource for evangelization and making disciples for Jesus Christ.

The end time of pastoring Epworth came in a bizarre series of events. I had indicated to the district superintendent my desire to remain at Epworth when the appointments for 1973 were made. The pastor-parish relations committee had also asked that I return.

While I was at my desk in the first part of May, my secretary advised me to call Dr. Sprouls, who was in a cabinet meeting with the bishop. Naturally I immediately called the bishop's secretary, who said she had no knowledge of Dr. Sprouls wanting to talk to me. She delivered a note to him, and he came to the phone. Our conversation was awkward, to say the least. He had not called me. Someone had pulled an embarrassing prank on me. I had heard such a thing had been done to others "in fun." It was not funny for either Dr. Sprouls or me.

I apologized for calling him out of the cabinet meeting. He was most gracious and understanding. He went on to say the cabinet was working on appointments and that I was still slated to remain at Epworth. I was pleased to hear I would be returning.

The United Methodist system of appointing all pastors yearly makes for surprises at times. Late that very afternoon, Dr. Sprouls called me at home and chuckled as he said, "Ray, this really is your district superintendent!"

We both laughed. He then told me that some of the appointments had not held together and that I was the pastor the bishop and cabinet wanted to send to New Haven Church in Tulsa. Never once had I ever hesitated to go where I was sent and to stay until I was sent elsewhere.

"If that is where the cabinet and bishop want me to go," I replied, "I would be pleased to do so."

Dr. Sprouls thanked me for being willing to move.

It had been an up and down experience during the daylight hours of that one day. Quite by accident, I learned who had perpetrated that joke on me. It was difficult for me to resist jumping on him for such a sorry stunt. I never indicated to him that I knew. Long since the sting has gone out of me, and I am glad.

The family all began to think about moving to Tulsa after only 29 months with the courageous and fun-loving members of Epworth Church. I knew nothing about New Haven Church, not even where it was. I knew, however, that when we arrived, a fine congregation would be waiting to receive us and to love us. That would be enough for a beginning.

We departed Epworth Church feeling it was a stronger congregation and that our journey of faith among the members bore indelible marks of love and friendships that would last our lifetime. And beyond.

I had started out at Epworth feeling I stood in the shadows of eminent pastors. I departed Epworth feeling I had cast merely a shadow among an eminent congregation of dedicated followers of Christ.

11

Journey of Sadness and Celebration

Our first worship service at New Haven Church in Tulsa was June 10, 1973. From the call to worship to the benediction, it was an experience of inspiration. All the pews were filled, including those in the balcony. Splendid music and singing uplifted and thrilled us. The congregation seemed spiritually alive and joyful. Every person present for worship must have stayed for the reception immediately following. The people greeted us with genuine warmth and welcome.

We went home wrung out with emotion and gratitude for having been appointed as the pastoral family for such delightful and dedicated people. That first Sunday, which started out as a most wonderful day, however, would end as the absolutely saddest day for our entire family.

Late that afternoon I returned to the church to check on the evening activities. A short while later, one of our members escorted to my office a major in the United States Army who needed to talk with me. In full military dress, he expressed his deep regret for having to inform me that our son, Dana, had been killed in a motorcycle accident just a short way from the military post where he was stationed.

Dana had ridden to a nearby convenience store to buy some miscellaneous items. As he returned, he came to a curve in the road where sand had accumulated on the pavement. As he leaned with the curve, the cycle began to slide sideways, drawing him under an oncoming pickup truck and out the passenger's side behind the front wheel. Even though Dana had his helmet on, death came instantly from massive head injuries. It had happened at the same time our family greeted members in a reception line earlier that morning.

The driver of the pickup truck was a 16-year-old boy out with his father. The police furnished us with the accident report, which concluded, "No one was at fault since neither driver caused the accident nor could have prevented it."

I was shocked and shaken to the very depths of my soul upon hearing the tragic news. I had a compelling need to go into the sanctuary to pray at the chancel. I thanked God for the fine son we had for nearly 20 years. Strangely, perhaps, I felt no anger. Nor was I desirous of settling blame. I remember praying for the young driver of the pickup truck and his family. Looking back, I think that brief time of prayer settled my own soul for the ordeal of having to go home to tell Lavelle and our other two sons the horrible news. I cried out for God's spirit to be with us and to hold us. As we gathered the family, we knew the Holy Spirit was giving us strength in the most agonizing hours of our lives.

Within minutes, Dr. John Russell, our new district superintendent, was in our home praying for us and supporting us in every way. Within hours, friends from near and far came to love us and to encourage us. Bishop Paul Milhouse called from Oklahoma City to extend his heartfelt prayers and concern for us.

Later that night, a reporter from the *Tulsa World* newspaper called to ask for a statement from us to be published in the next morning's edition. "How in the world does one in the crush of such an experience make a statement?" I asked myself. In that heavy and horrible moment, I managed to speak these words: "Lavelle and I and our two sons believe all the moments of life are in God's hands. So we have committed this, our most difficult moment, to God's care and keeping." It was all I could think to say. Now, after nearly 29 years, I've found those words had been enough. They said all that was in our hearts.

We arranged with the military for Dana's remains to be delivered to Tennessee for the funeral and interment. At that time in our lives, we fully intended to return to Tennessee upon our retirement. The memorial service and committal would be several days later. It would take that long for the funeral home and military to finalize arrangements.

When Dana's remains arrived at the funeral home in my hometown of McKenzie, I was advised immediately that we would not be able to view our son's body. The head injury had been so extensive as to preclude any semblance of recognition. At the time Lavelle was with her folks in Atwood, Tennessee, awaiting word from me about when the body arrived.

It was another incredibly hard moment for me, especially as I drove the 15 miles to tell Lavelle in person. For years I had been about the pastoral ministry of informing families of untimely deaths of their loved ones in similar circumstances. Now I had to inform my own beloved wife and sons that we would not view our son's body.

As I drove, I called out to God again for strength and help. Suddenly, many of the funeral passages of scripture I had used in funerals over the years passed audibly over my lips. It was as if God were saying to me, "You believed these words when you spoke to others in their grief. Now apply these passages to your own pain, and be comforted and strengthened!" Though it was another wrenching moment for us, I was able to share another piece of painful news.

Time has never closed the gaping hole Dana's death tore in our souls some 29 years ago. Time, however, has brought healing. That healing began several months later as we decided to make something good and lasting come out of Dana's death. We established the Dana Owen Scholarship Fund at Oklahoma City University. Dana had completed one year of study there and was committed to return after his tour of duty to complete his degree in law enforcement.

Regularly over the years we have received notes and letters from student recipients of the scholarship assistance. With each letter or note comes the recurring sense that Dana goes on living through those students. We again and again are made thankful for his brief and exemplary life among us.

Upon our return to Tulsa, the New Haven congregation went all out to minister to us. The lay leader encouraged us to take several days off for rest and recuperation from the staggering ordeal we were still enduring. He had even made tentative reservations at a lodge for our extended time out. It was a sensitive and caring thing for the church to do. We were deeply moved by the gesture of love, but we declined the offer. We had already decided to get on with our lives and the ministry at hand. Additional delays would only extend the time of adjusting to our loss. Not only that, but New Haven needed to get on with its ministry in the community. Within a short time we knew we had made the right decision.

Not long did it take us to realize New Haven's spiritually energized congregation of more than 1,300 members had a promising future in making disciples of Christ in large numbers. The fairly young congregation was located in the rapidly developing quadrant of southeast Tulsa. My predecessor, the Reverend Howard Plowman, had given good leadership in preparing the church to move forward in growth. The congregation's makeup was well balanced, with the largest segment being families with children still at home. It was a good sign of future strength.

The colonial-style facility stood boldly and elegantly in the center of the parish. Already the facility was severely strained. The sanctuary provided adequate space for worship by having two services on Sunday. A connecting corridor led to a two-story building consisting of offices, a small kitchen, and fellowship hall on the ground floor. The second floor provided rooms for several Sunday school classes—all of which were already overcrowded. The glaring, urgent need for the new building phase was self-evident. Some serious talk of moving ahead had taken place before my arrival. Yet no official decision had been made. Lest the church lose momentum and become stymied, it was critical that decision and commitment be made to undertake the new building phase immediately.

New Haven staff members were all quality persons who were in favor of moving forward. Berle Nash, director of music ministries, was an accomplished musician and choir director. She was also a delightful and fun-loving team player. The Reverend Richard House, the associate pastor, was an informed and supportive strength in staff relations. An able preacher, he was of tremendous help to me in getting the church to move on. Well-educated, he was looked upon with respect and was a leader of promise for the future. Richard went on to serve as a district superintendent and pastor of premier churches in Oklahoma. David Burris, director of youth ministries, went on to become a prominent pastor and delegate to the South Central Jurisdictional Conference. David was beloved by everyone, especially for his talents in leading and inspiring youths.

It also didn't take long for us to realize the parsonage was inadequate for our family of four. Though a lovely home, it consisted of three small bedrooms, a living area with adjoining breakfast nook, and a kitchen. The tiny kitchen was built on both sides of the narrow passageway to the garage. One could stand at the sink and reach anything on the opposite side of the room. The need for an adequate parsonage had been talked about before my arrival. Yet, again, nothing definite had been decided. Time was ripe for some definite decisions and commitments on these two pressing needs.

Soon working committees were appointed to address the needs for a new addition to the church and an adequate parsonage. Reports for administrative board action would come as committees were ready to make recommendations.

Adding to the urgency of getting another parsonage was an invasion of tiny sugar ants in the kitchen. They posed no danger, but they were definitely a nuisance. It was an everyday battle to keep the ants under control.

At the board meeting a few weeks later, the purchase of an adequate parsonage was the major item of business. The committee had reported nothing about the ants' invasion, but it recommended an immediate purchase. Few questions were asked, and little discussion took place. It was obvious the board was in full agreement with the committee. I was invited by the chairperson to make any additional comments. Because the board was in high spirits and always fun-loving, I stood up. Everything got quiet, as if the members weren't quite sure they wanted to hear any more points of view. They were ready to vote. I thanked the chairperson and said teasingly, "I hope you will authorize the purchase of a larger parsonage. Not just because we need it, but mostly because we can't spare the space the ants are taking up running about in the present one."

I thought the board would break up from the laughter. The vote was taken and approved unanimously. Then some member shouted out, "Never underestimate the power of sugar ants to prod the board of a Methodist church to make a decision!"

The board of trustees was authorized to find an adequate parsonage and to purchase it without having to bring it back to the administrative board. Three months from the time we arrived, we moved into a beautiful and spacious four-bedroom home that would provide plenty of room for sugar ants to romp and rove, should any show up.

With public schools opening in the fall, the activities and programs of New Haven quickly increased. I invited the men of the church to be my guests for breakfast at the church at 6:30 a.m. on a Tuesday morning. I promised to furnish a full breakfast for them. A dozen or so hungry men showed up expecting a "C-ration" type breakfast prepared by a former Army mess sergeant. They had to repent after enjoying a full from scratch breakfast instead.

I presented a plan for their consideration. I challenged them to meet with me every Tuesday for breakfast, devotions, and prayer. The meeting would be for one hour, with three segments taking 20 minutes each—eating, devotions, and prayer for New Haven's ministry and outreach to the area. We would dismiss sharply at 7:30 so everyone could be on the job by 8:30 a.m.

I encouraged them to make the Tuesday prayer breakfast a weekly priority. I also urged them to help get all our men involved. I assured them that men witnessing and working for New Haven was absolutely crucial to the church's overall ability to reach men and keep them involved with Christ.

Those present took up the challenge. Each week new faces showed up. Soon 40 or more were gathering to pray for one another and for God to help them witness for Christ to other men. Soon different teams of men took turns preparing the meal. The prayer breakfast had become their own ministry.

The prayer breakfast became a powerful spiritual influence in the parish as well as in the congregation. The weekly meeting served as a major port of entry for new member-families to get involved in New Haven's ministry and mission.

By the end of the year, the congregation was moving forward and growing stronger in all its vital signs. Worship attendance was up significantly. So was Sunday school participation, which necessitated a few classes having to meet in nearby members' homes until the second phase of the facility could be completed. Youth ministry, too, was growing. Giving was noticeably up, as were ministries of outreach. A deliberate and comprehensive means of assimilating new members was working with more than 100 people by years' end.

In the six churches I had served before, I had been able to keep informed of all activities going on in the congregation. At New Haven, however, the congregation challenged me to the extent of my having to play catch-up on all that was taking place. Regularly and frequently someone would catch a vision for a new ministry. Soon a group would bring that needed ministry into play, with a leader already identified. It was a thrilling and remarkable characteristic of New Haven.

Pressure increased for additional space by spring. The change-out of associate pastors in 1974 deflected some of the pressure. The Reverend Richard House was appointed to his own church in Blanchard, Oklahoma. The Reverend Gary Graham was appointed to New Haven. He and Margaret received a splendid welcome and were put to work immediately.

The feasibility committee appointed earlier was ready to report its findings and recommendations to the administrative board. Word leaked out that the committee would recommend strongly that the second building phase get under way. The recommended addition would almost double the existing space. Preliminary costs estimates, furnishings, and necessary remodeling would likely cost $700,000. It was a huge financial undertaking in the mid 1970s.

Yet the board never blinked or took a deep breath of surprise. The motion to move forward was briefly discussed. Few questions were raised. The motion was adopted almost unanimously. A building committee was appointed to work with the board of trustees to hire an architect for preliminary drawings and to formulate a financial plan to support the project. The long-range target date for completion was summer 1976.

Later that year I made two trips outside the country. The

World Congress on Evangelization took place in Louzanne, Switzerland. As the chairman of the Oklahoma Conference's Board of Evangelism, I was a delegate invited to attend. Thousands of leaders in evangelization met for several days of preaching, praying, sharing, and formulating a worldwide plan. Each represented denomination was challenged to take most seriously its call to "go make disciples of Jesus Christ."

The Billy Graham Association, along with judicatory leaders of world church bodies, put the event together. From all parts of the globe came renowned church leaders, including United Methodist bishops. At mealtimes we all ate together in a common dining facility. I felt so insignificant, sitting daily among world church leaders. Yet in every sense I was treated with respect and accepted as a fellow leader. We sang together and worked toward a common strategy until the final plan was greeted with excitement and commitment. It had been a grueling, energy sapping, and spiritually renewing 10 days of inspiration.

Near the end of the congress, a group of us took a train to Zermott and a visit to the breathtaking view of the Matterhorn. Its awesome and majestic presence is still hard for me to describe. My trip to the congress was truly a gift for a lifetime.

I was asked to serve on the Louzanne Committee, the follow-through group for the United States section. I attended the first meeting of the committee later that fall in Chicago. Upon learning the committee's work would require large chunks of time, I regretfully had to resign. There was simply no way I, as a pastor, could contribute the necessary blocks of time away from my church. The committee thanked me and understood.

In late fall I traveled to Israel for the meeting of the United Methodist Council on Evangelism. I was a delegate, since I was chairman of our conference board of evangelism. The board at New Haven was pleased that I had been invited and encouraged me to go. The trip was a whirlwind journey to Jerusalem for four days of finalizing evangelization strategy for the United Methodist Church. The other four days we visited biblical points of interest from Caesarea to Bethlehem. It was my first trip to Israel. Both parts of the trip added so much to my increasing understanding of the global nature of the United Methodist Church.

Upon my return, architectural drawings were waiting to be presented to the administrative board. They were handily approved. Specifications and details were sufficient to let out for bids. Concurrently, a church bond sale for raising the $700,000 cost was approved. Most of the bonds were sold to members of the congregation, with maturity dates ranging from three to 15 years.

By the time architectural plans were brought to the board for final approval, the total bond issue was essentially sold. As is always the case, the bids came in significantly higher than the total bond issue. Adjustments and cost cutting alternatives had to be taken. For the most part the initial cutbacks went well, until it came to the staff office area.

The suggestion was made to reduce staff space equally for each staff person, including the two areas for pastors' studies. It was the wrong place to start. My present study was totally inadequate, and what was suggested was unacceptable from my point of view. I realized that now would be the only time the church would provide permanent space for all the needs of the pastors in the future. I was firm in my view that we should not cut space or reconsider what a pastor's study should include.

A prominent member and businessman spoke rather stoutly, saying his own office was not as large as the pastor's and he seemed to have plenty of room. I did not want to confront this highly visible and successful man whom most everyone, including me, held in high esteem. Still, I felt we had to face this issue and get beyond it.

So I said to this good and faithful member, "I do not have any idea how much space you feel is adequate for your particular business. I do know what is adequate for a pastor in a church this size for the future."

I felt no anger, but I was firm.

The cutbacks and revisions moved on to the rest of the building. It had been a long, tedious, and tiring meeting, but we did the job that had to be done. When we adjourned, everyone lingered to chat and to congratulate one another.

I looked up to see the businessman coming toward me in long strides. Several noticed his direction. Arriving, he reached out his hand and said, "Preacher, you are absolutely right. I know nothing about how much space our pastors need to fulfill their responsibilities. I do know all of us want you to have sufficient space to do your job well. You have my full support and thanks!"

What a gracious gesture he had made. Then and there I knew I was privileged to be pastor of New Haven Church. This man's gentlemanly comment further solidified the congregation's full support for the expansion project. My admiration for him only increased from that point.

Out of that exchange I realized I was growing on several critical edges of leadership and effective ministry. First, I realized the congregation expected me to hold strong convictions and to express them when situations called for them. That was borne out by comments from other leaders.

"We need decisive leadership from our pastor," one person said. "Don't hold back in your convictions. If we disagree with you, we will work through it together. We trust your leadership!"

Her comment reminded me that sincere differences of convictions were helpful in reaching clearheaded decisions for the church.

Another edge of critical growth going on in my leadership was sermon preparation and preaching. From the outset of my ministry, I had written a full manuscript. I still do. It took several rewrites to get the sermon where I wanted it to be. But preaching from the full manuscript seemed to limit not only what I said but also how I said it. All the while, I was reading several books by prominent pastors on preaching without notes. I started to outline the sermon and preach from that. But I still felt limited, largely because the outline was almost as long as the manuscript. I started then to preach from key phrases, but I still hadn't found "my way" of preaching. Down deep in my soul, I wanted to preach without notes.

One Sunday I robed up hurriedly, picked up one of my Bibles and followed the choir into the sanctuary. As the choir sang its anthem I realized I had picked up the wrong Bible, leaving my notes in the one on my desk. I felt panic. No time to go back to get it. All I could do was pray, "Lord, help me!"

I never mentioned it to anyone—not even Lavelle. Within a

month the congregation knew something was different in my preaching. I was asked by a member if I were preaching without notes, since I never looked down. I had to confess. The word got out. One of the most endearing compliments regarding my new style of preaching was made at a Sunday school class party.

One man said, "Ray is so full of his sermon on Sunday, you can punch him anywhere, and it will squirt out!"

The compliment was a keeper. In a way, he was right. After writing the manuscript several times, I had actually internalized it. All the sermon needed was a little prodding, and it would flow out.

Concurrently, I was experiencing critical growth on a third edge of my ministry. I became inwardly aware that I was not getting to know the families in the church in a pastoral way. Our membership was growing. The faster it grew, the less able I was to know the members' needs and struggles as well as their joys and celebrations as growing disciples. It became a frequent concern that I lifted up in my prayer-closet time. Gradually, a plan began to come together.

I went on a prayer retreat for four days. In preparation for it, I sent a letter to all member families, inviting them to share with me prayer request for any concern, personal struggle, or need that I could pray for in my time apart. In the letter was a blank card for their specific requests. Included also was a stamped, self-addressed envelope to me personally that would go to a post office box number I rented to receive their requests.

I made five specific commitments in each letter:

1. Whatever requests were made would be strictly for my eyes only. I alone would pick up their letters and secure them until I opened them in the seclusion of my prayer retreat.

2. At the retreat I would read each request and give to it my own thoughts.

3. I would pray for God's spirit to draw near and guide the writer toward resolution.

4. I would search for a scriptural passage that would be of benefit for the writer to keep in mind. I would pray specifically by name for the one making the request.

5. When the retreat was over, I would take all cards and envelopes and burn them, so there would be no chance of the request ever being known.

The number of requests received simply overwhelmed me. The retreat would require sustained and uninterrupted time. I chose the location. Only Lavelle would be able to reach me. Emergencies during the four days would be handled by the associate pastor.

I must say those days in the prayer retreat enhanced dramatically my understanding of the value of pastoral care in my ministry. I was humbled by the trust and eagerness of the people to pour out their innermost heart and soul concerns. The specificity of most requests was raw and real.

That first afternoon and night I was unable to find a stopping place. Except for necessary breaks and one meal, I was still going through requests at 2:30 a.m. The second and third day it was the same, except that I did go to bed a bit earlier. By midafternoon of the fourth day, I had processed the last request. I returned home exhausted but far more aware of God's activity in the lives of the congregation. I was far more informed about the enlarged responsibility I had as a pastor and spiritual leader. As a disciple of Christ myself, I was merely seeking with those 300 families to make my personal walk with Christ more real and productive.

At the following two worship services on Sunday, I gave a general overview of the retreat experience, without reference to any specific request. Several times I had to pause because of emotion. I knew I was a different person because of those four days apart in prayer. Later I came to know the congregation was already seeing that change. For weeks the overview was received with continuing expressions of gratitude.

Nine years earlier, while serving the Antlers church, I had decided to take literally Jesus' admonition: "when you pray, enter into the closet...." It started out as an experiment in prayer. It turned out as an ongoing, enlarging experience in prayer. I discovered a new and exciting dimension of praying in absolute seclusion. From that time on, I found my own "prayer closet" in which to commune with God.

As a result of the prayer retreat, I yearned to develop and

preach a series of sermons on what I was discovering about "closet praying." In those seven sermons I simply shared with the congregation the findings and learnings I was gaining about the place and value of prayer in a disciple's life.

Apparently the series was much appreciated, since immediately it was suggested that the sermons be published. One businessman called to say he wanted to pay the publication costs. Two conditions he insisted on making in return: (1) that he would remain anonymous and (2) that the book be professionally published in hardback.

In 1975, *Probings In Prayer: Why the Closet* came off the press. The book appropriately was dedicated to the congregation of New Haven Church. In 1983 a second printing was published. Now, even in retirement, I am still discovering mysteries of praying in the seclusion of a closet.

Invitations began to come in to hold prayer retreats in local churches. On my way home from such a church retreat in western Oklahoma, I stopped at First Church, Stillwater, for a brief visit with Dr. Lloyd Peters, a dear friend and mentor of long standing. He was serving as senior pastor of that great congregation. He had been diagnosed with the beginning stages of Hodgkin's disease. It would be good to see him and to be uplifted by his strong faith and practical wisdom. We had a marvelous visit as we talked about several things.

His stature as a church statesman and leader had resulted in his being elected several times as a delegate to General Conference. It was certain Lloyd again would be elected to the delegation for the upcoming 1976 General Conference.

Without warning, Lloyd brought up the subject of the elections.

"Ray," he said to me bluntly, "you will be elected a delegate this time to the Jurisdiction Conference."

Before I could respond to his prediction, he said further, "Your leadership in the Oklahoma Conference has certainly made you a viable candidate. That will be the first of many elections for you in the future. Just remember this: None of us *deserves* to be elected to represent the church at that level, but some are *worthy*."

His few words amounted to a short course in common

sense, the value of humility, and the true boundaries of expectations—all bundled up into a principle to govern my conduct in matters of church politics. That day I realized the vast difference between seeking to "deserve" some honor and living in such a way as to be declared "worthy" of such honor by one's colleagues. Lloyd Peters' words served regularly in the future to curb any erupting tendency toward self-importance on my part.

At a meeting in Oklahoma City two weeks later, Dr. J. Clifton Sprouls—my former district superintendent—told me I would be elected. I was still somewhat skeptical. When the annual conference session convened, the first ballot was taken. It included my name far down the list. At the evening break Tal Oden, a dear friend and longtime lay delegate to General Conference, said to me with his mischievous grin, "Ray, you will be elected to the Jurisdictional delegation on the 16th ballot."

I chuckled and said, "And how would you know that?"

He grinned and walked away. I was elected on the 15th ballot.

That, too, was a humbling experience, knowing friends and colleagues trusted me to represent them in the business affairs of the eight-state area of the South Central Jurisdiction. The jurisdictional conference convened in Lincoln, Nebraska, in July 1976.

Most every pastor accumulates incidents so bizarre, so instructive, and so comical they are worth passing on. Such an event came to me late one Saturday night as I sat in the den reading a book. Long since, the family had gone to bed. Suddenly I was seized with jolting and writhing pain in my lower back. It was the most memorable and miserable moment I had ever known. I stood up, only to feel the stabbing pain again. As it worsened, I sat down again. I talked to myself and stretched out on the couch. I even squatted down and duck-waddled to muffle the rising pain. Nothing was helping.

I went to the bedroom and roused Lavelle. She was not much impressed with my agony.

"Take some aspirins and come to bed," she said.

I did the first but not the second, for fear I'd never get up again. Returning to the den, I went through the routine again, adding finger rubs as far as I could reach. No relief. I went again to the bedroom to tell Lavelle I was in sheer agony and that the aspirins hadn't helped. This time she at least turned over groggily and told me the aspirins had not had time to ease my pain. Back to the den in aloneness, to suffer my excruciating torment. By then it was way past midnight.

Once more I returned to the bedroom.

"Get out of the bed," I said, "and call the doctor you work for before I die! It's not right for you to sleep while I'm hurting so!"

Mumbling something I couldn't decipher in my agony, she finally called Dr. Don Loveless and explained my situation. After two or three "Uh huhs" and "OKs!" Lavelle said to me: "You're probably having a kidney stone attack. He said for you to go to the emergency room at the hospital. He'll call ahead to brief the personnel and arrange for a urologist to see you. You can drive yourself, and you are not dying!"

I felt helped but also hurt. Lavelle was sending me off alone in my most horrible ordeal. Not only that, but my doctor wasn't even coming to the hospital. I think one of my eyes was crying from the pain while the other eye was leaking tears that the two people I thought would always be there for me weren't.

I dragged myself to the car. By the time I arrived through potholes and street construction bumps, I walked into the emergency room—pain free. I told them who I was and sheepishly said, "The pain is gone. Is there any reason now for me to stay?"

Unimpressed, the nurse said, "Get on the gurney!" She then pushed me behind a thick curtain and parked me along the wall. Handing me a paper gown, she said coldly, "Take off all your clothes and put on the gown. The pain will definitely return. The doctor is on his way and will be here in 20 minutes."

Just like that, she disappeared through the curtain.

I fumbled to close the back of the paper gown, but it wouldn't cooperate. The nurse had been right. The pain came back in multiplied proportions. It was past just being unbearable. I rolled to one side and then the other, moaning in both directions. I sat up and talked to God and myself but only heard from the latter. I must have agonized for half an hour, at least. I rolled over to face the wall and saw a red button with a sign that read, "Push if you need help!" Well, I needed help in the worst way as I held the button down.

The nurse came and asked, "How are we doing?"

I didn't know how she was doing, nor much cared. As for myself, I was hurting, really hurting. A bit impatient, I asked, "When is the doctor going to get here?"

Quite coldly she replied, "You have been here only 10 minutes!"

I found her words to be unbelievable in my torture. She then told me the technician was on his way to take me for a full body X-ray.

"By the time you get back, the doctor will probably be here," the nurse said.

As she was leaving the technician arrived, rolled me up the hall, and pushed my gurney alongside the huge X-ray machine for a full supine-position X-ray.

"Just slide yourself off the gurney and onto the slab of the machine," he said.

I raised myself up on elbows and slid onto the slab. The gown at the back did not follow. My bare backside plopped down onto the icy cold slab. For a second I forgot my misery as I almost jumped back onto the gurney, where half my gown was still stuck. Things were not improving. The X-ray done, I was rolled back to that place where the "press the button" was located. I was about to press that button again when the doctor came in with X-rays in hand.

"Well," he said, pointing at the picture, "You have a kidney stone."

Bleary eyed, I could hardly see the tiny white dot at the end of his finger.

"We think we can take care of it by keeping you overnight and letting nature take its course," he said. "I'll give you an injection of Demarol for the pain and send you to bed upstairs."

I had not the will to resist.

With that, he injected me. I told him I needed to call my wife.

"Do it quickly!" he replied. "You'll be asleep in a few minutes."

"Lavelle is probably so sound asleep she won't hear the phone," I thought to myself. "Then I'll be out like a light, and she won't know what happened to me."

She answered, and I told her to call Buddy Bolin, the associate pastor, and tell him he had to preach both services later that morning.

"You want me to call him at this hour?" she asked.

"I certainly do!" was my response. "After all, it's only 2:30. That gives him six hours to prepare. Just tell him to do the best he can. That's what I'm doing."

I felt better as the medication took effect. My last thought was that if there were such a place as purgatory, I had already suffered sufficient torment to expiate all my sins and qualify me for heaven forever.

I went home the next day, still mystified at how such a tiny stone, which the doctor had given me as a souvenir, could cause such writhing and contorting pain. Then I looked at it with a magnifying glass and knew why.

Another pain that most every pastor in the United Methodist Church dreads is the annual campaign to underwrite the congregation's budget and worldwide mission costs for the coming year. Plenty of "bound to succeed" programs are always available. They include specific timelines and required solicitations from the members.

Letters and pledge cards are sent out to every member. Such cards are to be turned in on a certain date. Follow-up contacts are made to those who fail to respond. Invariably, the adopted budget has to be adjusted downward. Invariably, too, a number of members grumbled, got angry, and refused to pledge. It seemed we spent one half the year dealing with several members disgruntled at being asked to pledge and the other half developing a budget for the coming year.

I expressed my frustration to the finance committee about the rut we were in and said we needed a new approach. The committee agreed and asked me to work on a better way to go at the budget. The old saying is true: "Suggest something new and you will be tagged to show how."

It was time for me to head to the prayer closet in a hurry. Drawing upon my experience in closet praying, the prayer retreat, and sheer daring, I took back to the committee a new way of underwriting the budget. It was such a bold undertaking that the committee was more than a bit apprehensive. Even so, the members said, "Let's do it!"

The plan called for a series of sermons based on Genesis 8:22, regarding the principle of "Seedtime and Harvest." The series was preached. The congregation was challenged. And I was a bit anxious.

A letter of information and instruction went out to each family. Enclosed with the letter was a commitment card and a stamped envelope with the family's home address. Each family was asked to discuss and pray about what it should give. On either of two Sundays the family would take the sealed letter to church and drop it into a sturdy locked box, symbolically "planting" it. The box containing all commitments would then be secured in the church's safe.

No one would know what any family's commitment was. Nor would the church know what the total commitment was to the budget. Only weekly receipts would be known.

Our "not knowing" gave many of us leaders a bit of pause. We were forced to trust the membership. I received a fair number of communications from faithful and generous members expressing their anxiety. One made it clear that what we were doing "smacked of the lack of common sense!" I must confess that such comments from responsible and faithful members gave me much to consider. But we persisted in faith.

In October of the following year, the envelope with the commitment card sealed inside would be mailed back to the family. There would be no quarterly statements. Each family would be on its own honor to make whatever response it felt appropriate.

The new year came. We were on a different track, receiving funds sufficient for the church's ministry. On the third Sunday of the new year, I was delayed in getting back to the staff office area to remove my robe and proceed to lunch. As the last person greeting me left, the business manager came rushing up to me and said, "Preacher, what does this check go for? There's no instruction given!"

He showed me the check for several thousand dollars.

"Well," I responded, "since there is no direction, put it in the general fund."

Never before had I seen a check that large just dropped casually into the offering plate. As we walked back to the office area, he said to me, "If this is an indication of what this year's giving is going to be, it will be a blowout year!"

A few days later I called the donor and asked if we could have lunch. He was a young junior executive officer in a large company. He was pleased to have lunch the next day. I expressed to him what the business manager had said. He chuckled with me. Supposing the check was his lump sum gift for the year, I thanked him and asked why the leap in his commitment.

"Oh," he replied, "that's not our pledge for the year. That check is the tithe off the bonus I received for last year. My wife and I decided to give the check in gratitude for a second blessing we had from last year. Our commitment for this year is in that 'seed box' at the church."

He never divulged the amount on the card, and I did not want to know. In time I would come to know that his "tithe" check alone amounted to more than three times his previous year's commitment. Not only that, his sealed commitment for the coming year turned out to be 10 times the amount given the year before.

Something had happened to that couple. Something also happened to many other members. Board meetings during the year were different. There was no bad news about shortfall. All we had were the receipts of the congregation's support for the church's ministry. The following October the envelopes with pledge cards were mailed back to the families for "checkup on themselves." At year's end all bills had been paid, including outreach ministries locally and all over the world. We were truly on a spiritual track when it came to underwriting the annual budget.

At the 1976 annual conference session I was elected conference missionary secretary. As such, I was responsible for the movement of missionaries around the conference during their furloughs from overseas assignment. I was also responsible for getting local churches to help support missionaries in other parts of the world. It was a challenging but gratifying four-year assignment. I also coordinated with the General Board of Global Ministries on various programs.

At the same session of the annual conference, I was elected chairperson of the ethnic minority local church committee. My assigned responsibilities were to work with the African American and Native American churches in securing conference grants for programs and church facilities. The Minority Fund also furnished supplemental salary support. While the amount of funds to be distributed upon certified need were modest, we were still able to make significant improvements in both the Oklahoma and Indian Missionary conferences. Not only that but I got to know and admire many dedicated leaders in both ethnic communities. My job, I felt, was a gift of privilege.

In late summer of 1976, the New Haven Church building expansion was completed. Bishop Paul Milhouse came to preach and to consecrate the new facilities. Dr. Lester Meyer, our able and highly regarded district superintendent, assisted the bishop in the consecration service. At last we had the space to accommodate increasing needs for ministry.

In July I attended the South Central Jurisdictional Conference in Lincoln, Nebraska. It was an informative, inspiring, and enjoyable experience. I was deeply honored and grateful to be a part of the 360 delegates who carried on the business at hand. It was especially thrilling to cast my ballots for the election of bishops Monk Bryan from Missouri, Kenneth Hicks from Nebraska, and J. Chess Lovern from Oklahoma.

Later, as missionary secretary, I undertook to inform the annual conference of the opportunities it had to strengthen the African American church in the conference. I shared my vision with Dr. Bonner Teeter, who was chair of the conference board of missions. I proposed producing a slide presentation on the black churches and challenging Oklahoma Conference churches to get involved in meeting many of the black churches' needs.

Dr. Teeter agreed that the effort was indeed worth undertaking. He authorized my travel expenses to be paid by the Board of Missions. I traveled with different African American pastors to take pictures of facility needs and opportunities for developing leadership. It was a greater job than I had imagined. When the visits were all made, pictures taken, and initial needs established in local churches, it was time to put the presentation together. I showed it to the Board of Missions. Members agreed it should be shown at the annual conference session of 1977.

In mid-May I spent a day in Oklahoma City meeting with the conference council on ministries. It was a full day of hard work, finalizing programs and budgets to be presented for approval at the annual conference session. By chance, I happened to sit beside Bishop Milhouse all day long. We had several brief exchanges during the day.

Arriving back home, I walked through the door to see Lavelle holding the phone. "Bishop Milhouse is on the phone and wants to talk with you!" she said.

Bishop Milhouse was noted for speaking softly and getting to the point quickly. Without ado, he said, "I want to invite you to become a part of the cabinet."

I was surprised. He had given no hint of such a notion as I sat beside him all day. With sincere and expressed gratitude, I accepted the invitation to be the district superintendent of the Bartlesville District.

At the time, Lavelle worked as a doctor's assistant. Since the appointment would be made soon, I asked Bishop Milhouse for permission to advise Dr. Loveless confidentially of our impending move.

"Yes," he said, "but don't tell it to anyone else until I have everything worked out."

The conversation took no more than three to four minutes. Yet how dramatically changed my life became in those minutes. I was moving out of the familiar territory of pastoral ministry into the administrative leadership of the annual conference. Certainly I would be outclassed among highly regarded leaders and mentors I had looked up to for years. Not only that, I would be the youngest member of the cabinet. The whole idea was both humbling and challenging. I knew the prayer closet would be a place of more frequent visits and longer stays.

We had come to New Haven four years earlier. My tenure had been the longest of my career to that point. I would have been pleased to stay much longer, but the call came to move, and I accepted it. That was the vow I had taken willingly at my ordination. The itinerate ministry of the United Methodist Church was the lifestyle I had chosen in response to God's call some 19 years earlier at Highland Park Church.

We arrived at New Haven to meet head-on the saddest days of our lives. We would be leaving New Haven with nothing but joy and celebration. Our tenure with New Haven had become a journey of milestones.

After a thoroughly conspired "Roast Ray" farewell dinner headed up by Associate Pastor Buddy Bolin, we said our farewells, with occasional tears. The following morning we departed New Haven for Bartlesville.

The 45-mile move north to Bartlesville was brief in time but so rich in memories. It was time sufficient to celebrate the ministry we had among some of the finest people we would ever serve. The brief drive, too, was sufficient for me personally to reflect on my new responsibilities of supervising 45 churches and more than 40 pastors. The closer we came to Bartlesville, the larger those responsibilities loomed before me. It all became a bit scary by the time we arrived at the district parsonage.

12

Journey of Enlarged Leadership

U pon our arrival at the district parsonage in Bartlesville, we found no welcome committee waiting to greet us. No food was in the refrigerator for convenient first-day meals. These were merely initial reminders that our journey of enlarged leadership would be quite different from the pastoral settings of the past.

The parsonage was a spacious and lovely home with four bedrooms and two-and-a-half bathrooms. The smallest bedroom at the front of the house served as the district office. It was immediately evident that this arrangement was not the best. Anyone needing to meet with me would have to cross the hallway that led to the other three bedrooms. Any committee needing to see me had to sit in the living room. That meant there would be very little privacy for the family.

Besides that, the office barely had space for me to walk around my desk and the one guest chair. Shelving and cabinet space framed a window behind my desk. The countertop barely had room for the telephone and my portable typewriter. A closet provided very little space for files and record storage. The parsonage, though otherwise spacious, was simply not arranged to provide basic needs for a district office.

Not only that, but I had no on-site secretarial help. There I was, promoted to larger leadership but without on-site provisions to carry out such leadership. Half humorously, I muttered to myself, "This misplaced office with too little space and no secretarial help—and no place to put it if I had it—gives me a number of priorities to work on forthwith!"

During those first few days of discoveries and surprises, I learned that the treasurer of First Church downtown administered the designated District Administrative Fund. I had to request money from the treasurer for everything from rubber bands to office machines.

A day or so later I directed the treasurer to transfer the District Administration Fund to an account I had opened at a bank much more convenient to the district office. The fund was transferred, balanced each month, audited annually, and reported each year to the district conference.

A day or two later still, I was advised that the church downtown would be pleased to continue affording the district superintendent some secretarial help, along with the use of the church's office machines to print and copy letters and other materials needed. I then understood why the district office was so barren of basic office equipment.

While I sincerely appreciated the church's continuing offer, I found the situation inadequate. Too much of my time would be taken up with any number of daily trips downtown to the church for any number of reasons. More importantly, the affairs of the district office needed to be exclusively the business of the district office. Exposure of letters, information, and numerous other materials made confidentiality and accountability horrendously difficult.

I asked the chairperson of the district board of trustees to call a meeting at the district parsonage. That way the trustees could see for themselves the full situation. Upon inspection, the board agreed to address the space needs for the district office. One option was to remodel the double garage into the office area. A second option was to rent sufficient space away from the parsonage. A third option was to build onto the existing parsonage. The third option was adopted, since we had ample yard space. The addition would adjoin the side of the garage. Such a plan would add beauty to the front of the house and look like an original part of the residence.

The extension would have its own entrance into the office area. The secretary's space would be in front, furnished with all necessary equipment for an efficient and attractive work place. The superintendent's office at the back would be furnished for small committee meetings. Plenty of bookshelves, cabinet space, and countertop area would all be built in.

Between the two offices were the restroom, an under-the-counter refrigerator, and lots of space for keeping records and office supplies. One special feature was that the door leading into the garage, and thus to the parsonage, could be secured from traffic in either direction.

An architect was hired to detail the plan. A loan was secured to build the office and was paid off in quick order. The new district office afforded not only needed space but also an environment conducive to efficiency and pride.

I hired Lavelle as my secretary at the handsome salary of $50 a month. By the time we moved from there, she had advanced to $150. In addition to her bearing the secretarial load, she managed to type, edit, and perfect three manuscripts for publication. She was beloved by the clergy families and laypersons all across the district. I must say Lavelle was the finest secretary I ever worked with. And the most fun. Occasionally, we played golf together. Afterwards we would have lunch at a favorite country-cooking restaurant— the cost of which came out of our family budget. So did the golf fees.

On our very first outing, Lavelle hit the ball off the tee on a par-three hole onto the green. The ball bounced off the pin and came to rest about a foot away from the hole. She made a birdie from there. But the joy and excitement of her achievement gradually wore off. Afterwards, every time we played golf she became more frustrated at not being able to replicate hitting the pin from the tee on that same green.

In time she quit playing golf altogether. Too much success too soon, I suppose. Unlike most golfers, she had the good sense and courage to quit playing while on a streak of one birdie. And before her game went to pot.

As a district superintendent I was rapidly learning just how extensive and essential my new job was. The district superintendent's office is actually an extension of the bishop's office and authority. The superintendent is in charge of the overall ministry within a particular geographic area.

Indeed, my new assignment was quite different from what I had known as a pastor. While I greatly missed the daily interchange with staff and local church members, I was enjoying the challenge of being engaged in a broader ministry.

Once settled in the parsonage, I visited each district church during the summer of 1977. I met with pastors and laity for a time of listening to their concerns and needs. I then shared with each congregation my own hopes and vision for the district.

The brief time given to visiting and getting to know the people proved to be invaluable as we worked together. By the time of the fall round of charge conferences, we all realized how priceless had been the time we had spent in the summer visiting and sharing. Most of the charge conferences went extremely well. They were productive and inspiring.

The district's year-end report indicated the churches had given a fine account of themselves. One thing that troubled me, however, was that several of our churches needed to reach a higher level in their payout of apportionments and fair-share goals. Funds collected for these items underwrote the cost of ministry outreach from across the street to across the world.

I knew from experience that when United Methodists really understood how much good their apportionments accomplished, they would want to pay them in full. During some of my summer "in between time," therefore, I developed a booklet that described the ministry each item funded. It took awhile and required a great deal of research.

For instance, one apportionment went to support the 12 Methodist African American colleges. Apparently, because there was no such Methodist college in Oklahoma, the apportionment was poorly supported.

By June of 1978 the booklet *Our United Methodist Ministries* came off the press. The booklet described nearly 50 vital ministries for the churches to support more deliberately. Each fund item was described, then dramatized by a cartoon character, "Marvin Methodist." Lisa Shriver, an outstanding and creative high school student, drew the cartoons.

We distributed copies of the booklet to pastors and congregations. We asked each church to spend a whole administrative board meeting on discussing the booklet before the charge conference met to approve the forthcoming year's budget. Most of the congregations cooperated. The response was inspiring, and the churches reached a higher level of giving.

At the next cabinet meeting I gave a copy of the booklet to each superintendent, explaining its use in our district. The booklet was well-received, and several colleagues wanted to use it in their districts. At the time, Dr. Clif Sprouls was serving as secretary and treasurer of the annual conference. With his gracious support and leadership we were able to make more copies available to the other district superintendents.

I do not know what the results were in other districts. I do know Bartlesville District churches paid more every year from then on. I know, too, that the booklet became known across the annual conference as the "Little Green Book."

In December of 1978 word was spreading that Oklahoma City University was desperately struggling to survive. The law school was in serious jeopardy of losing its accreditation. A deficit of $1.6 million was projected for the 1979-80 school year. In addition, a $1 million loan payment was due. In March 1979 a state of financial exigency was declared regarding the university.

Rather quickly, an editorial in Oklahoma City's *Daily Oklahoman* declared that the university would not recover and that the community would not support the school sufficiently in the future for it to survive. The editorial called on the trustees to offer the entire campus to Oklahoma University as its Oklahoma City campus.

That editorial evoked what became the famous response from Bishop Paul W. Milhouse. Softly but firmly he said, "Well, we are not going to do that!" "We" because the cabinet fully supported the bishop in keeping our United Methodist school. Pastors and laypersons alike rallied behind the bishop to save the university.

By the time the Oklahoma Annual Conference session met in May, Bishop Milhouse had secured confirmation that the school needed $3 million to put it on promising footing. That would provide time to secure its future.

At the Tuesday evening session Bishop Milhouse set aside the printed agenda to inform the 1,200 lay and clergy conference members of the situation at OCU. Courageously he said, "I did not come to Oklahoma to close Oklahoma City University." He then asked the conference leaders to pray for the school and to help raise the $3 million. Further, he asked them to set the pace for the campaign by being ready the next day to make a pledge for the university.

At 4:30 p.m. the following day the pledged amount was awesome. Nearly $200,000 had been pledged by conference participants alone. Following that, the annual conference voted to increase its annual apportionment to the university to $750,000 a year. Immediately it became abundantly clear that the United Methodists of Oklahoma were not about to let the university close its doors. In addition, each district superintendent was to go home and canvass the congregations and individuals for pledges.

Mainly because of the bold and courageous leadership of Bishop Milhouse, Oklahoma City University was turned around and put on a much more promising course. Dr. Jerald Walker, a graduate, was elected its president. His visionary and dynamic leadership gave immediate evidence that the university was there to stay at 23rd and Blackwelder.

At the same annual conference I was elected a delegate for the first time to the General Conference, which made me automatically a delegate to the South Central Jurisdictional Conference. Both would convene the following year. It was difficult for me to express what I felt concerning the trust my fellow clergy colleagues had vested in me.

That summer I finished the manuscript of sermons and lectures on *Seedtime and Harvest*. It would be published in 1980. Dr. James Buskirk, dean of the seminary at Oral Roberts University in Tulsa, invited me to give a series of lectures on the subject the following summer. I was pleased to accept the opportunity.

One night, as my writing on that manuscript took me past midnight, the telephone rang. I assumed it would be bad news. I answered the phone and heard a woman's voice ask, "Is this Brother Ray Owen?"

I answered yes.

"This is Celia Cox," the voice then said. "I just talked to Dad and told him I was called to ministry and wanted to know what I was to do next."

This was the little girl I had helped to get her kite flying back in 1961 at Highland Park Church.

"Dad told me to call you right now and that you would know what to do," she said.

What a thrill! We talked for a few minutes, then I advised her of the steps necessary to enter the ministry.

A few years later I learned she had graduated from Candler School of Theology at Emory University in Atlanta, Georgia. Later still, I learned she had been appointed as a staff member for the Southeastern Jurisdiction at Lake Junaluska, North Carolina. In 1997, while attending the Council of Bishops meeting there, Lavelle and I had lunch with Celia. It was a delightful and sometimes emotional time for all of us. I understand she is now serving a church.

What a tragedy indeed it might have been, if on that kite-flying Saturday some 20 years earlier, I had excused myself from Cecil's request to talk with me.

In December Dr. Jerald Walker was officially inaugurated as president of Oklahoma City University. On that occasion the university bestowed upon me the honorary degree of Doctor of Divinity. I was immensely honored and grateful, especially since our family ties to Oklahoma City University were becoming more and more significant. At the time, Darryl was enrolled as a student.

Our district congregations came to the end of 1979 in high spirits. Most of our churches were growing in membership, attendance, and participation in outreach ministries. We saw ourselves as a team of 45 churches engaged in the basic business of witness, spirituality, and making disciples—which is the very essence of Methodists' "connectionalism." We all had much to celebrate, for achievements took place throughout the year.

My journey of enlarged leadership was indeed proving to be different from the pastoral setting. I found it to be extremely challenging, yet so very rewarding. The superintendency was filled with opportunities to shape visions and be creative in bringing those visions into reality.

The year 1980 came at me in a full rush. Keeping abreast of responsibilities in the district and at the cabinet meetings made for little time left over. I attended the General Conference in May in Indianapolis. It was indeed a unique experience of long days, preaching and praying, worshipping and studying, receiving and renewing, debating and legislating, discussing and disagreeing, concurring and compromising—and through it all, loving and respecting one another until the 11-day marathon came to an end.

The 1,000 delegates from all over the world departed bleary-eyed from exhaustion—yet energized and joyous of heart at the direction set for the church in the next four years.

Following the General Conference, the Oklahoma Annual Conference session convened the last few days of May. The report from Oklahoma City University was upbeat, showing many signs that the school was regaining its financial footing.

In June my book on *Seedtime and Harvest* came off the press, just in time for the lecture series at Oral Roberts University. I really enjoyed the experience, and others told me the series went well. Later that summer the seminary made the book required reading for all seminary students. Not only that, the university paid for the remaining stock of the edition for further distribution.

While we were on a brief vacation in Tennessee in June, my father fractured his hip. He was 86 years old, and after the accident, he was confined to a nursing care facility for the rest of his life. He never lost his dry sense of humor. But it was still sad to see his will to walk again slowly disappear.

In July the South Central Jurisdictional Conference met in Little Rock. Five bishops were retiring, which meant we would be electing five new bishops.

Those elected were W.T. Handy from Louisiana; John Wesley Hardt from the Houston Area; Ben Oliphant from Dallas; Louis Schoengerdt from the Missouri Area; and John Russell from the Oklahoma Area. The following September 1 Bishop John Wesley Hardt became the episcopal leader of the Oklahoma Area, which included the Oklahoma Indian Missionary Conference and the Oklahoma Conference.

After 12 very fruitful years of quality leadership, Bishop Paul Milhouse was one of the five to retire. He immediately became the bishop in residence at Oklahoma City University. While in that position he wrote *A Miracle on 23rd and Blackwelder.* The book gave an excellent account of the university's long struggle and its three attempts to become a viable Methodist school over its 75-year history. I felt privileged to serve as a trustee of the university from 1977 to 1981, during its latest miraculous recovery.

In August I was the preacher for the annual United Methodist Men's Retreat, held at Canyon Camp in western Oklahoma. I am sure I received far more from that event than I was able to give. The relaxed yet intentional focus on spiritual life in the men made every aspect of the retreat rich in fellowship and exchange. The service on the last evening was especially inspiring, as some 200 men took turns at the chancel rail committing their lives anew to God in their walk of discipleship. I came home spiritually and inwardly renewed and energized.

After a full schedule of charge conferences in the district churches during the fall, I was ready for a less frantic pace during Thanksgiving and Christmas. It was then that I wrote and printed a booklet on *Joseph and the Birth of Jesus* as my Christmas gift to each clergy family. It was not meant to be a factual account of the biblical events surrounding the birth of Jesus. Nor was it meant to be scripturally precise regarding the behavior, beliefs, and struggles related to Joseph.

I read the book to the families after dinner, and then I distributed autographed copies to each. The booklet added to the Christmas season. Many of the families asked about purchasing additional copies for Christmas gifts to friends and family. In short order, the original copies were depleted. In 1982 a second printing was published. Occasionally, even now, I get inquiries about the booklet. As far as I know, only a dozen or so copies still exist.

A few weeks into 1981, I experienced a near-death situation. For several days I had been feeling poorly. My energy decreased daily. I first thought it was another passing siege of sinus misery. Because it persisted, I thought it was the flu. All the while I was taking aspirin, a mild nasal spray and lots of liquids. I got worse—weaker and weaker. Yet I was not hurting anywhere in particular.

Finally I agreed to Lavelle's calling the doctor. She explained to him my symptoms and increasing weakness without specific pain. Immediately the doctor instructed her to bring me to his office. A wheelchair would be waiting on the ground floor for moving me up the elevator. He did not want me to walk, since he was sure I was losing blood internally.

Lavelle loaded me into the car and broke the speed limit all the way to the doctor's office in Tulsa. She had worked for the doctor for several years and had seen the danger surrounding my situation. The doctor looked at me, took a blood count, and sent me forthwith to the emergency room for admittance. My blood count was dangerously low. Apparently the aspirin had caused internal bleeding. Later it was determined I was probably allergic to aspirin, although I had taken it all my life for minor aches and pains.

I received several units of blood and was ordered not to get out of bed and walk around. Lavelle returned home once the doctor said I would be all right for the night. The crisis came late that night when I went into "code blue." I had buzzed the nurse's station because I was becoming nauseated. A voice said, "We'll be there shortly." Again I buzzed, and again I was told the same thing. Once more I buzzed. By then I had to get up and sit in the chair beside the bed. As I sat down, I regurgitated a huge amount of blood. My roommate yelled for the nurse. I remember a male nurse and two others rushing in and putting me onto the bed. The last words I heard were, "I can't get a pulse!"

The next morning I woke as my doctor was examining me. He was not happy when told I had called for help several times before the nurses finally got there. Nor was Lavelle happy when she walked in and learned what happened and that she was not notified of my code blue ordeal.

I stayed in the hospital six days. I recovered speedily in fine fashion, although I was on medication for several weeks following.

Later, as I reflected on that ordeal and hearing the words, "I can't get a pulse," I realized I had come through a near-death situation. At the same time I discovered something about dying. I realized that if death was merely "slipping away" in utter peace as I had felt I was doing, then death is not some fearsome experience to resist. Rather, it must be a moving onward, calmly, into yet another dimension of life's journey.

As superintendent I shared communal and spiritual lives with 40 clergy families in the Bartlesville District. We took advantage of every opportunity to meet, to share a meal, and to talk about what was going on in our churches and in our families. In those settings we certainly lived up to the old saying that when preachers and their families get together, they have more fun than just about any other group. Always we had fun as we shared the latest parsonage happenings since last we met. Many of the spouses could relate a story so vividly that it breathed and walked. Here's a typical example of how clergy families keep one another alive with laughter, love, and amusement.

I had the opportunity to help a young couple, John and Tina. They were from out of state. John was serving a small church as a student pastor while he attended the seminary at Oral Roberts University in Tulsa. Two years earlier John called to ask if there was a student appointment available in my district. All I had was a small church that didn't pay much of a salary. It did have a nice parsonage, which would help their monthly expenses. I offered to place him there. I had not forgotten how tough Lavelle and I had it while I was attending seminary. John accepted the appointment but only after praying for God's will in the matter.

For two years John had done a credible job, even though the couple was still struggling to make financial ends meet, especially with a small child. Yet they never complained. Both he and Tina were deeply committed and spent much time together in prayer, trusting God to provide.

At a cabinet meeting I learned that another church had come open. The appointment would provide a nice raise for John. I asked the bishop to appoint John to that church. My request was granted, provided John would move. When I returned home, I called John and offered him the church, with a raise in salary. He seemed quite pleased about the offer. But as I expected, he wanted an hour or so "to pray for God's will in the matter" with Tina.

Now Tina was a delightful person, who was also practical from the top of her head to the soles of her feet. I could tell Tina was overhearing the conversation. Before I could respond to John's request to pray, I heard Tina say, "You go pray, John! I'm packing! Tell the superintendent we'll take it!" John then said to me, "We'll take it!" I supposed his response was made on the assumption that "God's will" had already clearly spoken in Tina's practical words.

Every time the district families got together thereafter, John would be joshed about whether he had heard "God's will" any more through Tina's words. John would just grin and shake his head in response.

Since as a superintendent I no longer had a congregation as such, I made the 40 clergy families in the district my parish. I divided the pastors and their families into a monthly prayer list.

Each day I would, in thought, bring a pastor and his family to my "prayer closet." I prayed for their work and participation in the church, calling the names of each child, the pastor, and spouse. Most of the time I would address some family situation, like John and Tina's financial struggle or illness of a family member. Afterwards, I wrote a card with a brief overview of my prayer for the family. Lavelle would mail the card that day.

The results were heartening. Soon families were praying for each other and keeping tabs on those who were ill or facing some challenge or grief in the loss of a loved one. It was quite amazing how often someone told me that the card had arrived in a timely situation. Our regular meetings became a forum for reporting to the rest of the families and requesting prayers from the group for upcoming needs, events, and hurdles to get through. In an obvious way this praying for one another nurtured us in our prayer life and in our spiritual growth.

In May of 1981 I preached a revival at First Church in Lawton. Larry Becker, a longtime and valued friend, asked me to be the preacher. Of course I accepted. While there, I met an old-time friend from my time in Korea nearly 20 years earlier. He had long since retired from the Army and was a member of First Church.

He had played a vital role in all the mission work the Protestant Men of the Chapel had precipitated and participated in while we were in Korea. He was indeed a splendid specimen of a career military Christian gentleman. We recalled so many experiences we had shared in Korea. We recalled the names of as many of the other G.I.s as we could who had been a part of our mission work. He was one of the men who accompanied me when I preached in that Korean prison in Pusan, the visit "Willie" had sprung on me. Our getting to see each other enhanced the value of the revival.

One afternoon I asked Larry if the Highland Park Church was still standing. He said it was, though it had been condemned for several years after its turnover to the Oklahoma Indian Missionary Conference.

I got into my car and drove the short distance to see it for myself. That afternoon I would pay the first of two of my last visits to the church. Each would be brief but oh so lasting in the spiritual impact upon me.

Indeed, the church building and property were in sad shape. I parked near the front entrance. For several minutes I just sat there in silence. I remembered so many events, situations, and celebrations during my "twice made" pastorate. I recalled the day I delivered my very first sermon, the Sunday evening singing, the prayer time at the church, the baptisms. I saw afresh the faces of Jack Lyons, Cecil Cox, and Robert Young—all of whom had become preachers. My mind then settled on that last but unforgettable handshake with the Reverend Herman Snodgrass. His last words resounded in my soul as clearly as they had reached my ears two decades earlier: "Ray, as long as you live, I will go on preaching through you."

Instantly I was gripped with a compelling sensation of Brother Herman's presence. I got out of the car, stretched out my arms, lifted my face toward heaven, and, with tears in my eyes, shouted out, "Brother Herman, you are still preaching through me!" It was one of the most profound and spiritual moments of my lifetime.

Years later I would understand even more fully Brother Herman's words. It would come on the occasion of our two sons' ordination as elders (Darryl in 1988 and Dyton in 1992).

In anticipation of their upcoming ordinations, I wrote each one a letter of congratulations, commendation, and perhaps a bit of counsel. I am not certain I used the words "As long as you live, I will go on preaching through you." If I didn't, I'm certain I whispered them as I added my hands to those of Bishops John Wesley Hardt, Dan Solomon and other elders when each son received his ordination and was received as an elder in full connection within the ministry of the United Methodist Church.

In June 1981 our family took an extended vacation in Tennessee with our folks. Dyton always enjoyed being back home with Lavelle and me. He was especially eager to spend time on the farm with Lavelle's folks.

For quite some time my mother had indicated she would like to come to Oklahoma someday for a visit with us. Always, however, there was some reason it was not the right time. Well, that summer we convinced her it was the right time. She could come home with us and stay as long as she liked. When she wanted to return home, I would drive her back to Tennessee.

Mother decided to come with us, since Dad was being well attended and P.J. would be checking on him almost every day. Though not in good health, she made the trip in good shape. She enjoyed the many sights around Tulsa, Bartlesville, and northeastern Oklahoma. She seemed to enjoy her stay of about a week.

Late one afternoon she said she needed to walk if there was a nearby place to do so. Well, the community in which we lived had wide sidewalks on level grounds. Many homes had beautiful flowers in their yards, which she surely would enjoy. So we began a casual walk through the community. Rather abruptly, while holding onto my arm, she began to say things about herself that I had never before heard. She told me that when she was a young girl, she had dreamed of being a missionary in some faraway place. Apparently she had secretly harbored that dream for many decades. She said that because she married young and the children came along, she knew being a missionary would not be possible.

As we slowly walked along, she said, "When I finally realized I would never be a missionary, I prayed that one of my children would be called to preach or to be a missionary."

Then she stopped dead still, squeezed my arm and said, "Son, you are the fulfillment of my dream! I am so thankful."

It was a precious and sacred moment for both of us, I believe.

The next morning, as if she had done what she had come home with us to do, she said, "I think I need to go home, if you can drive me."

The all-day trip with just the two of us was a special time. We talked of the siblings' growing-up years. We also talked about some of the spiritual heroes I knew as a boy in New Valley Church and later in First Methodist Church in McKenzie, where I grew up. She told me about the tough and spiritually testing times during the Great Depression, never letting us children know. I don't recall our ever having such an unhurried block of time for us to talk and share.

By the time we had arrived at our home place in McKenzie, I realized my mother had been a "missionary" all of her life. When someone down the street was ill, she would be there with a hot dish of food or a pie. When someone in the neighborhood died, she would call all the people on the street and collect money to send flowers or a memorial for the deceased. Time and again when we departed after a few days of vacation with our folks, I would hug her goodbye, only to find later a few bills she had subtly slipped into my shirt pocket. She prayed for a lot of people who were ill, troubled, or in need of a word of encouragement. Giving, praying, encouraging, and caring—those are just a few of her credentials as a missionary-in-residence in the territory of her own community. I was the one on that sidewalk stroll who had far more reason than she to be "so thankful."

A joyous interlude in the busy summer was the marriage of our son, Darryl, and his wife, Denise. I served as father and official agent of their marriage—either of which would be blessing enough. To be both was indeed a double joy.

Soon after Darryl's wedding, Lavelle, Dyton and I went to Honolulu, where the World Methodist Conference of 1981 convened. For a second time I was a delegate. As always, the world meeting of some 70 Methodist denominations was an experience to cherish.

While there, Dyton met the eminent Harold Beck, professor of Old Testament and Hebrew at Boston University. They struck up a friendship, which wound up with Dr. Beck inviting Dyton to have breakfast with him one morning. It was a gracious act for a man of his stature to even talk to Dyton, let alone take the time to visit over breakfast with a young man yet to discover his own direction in life. It is precisely that sort of graciousness that moves an already prominent person toward greatness.

The rest of that summer was rather uneventful. That was good, in that it afforded me sufficient time to prepare for the fall round of charge conferences in the district churches. It also afforded some quality time with Lavelle.

Dyton started his final year in high school with an after-school restaurant job he had held since his sophomore year. A few months after he first took the job, he came home upset and said flat out that he was quitting. We were surprised. When we asked why, he said the owner had come in, obviously was under the influence of alcohol, and started yelling and cursing at the employees. His temper apparently had exploded after he had lost money in a card game. The man's rage continued for some time. By closing time, Dyton had had enough. He was going to quit.

I suggested he let me talk to the boss first, and Dyton agreed. I called the man and calmly advised him that he was about to lose a very fine employee. I said Dyton was not accustomed to people cursing at him and bawling him out because "things for the boss" were not going well. I told the man I would not allow my sophomore son to work anyplace where alcohol influenced the demeanor of the boss.

I was surprised at how calmly I had stated my case. The man apologized and said he would like very much for Dyton to continue working at the place. He said he would apologize to Dyton when he came to work the following day. We both felt good about our conversation's outcome. Dyton went back to work and stayed at the job the rest of his time in high school and during Christmas vacations and summer breaks in college.

Several years later, Lavelle and I went by that restaurant for a hamburger. When Paul, Dyton's former boss, saw us, he came right over and asked how Dyton was getting along. We told him Dyton was a pastor. We were quite astonished when Paul said what a positive and significant influence he had been in Dyton's becoming a minister. Lavelle and I both thought he must have forgotten a thing or two when it came to his actual influence on our son.

As the fall schedule of charge conferences fell into place, the sad news came that Lloyd A. Peters had succumbed to Hodgkin's disease. His battle to live had been long and strong, but death came peacefully at age 62. All of us on the cabinet felt the immense loss. Lloyd had given so much to Oklahoma Methodism. He possessed a brilliant and analytical mind, a gift for leadership, and compassion to reach out to encourage young pastors in their initial steps toward ordination. His knack for teasing made it a treat working with him. He relished the brisk interchange of ideas and conversations. I knew I would miss his genuine friendship and counsel for the rest of my ministry. I counted being on the cabinet with him among the highlights of my learnings. I am sure the other superintendents felt the same way as we served as honorary pallbearers.

It never dawned on me that Lloyd's death would trigger my own move off the cabinet. Several days after the funeral, Bishop Hardt apparently planned to appoint Dr. Argus Hamilton Jr. to the South Oklahoma City District, where Lloyd had served. That meant First Church Bartlesville would be open. Bishop Hardt asked me if I would go behind Dr. Hamilton as pastor.

Apparently the bishop had given much thought to the matter and wanted me at Bartlesville First. It was a real surprise to me. I had not expected to move, since I had served only four and a half years of the usual six-year district appointment. Not only that, it was somewhat unusual for the superintendent to be appointed to the largest church of the same district.

As always, it was my desire to go wherever I was asked. If the bishop wanted me to go, then I was certainly grateful. After all, I had a good relationship with the leaders of the congregation of about 3,500 members. Also, I was well acquainted with the entire staff of some 20 able persons. So I said to Bishop Hardt, "I would be pleased to go wherever you want to appoint me."

I did get to hand back to him some words he had said when he was elected a bishop in 1980 at Little Rock. Our delegation had worked hard to get him elected and assigned to the Oklahoma Area. As chair of the strategy committee, Lloyd Peters had steered our delegation through the process. I and two other delegates on the strategy committee assisted Lloyd.

Upon the announcement of Bishop Hardt's election, I made my way down the aisle to congratulate him. As we shook hands, he said to me, "I just hope all of you know what you have done!" We both chuckled and felt hopeful he would be assigned to Oklahoma.

Now, upon his appointing me to First Church, I said to him, "Bishop Hardt, I just hope you know what you have done!" He asked me to say nothing about it until the next cabinet meeting, when he would announce it. Moving day would be January 1, 1982. Dr. LeRoy Sewell, another longtime and dear friend, was appointed the new superintendent for the Bartlesville District. I was thrilled. LeRoy had played a large role in my ministry across the years. He had served as conference secretary of evangelism throughout the time I served as chairman of the Board of Evangelism. Working with him again would be a real treat.

Those last weeks of 1981 were hectic in every direction. Wrapping up all the fall's business and processing all year-end reports kept me in a stir. In addition to all these responsibilities, we had to pack for the three-mile move across town.

Suddenly the day of moving was upon us. Though a bit harried, I did feel my journey of enlarged leadership as super-intendent had stretched every fiber of every capability I possessed. The four-and-a-half-year journey had resulted in positive productivity across the broad spectrum of ministries in the United Methodist Church. As I had heard it said by someone somewhere in the past, so I said to myself as I backed out of the driveway: "I feel pretty good about the job I did here!"

Now it was time—time to move across town into what later I would call my journey of forging mettle and maturation.

13

Journey of Forging Mettle and Maturation

While I was growing up, the front porch of our home served as the setting for family conversations and visiting. The two metal chairs, the glider, the porch swing, and Mother's many pots of blooming flowers made the porch a pleasant and special place for relaxing and chatting with passersby.

Late one afternoon my father and I were talking about life in general and some of the essential lessons it teaches us. Well into his 60s at the time, Dad remarked, "A man doesn't know what's what until he gets past 50."

I thought his comment was a bit exaggerated and somewhat humorous. After all, I was in my mid-20s. I was married and the father of two sons. I had returned recently from my tour of military duty in Germany. Already I had seen a sizable chunk of the world. My exposure to various cultures and life-informing experiences was significant. Indeed, I felt I knew "what's what" even though I was only about half way to 50.

Time would come, however, when not only would I put much greater value on my father's words, I would come to agree fully with his insight and wisdom. Twenty-four years later, on January 1, 1982, that time began as I took the reins as senior pastor of First United Methodist Church in Bartlesville, Oklahoma. My age was 49 years and eight months. By the time those four remaining months had taken me to age 50, I had realized *"what's whats"* do not stop at one's mid-century birth-day. In fact, as more months became years, I was convinced *"what's what"* was an endowment with distributions delivered throughout one's lifetime.

Reflecting upon my past, I thought about how every church I had served contributed its particular version of *"what's what."* My pursuit of three educational degrees to prepare me for ministry, the lingering and crushing debt left by that pursuit, the scars accumulated from having climbed high and hard mountains, those darksome days I spent in the valley questioning my calling and doubting my leadership, the sacrifices made by Lavelle and our sons—all these and many more made up a long list of *"what's whats."* Each appointment forced me, as Longfellow put it, "to grow some new wood" if I were to become effective in ministry.

Bartlesville First Church was the eighth appointment of my career. The city of some 36,000 residents served as the corporate headquarters of Phillips Petroleum Company. Consequently, the 3,500-member congregation was highly educated. The per capita income for Bartlesville was greater than most areas in the country. Many of the top executives and leaders were dedicated and actively engaged in the ministry of the church.

In every sense of the word, First Church was a premier appointment, except for one thing—its potential. Little wonder then that my nearly 11-year journey with the congregation would forge my mettle and maturation as pastor, preacher, teacher, visionary, and leader.

My first worship service proved memorable for many reasons. One came after the service as I met "Bill," a typical curmudgeon. As I greeted the departing worshippers, Bill took my hand and introduced himself. Without hesitance he said to me, "Well, I say this much, you are a hell-of-a-preacher!"

No one had ever described my preaching in such a graphic and colorful way. Those in line nearby just shook their heads and looked down in some dismay. I wondered why. Apparently, Bill had expected some sort of shocked response from me.

I chuckled and replied, "Well, Bill, I thank you for your

backhanded compliment. I think!" Those in line snickered. I then knew why.

Bill could be just as cutting as complimentary. A year or so later in a similar setting, Bill shook my hand, looked me in the eye and said, "Preacher, when the great sermons of Ray Owen are published, this one today will not be one of them!"

I would learn Bill was a businessman who grew up in First Church. His parents had been stalwart Methodists in decades past. Bill knew just about everybody in the entire area. He thoroughly enjoyed challenging the power brokers, decision makers, and gossip mongers with equal severity. He seemed to delight in cutting across the grain of community mindsets and in shaking up the orderliness by which things got done. Some people, however, looked upon Bill as a genuine community treasure. In time I would, too. Bill was a devoted churchman who fervently supported the mission and outreach of the church.

The following Tuesday morning I went to the Men's prayer breakfast, made up of four older members. For years they had been meeting quietly every week over coffee and donuts. I had attended twice while I was district superintendent. These men had been meeting faithfully to pray for the church, for its staff, and for revival in the city. I expressed to them my sincere gratitude and my full support of their dream of growing into a citywide prayer breakfast. I was deeply moved as one of them said with tears in his eyes, "This is what we have been praying for also."

We patterned the prayer breakfast after the New Haven model. In time, the group grew to more than 50 members, with about 40 in regular attendance each week. The breakfast became a vital part of my own spiritual nurture. I am now convinced that First Church would not have tackled many of the achievements it reached had it not been for the spiritual empowerment and spiritual leadership of the men in that weekly prayer breakfast.

The first priority on the list of things calling for the pastor's leadership was raising $108,000. That was in addition to the $500,000 budget for 1982 that had just been underwritten. The additional funds were to go toward implementing the new conference pension plan for pastors and church staff employees.

The existing plan simply was inadequate for the basic needs of pastors in the future.

Leaders from the 45 congregations in the district had recently met at First Church in Bartlesville to discuss the new plan. Bishop John Wesley Hardt had explained it and followed with a strong challenge for each church to raise its goal.

The first Sunday we received pledges, First Church raised more than $110,000, $2,000 above its goal. The drive closed the following Sunday with First Church pledging more than $135,000. The way it went beyond its goal served as defining and convincing evidence of the greatness of First Church. Again and again I would learn that the congregation seldom settled for giving the minimum asked of it.

Before my arrival at First Church I had been elected chairperson of the Methodist Children's Home in Tahlequah, Oklahoma. My term would end following the late spring meeting of the board. It had been a gratifying experience to have been part of the genuine love and care given 24 hours a day by house parents to children in crisis and need.

Though the home had an endowment of some $3 million and was the recipient of a conference-wide annual offering from the churches in Oklahoma, it still struggled to make ends meet. Maintenance costs for the campus alone were enormous. I still remember the anxious feeling I harbored upon being elected chairperson of the board.

My first official act was to sign two $100,000 loan notes. One was to fund operational expenses during regular cash flow shortages. The other was to remodel and upgrade four "family" residences, each housing six children and two house parents. Handing me the gavel, my predecessor said to me teasingly, "Welcome to the challenge, Ray!"

It was indeed a challenge. Even as the brand-new chairperson, I served notice that putting the home's financial affairs in order would be an immediate objective of the board. Interest paid on notes during cash flow shortfalls siphoned off money from the children's needs.

For some time before that, Bishop Hardt had put a high priority on making the Oklahoma Methodist Foundation a greatly needed instrument of the annual conference. He appointed Dr. Elwyn Thurston full time director. Almost overnight the foundation took center stage for financial services to the annual conference.

Although the Children's Home's $3 million endowment was quite substantial, the funds were scattered in bits and pieces in banks and other institutions, drawing minimum earnings. Dr. Thurston and I talked about bringing all the home's endowments into the foundation. That would result in far better earnings and would guarantee accurate records of distributions and accounting.

What a delightful experience it was for me to put my signature on documents that would transfer and consolidate all endowed funds of the home into the foundation.

"Ray, how does it feel to transfer $3 million solely by the weight of your signature?" Dr. Thurston asked me.

Feeling rather exuberant, I replied, "Elwyn, my Mama will be proud to know it took her son's signature to assign $3 million of Methodist money to ministry of children in need."

She was indeed impressed when I told her later.

My beginning months at First Church seemed to have been punctuated by Easter's record attendance of nearly 1,600. It had lifted the congregation onto a higher plateau of confidence and commitment to Christ. Soon thereafter, several ideas for new ministries surfaced and gained commitment of the church. All of them promised to position the church for greater visibility and significant growth in the future.

Among the first ideas was to sponsor a Jubilee '83 the next summer. Its purpose would be to rally United Methodists in the northeastern quadrant of Oklahoma for several days of preaching, praying, Bible study, teaching, and witnessing. It was no small undertaking. All 45 congregations in the district would have to support the endeavor. The jubilee would take place in the new Bartlesville community center, which seated nearly 2,000.

Sam Kamaleson, a world-renowned Methodist preacher, had committed to come for the event. Norma Zimmerman of *The Lawrence Welk Show* had agreed to be the guest soloist. George Hickman and dozens of other key leaders gave hundreds of hours to make the jubilee a momentous occasion.

Another proposal for emerging ministry gained the church's support when Joe Kaufman, an emerging leader in the congregation, presented the worship committee's recommendation to redesign the choir and chancel areas. That would accommodate expected choir growth. It would also provide increased visibility, which in turn would enhance the audio quality for music, singing, and preaching.

In a related project, the administrative board gave the go-ahead for a weekly two-part television ministry and authorized a professional study to determine if sufficient viewership warranted the telecasts. The first part would be a delayed telecast of the 11 a.m. worship service. Part two would be to televise a children's puppet ministry during the children's church hour.

Still another emerging project that gained interest and support was the construction of a high-quality retirement center, including an assisted-living facility. This idea had long been a dream of G.W. "Rich" Richardson, a well-known member of the church. Rich asked me to serve on the executive committee. The dream gained community-wide support.

Yet another recommendation was the development of a strong cadre of young leaders to take the church boldly into the future. That would help guarantee a continuing high degree of creativity as the church moved ever forward. Round-robin leaders who had served several terms were greatly pleased with the idea. Older adults were especially heartened to see young leaders take responsibility. With wide support, therefore, leaders like Tom DeSalme, Joe Kaufman, Doug Quinn, Bob Farmer, Lynn Railsback, Alan Freeman, Tuck Archer, John Perkins, John Bond, Cliff Stearns, and many, many others began to take the reins of lay leadership in the congregation.

One more proposal that gained full support was to fund a top-quality and competent staff to manage the broad-based ministry that would reach from the church across the world. I strongly expressed to the staff-parish relations committee that the cheapest money we could spend on staff positions was whatever it took to bring aboard persons who would do the job we expected to be done. The committee fully agreed. Already several staff vacancies waited to be filled.

In the grip of having completed my first year at First

Church, I already had collected several more of the *"what's whats"* my father had spoken of. I also had experienced a quantum leap in maturation—which was fitting me for the future.

By year's end we had set the church on a sure course and positioned it for a powerful and spiritual future in ministry.

Early in 1983, therefore, I set about to frame and formalize a vision for the church that would extend 17 years, to the end of the century. I asked myself, "If in the future we could present to God a truly great church, what would be its defining qualities and characteristics? What intermediate milestones would we have to reach along the way to make the church truly great?"

I jotted down numerous requirements, until they began to overlap and repeat. I then condensed the list into a dozen or so components. Armed with my ideas, I asked seven leaders of the church to ask themselves the same two questions and to list their ideas for a 17-year vision of ministry for First Church. When their reports came back to me, I would put together a draft vision for the future.

It was truly amazing how our insights melded in so many ways. This overlapping of our thoughts emboldened me to develop a vision worthy of courageous faith and God's blessing. The initial vision consisted of 14 components for presentation later to the administrative board.

I enlisted skilled persons to develop an audiovisual presentation. The dozen or so components would challenge the congregation as never before. When the board met in April, the presentation team was fully charged and ready. I explained the process by which the vision had been developed.

As I spoke, the dozen or so components came onto the screen with pictures, projections, and expectations of how each component would accommodate and enhance the whole. Following is the outline of basic components, and pieces of each:

- ❑ Children's Ministry—10 parts
- ❑ Youth Ministry—11 parts
- ❑ Adult Ministries—9 parts
- ❑ Young Adult Ministries—2 parts
- ❑ Family Life Ministries—9 parts
- ❑ Local Outreach Ministries—14 parts

❏ Worldwide Mission-Mindedness—12 parts
❏ Endowed Ministries—4 parts
❏ Institute of Discipleship—14 parts
❏ Membership Growth—6 parts
❏ Stewardship and Step-up to Tithing—6 parts
❏ Construction of Needed Building—2 parts
❏ Visions Oncoming—This component provided for expected "spinoff" visions, which were bound to emerge as primary components were realized. Each new spinoff idea would be reassigned to another component or become itself a new vision.

The 35-minute presentation went off without a hitch. I stepped to the lectern as the lights came on again. A thunderous standing ovation erupted and continued for some time. Before I could speak, Glenn Cox, a highly respected member and leader in the community, stood up and said, "Any preacher who would dare bring before old First Church such a vision ought to be appointed to the church until the vision is realized!" Another standing ovation.

Thus Vision 2000 was enthusiastically adopted as First Church's 17-year strategy, mission, and outreach. It was based on Habakkuk's words, "Write the vision anew, and make it plain, so that even a runner can read it...." (2:1-4) The theme of Vision 2000 was: "Either we shape the future, or the future will just happen to us!"

At the annual conference session in May 1983, I was again elected delegate to the General Conference the following year in Baltimore. Sterling W. Williams was appointed to First Church for his fourth year as associate pastor. Russell Cheatham was appointed as the church's second associate.

The rest of 1983 was a scramble, fueled by fervor and excitement, as components of Vision 2000 began to take shape. By June the church had purchased television equipment, provided for a small production room, and trained a crew of three volunteer cameramen. A professional survey indicated the need for the televised worship service in the community. Our first weekly telecast began the last of June. The children's puppet ministry began airing that fall.

Jubilee '83 in the summer proved to be a tremendous success. The entire area felt its impact. Bishop John Wesley Hardt held a cabinet session in Bartlesville and attended the opening evening service. More than 1,500 people came the first night. Many commitments to Christ were made in the course of the event. The lingering influence of Jubilee '83 continued to be felt throughout my tenure as pastor of First Church.

Later that summer I made a three-week trek to Kenya in East Africa. The Committee on Evangelism of the World Methodist Council invited six of us from the United States to participate in an African Methodist Area seminar on evangelism and making disciples of Christ.

The seminar was held at the Methodist Guest House in Nairobi and lasted well over a week. At the last session, Bishop Lawi Imathieu challenged pastors to double the membership of the Kenyan Methodist Church in three-to-five years. He also challenged them to pray that God would raise up twice as many preachers to serve the church in the same time span. It was an awesome vision and challenge for the 80,000-member church with 65 pastors. Later I asked my host pastor how in the world they were going to double the church's membership with only 65 pastors.

"Oh," he replied, "we are not going to double the membership! We can't! But with the power of Christ working through us, we will reach it! I'm convinced of it!"

After having seen for myself the number of people making profession of faith in churches I visited, I, too, believed the bishop's challenge would be realized!

The next day we departed for the Meru area of Kenya, where each of the six Americans would be appointed to a "preaching point" in a remote area. There we would preach, pray, teach, witness, learn, and make disciples of Christ for nearly a week. We were advised to drink only bottled water and to eat only hot, cooked food for the entire time we were in the bush country.

My preaching point was the Kaaga Church and several outlying smaller churches. Kaaga Church was considered the "mother church" of the Meru area. My host was Nahashon Gitonga, the pastor of Kaaga Church. He and his wife and two daughters composed a kind and grace-filled family. I was housed in a shed-like structure on the grounds of the parsonage.

Having received our assigned preaching point, Dr. Robert E. Fannin and I swapped precious essentials for our week in the bush. I gave him a number of my granola bars in exchange for several packets of hand-sanitizer wipes. Our bartering proved to be a far greater blessing. Our special friendship was struck.

Later we would discover how strangely our lives had paralleled one another over some 20 years. We discovered we had served in the military in Korea at the same time. Though we never met, we came home from Korea on the same troop ship. We both had been elected delegates to the upcoming 1984 General and jurisdictional conferences—he from the Florida Conference and I from the Oklahoma Conference. We would both go on to be elected Number 2 in our respective conferences in 1988 to the General and jurisdictional conferences.

Then for the 1992 General Conference, each of us would be elected as head of our delegation. At our jurisdictional conferences in July, we would be elected to the episcopacy within hours of each other, he from the Southeastern Jurisdiction and I from the South Central. No wonder we have become best friends, as have our spouses, Faye and Lavelle. We treasure every opportunity to spend time together.

In 1996 Bob and I would rejoice to greet a fellow participant in our Kenyan experience who was elected a bishop of the church, Nkulu Ntanda Ntambo. He still serves the Northern Katanga Area in the Republic of Congo. What an incredible and inspiring story is his very life! Bob and I were able to be with him in 1998 when all of us were in Angola for a meeting regarding the United Methodist Bishops' Initiative on Children and Poverty.

I preached three times at Kaaga Church the following Sunday morning. The early service brought hundreds of students, with many making professions of faith in Christ. At the midmorning service I preached to many more, again with many professions of faith. At the late morning service another large crowd came to worship. Again, several claimed Jesus Christ as savior and lord.

During the break between the midmorning and late-morning services, I stepped outside to gather my thoughts. As I looked down among the weeds, I found the ground had been dug to form the shape of a foundation for a building. By that time the lay chairman had joined me. When I asked him about the trenches, he told me that several years earlier the congregation had dug the foundation as a sign of faith that God would help them find the way to construct a much-needed Sunday school space and general-purpose building for fellowships and meetings. Without thought, I naturally asked how much a building so large would cost. He replied "about $50,000." I was surprised at how little the large building would cost, but thought no more about it.

In midafternoon I preached at Mweteria Church, a few miles from Kaaga Church. The crowd was smaller than at Kaaga. Yet several persons came to declare Jesus as lord of their lives. I was especially moved by the tender support and encouragement the older members extended to those who made decisions.

Early the next afternoon I preached at a new church. I learned later that 14 of those who came to the chancel to pray had made decisions for Christ. Late that afternoon I visited Kinoru Church, which was expanding its present church facilities. Several people were reported to me as having accepted Christ as their savior while praying at the chancel.

Around 5 p.m. the next day I preached at a church known as the Bean Field Church. No one was there when we arrived. My host said to me, "Most of the people in the church work in the coffee bean fields. In a minute or two they will be coming through the coffee bean plants from all directions to attend worship before going home for supper."

While we waited I noticed that the rather large building was still under construction. We went inside to wait for the congregation to arrive. To my astonishment, I saw a small, older building in the middle of the large unfinished building.

My host saw my puzzlement and remarked, "The congregation is building a larger church around their old, too small building. The membership is growing. They needed somewhere to worship until the new structure could be built. That way their excitement about their new church grows every week. When the larger building is finished, they will dismantle the old building and put in the flooring and furnishings."

I said to myself, "What a practical and sensible way to deal with keeping alive the dream of a new church home without ever having to move!"

Sure enough, we heard talking and singing as about 100 smiling worshippers came out of the field. Again, several were reported to have decided to give their lives to Christ.

A strange yet beautiful thing happened at the end of the service. Instead of a benediction, I was led to the entrance door to greet the departing, singing worshippers. As the first person came by, he shook my hand and took my left hand to form a line. As each person passed down the line shaking hands and blessing each person, another person was added to the "benediction line." It was an inspiring thought that every worshipper shook hands and greeted every other worshipper in a long snakelike line of swaying, singing people.

By the time our stay in the Meru area came to an end, we were all ready to return to Nairobi to prepare for our trip home. The Meru churches gave us a feast on the eve of our departure for Nairobi. The next day I became ill. At the airport Dr. Hanky gave me a large dose of antibiotics, which got me onto the plane for some long needed sleep.

The six of us from the United States had come to Kenya to witness and to share ideas for making disciples of Christ. I am sure all of us would agree that we came home having learned far more about sharing Christ and making disciples than we taught the African pastors.

During the flight home, my mind returned to that scene at Kaaga's foundation trench. Suddenly I was gripped with the notion that First Church, Bartlesville, could raise the $50,000 needed to build that much needed general-purpose building. My mind dwelled on the matter, and I prayed about how to introduce it to the congregation. Vision 2000 was already laying claim to significant future funds in addition to staff costs. Still, the idea persisted. It came to me that the Kaaga building would launch us vividly into the mission component of our Vision 2000. By the time I arrived in the United States, I made a personal commitment to challenge First Church to raise $50,000 for the Kaaga project. I had no idea how the congregation would respond, but I had immediate peace about the matter.

I have to say I arrived back home a different preacher, pastor, and leader. Having witnessed the risky, raw, and reckless faith demonstrated by Kenyan pastors, I determined to be bold of faith in leading the great congregation of First Church.

In my report to the congregation at worship two Sundays later, I ended by challenging the people to fund the $50,000 cost of building that facility at Kaaga. Having told them about the "dug trenches" of faith, I suggested we underwrite the cost by way of a three-year offering, beginning that day. It would likely take that long to plan, design the building, buy materials, and finish the construction. To my surprise, the commitment that day amounted to nearly 40 percent of the total cost.

I notified Bishop Imathieu and Kaaga leaders. Joy traveled heavily and happily between First Church and Kaaga Church. We had made visible and viable a tremendous aspect of "missions" to Vision 2000.

In the fall of 1983 the second segment of our television ministry was launched. The children's puppet ministry became an immediate hit and gained community awareness and support.

About the same time, our redesigned chancel and choir area were completed and dedicated. Their beauty and the improved sound quality met every expectation.

In late fall my book *Questions Which Shaped Destiny* was published.

One of our older and much beloved members remarked to me following the New Year's eve worship service, "This has been some memorable year for this church!"

It had been no less memorable for me personally.

Bethel African American Methodist Episcopal Church was just a few blocks from First Church. The elderly retired pastor and I had become good friends. On several occasions we talked of how our two congregations might work more closely. Nothing to date had become reality.

Bethel's big event for the year was its annual Founders

Day Celebration. The celebration's purpose simply was to give thanks to God for another year and to raise funds for the struggling congregation. The celebration lasted all day, with preaching, praying, and visiting that ended with an early-evening song and worship service.

Bethel's facilities could not accommodate the usual large crowd and activities. Good things came when I attended that event. First Church invited Bethel Church to hold its annual Founders Day Celebration in our large fellowship hall, which could adequately accommodate the gathering. The fellowship hall could also accommodate the closeout meal. And both the celebration and meal would include many members of First Church. As long as I was at First Church, Bethel's annual Founders Day Celebration took place in our fellowship hall.

The 1984 General Conference was in Baltimore. The homosexuality issue was hotly debated, but the church's position on the matter was left intact.

Later the 1984 Oklahoma Annual Conference session met. This particular session proved to be very special to me personally. Sterling W. Williams and Russell Cheatham were reappointed to First Church for another year as associate pastors. That was good news, since we had become a strong team. I was elected conference missionary secretary for a second time, after eight years. Also, I received the prestigious Harry Denman Evangelism Award. I had known and worked with Denman, which made the award even more humbling.

In July the 1984 South Central Jurisdictional Conference met in Lubbock, Texas. J. Woodrow "Woody" Hearn from Louisiana, Richard Wilkie from Kansas, and Walter Underwood from Houston were all elected to the episcopacy. Underwood had been my pastor in McKenzie, Tennessee, when I was in high school.

After a heavy travel schedule for several months, Lavelle and I, along with Darryl, Denise, and Dyton, vacationed in Hawaii. It was the first time in several years all of us could get away for family time. There hasn't been another time since.

For several months the Bartlesville community had been filled with much uneasiness. Boone Pickens of Mesa Partners had made a sustained hostile takeover attempt of Phillips Petroleum Company. In December the Mesa Partners called off the attempt after receiving a large sum from Phillips. Naturally, Phillips had to make some very hard decisions regarding its financial stability. A reduction in the number of employees, along with early retirement plans, got under way.

The church assumed all these actions would bring negative results to its financial outlook. We thought Vision 2000 likely would have to scale down its immediate goals and scale back its future commitments. None of that happened, which was another awe-inspiring sign of the faith of the congregation. It was also inspiring to watch the leaders and executives of Phillips face the challenge. Glenn Cox, executive vice president at the time, played a major role in the recapitalization of the company.

Year 1985 roared in with bitter cold, ice, and wind, which lasted for most of January. Everything slowed down, which added to the community's sense of anxiety and uncertainty about the future.

For much of the year I was overly filled with mood swings and emotional upheavals. Such swings are not unfamiliar to most pastors. In my particular case, however, the frequency and intensity of such swings seemed excessive. Not only would 1985's journey with First Church test my mettle. It would force me more deliberately to pay attention to my physical and spiritual health. Eagerly I looked forward to those "prayer closet" times to discern God's will and direction.

During a brief break in the terrible weather, we received word from P.J. in Tennessee that Mother was gravely ill. Lavelle and I departed immediately. On the way I called to check on her situation and learned she had died.

Upon our arrival in McKenzie, P.J. asked if I would tell Dad the sad news. Because he had been bedfast in a nursing care facility, Dad would not be able to attend the funeral. He took the news in stride. But his grief was deep as he said to P.J. and me, "Well, I will soon be joining her." He handled his loss and grief with the inward strength he had called upon to handle hardships throughout his 91 years.

Our grief as six siblings was profound and lingering. Yet countless comments that Mother was a good woman by friends, relatives, neighbors, and members of First Church in McKenzie comforted us.

As the weeks passed in Bartlesville, news came out that Carl Ichon, owner of Trans World Airlines, was attempting a hostile takeover of Phillips Petroleum. This second attempt filled me with what my grandmother called "the blues." Another emotional upheaval lodged in my soul as I envisioned even more people losing their jobs or having to retire early. I fretted about our possibly having to put Vision 2000 on the back burner this time.

My mood swing eased a bit when I learned that Glenn Cox had been elected president and chief operating officer of Phillips. I called to congratulate him and to assure him my prayers would be regular and frequent. I said I felt better about the Ichon takeover with him as president of the company. Finally I thanked him for his consistent faith and leadership in the church. His response was so typical of his commitment to Christ.

"You know," he replied, "the first thing I felt led to do upon being notified of my election was to come across the street to the church and to pray in the chapel!" His witness gave me heart and inspiration.

Ichon's attempt to take over the company failed but not without the heavy cost of additional layoffs and early retirements. There was no doubt in my mind that Glenn Cox had a lot to do with stabilizing the company through its second threat.

The murder of a middle-aged son of one of our member families tore into my soul with raging emotions. I was so disturbed that I could hardly think. Anger, disgust, sorrow, and compassion crowded into my innermost being. The 20-year-old suspect was arrested and held without bond in the county jail across the street from the church. I visited with him in his cell.

Trembling, he blurted out to me, "I need to be forgiven!"

It was an understandable plea. If ever I witnessed hell in a human life, it was in that young man's face. We talked for a while. I prayed for him, for his family, and the victim's family. I left him a New Testament and promised I would visit him again.

As I was leaving, he said to me, "Tell his family I am so sorry!"

Later that day I called the victim's father to convey the young man's words. The father was barely civil in response. It was too early for him to do more, with his son's body lying in state at the funeral home.

In midsummer I departed for a 21-day trek to Australia and the Fiji Islands. Again the World Council's Committee on Evangelism had invited me to be a part of the Australasian seminar on evangelization. Tuck Archer, a devoted member and leader in First Church, accompanied me. The event was patterned after the African seminar.

After 10 days of training, the American group went to Fiji to assists the church leaders in making disciples of Christ. My assignment was to Suva, the capital city. We arrived at Nandi Airport after midnight and traveled by van the rest of the night to Suva. Upon arrival, I was informed that I was to "preach to the nation" at 9:30 a.m. in Dudley Church. I was unprepared physically to preach.

During my introduction I learned that the Methodist bishop of Fiji could not be present because he would be on another island laying a wreath at the gravesite of an Englishman named Baker. Baker and several other young men had come to Fiji exactly 150 years earlier to found Methodism among a cannibalistic people. Baker was the only one to survive. The others simply disappeared, one by one. As the bishop laid that wreath, we were reminded that more than 90 percent of the indigenous Fijian people were Methodist in 1985. I was told that was the densest percentage of Methodist people in the world. What a rare honor it was for me to preach on that occasion.

Upon my return, emotional swings and upheavals continued. Dyton's recurring sieges of mononucleosis-like symptoms plagued him. Several doctors gave their medical opinions and wrote prescriptions. Nothing seemed to prevent recurrence. Finally we took him to Scott-White Clinic in Temple, Texas. After extensive tests, the doctors located and treated the source of his sieges. The stress we had endured for many months had at last lifted.

A few days after returning to Bartlesville, we were blessed

with the birth of Denae Rachelle, our first grandchild. The emotional high this time was purely positive. Our understanding of life moved into a new dimension.

Two months later word came that E.W., my oldest sibling, was in the hospital in Louisville, Kentucky, with advanced stages of liver cancer. P.J. and I visited him and found him upbeat but aware of the inevitable.

The last three months of 1985 were filled with several positive emotional experiences. I received notice that I had been nominated for membership on the executive committee of the World Methodist Council. I would be elected the following July at the World Methodist Conference in Nairobi, Kenya. It was an honor I was unable to grasp for a long time.

That same week, Joe Kaufman, one of First Church's outstanding leaders, dropped by to advise me that he and Sherryl had established a scholarship at Oklahoma City University in Lavelle's and my honor. My emotional quotient improved even more.

The year ended on another emotional high. A church conference was called in December. Every member was invited to attend. The board of trustees presented a resolution calling for a new building and major remodeling of the existing facility to accommodate the acceleration of Vision 2000. Originally this construction was not projected until late 1989.

There was little debate on the building program, estimated to cost $2.7 million. More than 90 percent approved the resolution. The congregation's vote served as yet another sign that First Church was fully in support of Vision 2000 as its strategy for ministry to the end of the century.

As I had entered 1985 filled with emotional sadness, I ended the year filled with gladness. One of the most important and gratifying things we had done that year was hiring Dr. Randy Thompson as minister of music. He was a godsend. Not only was he a highly talented musician, instrumentalist, and team player, he became one of my closest friends. Every staff person saw him in much the same light. No wonder, then, that First Church became a flagship example of a comprehensive music ministry. My fourth year journey with First Church had continued to prove my mettle and to hone my spiritual maturation.

In January 1986 Sterling Williams was appointed pastor of First United Methodist Church in Paul's Valley. Clint Purtell, a longtime respected friend, was appointed as senior associate of administration of First Church. It was a perfect fit for the church's growth needs. Mike Schlittler was appointed as the third associate for First Church. Mike had served as youth minister at Epworth Church some 13 years earlier. He would be minister of evangelization and discipleship. With Russell Cheatham already aboard, we were fleshing out pastoral leadership needs called for in Vision 2000.

Lavelle's mother suffered a fractured hip and was not doing well in the hospital. We drove to Tennessee. With Lavelle's presence and assistance and the help of her sisters, her mother stabilized and improved after being in the hospital five weeks.

In May we were back in Tennessee for me to preach at McKenzie First Church and to dedicate the Methodist Heritage Memorial given by the family to the church in memory of Mother. That event caused me to give thanks for so many ways that church had touched and influenced my life.

While in McKenzie I visited with my father for a long while. As usual he was alert, but he had obviously deteriorated since last I had seen him. We spoke of many things. He talked frankly of his dying and "going on to be with Lula," our Mother. Our time together was made richer by his calm assurance that death was not to be dreaded but expected. He said to me without ado, "I am fully ready to go!"

He was growing tired, so I stepped to his bedside and took his hand. I said, "Dad, I want to thank you for the life you have lived and for the example you have set for all seven of us children." I then prayed, kissed him, told him I loved him, and never saw him alive again.

A few weeks later I departed for Nairobi, Kenya, to attend the World Methodist Conference. I left a few days early to give me time to return to Meru to dedicate the new building at Kaaga Church, which First Church, Bartlesville, had funded. I was to be met at the airport by Francis M'Immanenie, who would transport me to his home in Meru for the night.

Several of my U.S. friends were on the same flight as delegates to the World Methodist Conference. Having landed in

Nairobi, I made my way to the passport check-in. A burly man stopped me and asked if I were Dr. Ray Owen. I said yes. He took my arm and asked me to come with him. I was mystified. My friends were looking puzzled at my being led away. The man identified himself as Richardia Gitonga, chief of security for the airport. He and Mr. M'Immanenie had separated so as not to miss me when I entered the terminal. We greeted each other. My friends were still looking on as Mr. Gitonga took my passport and my baggage stubs and asked me to follow him. My friends were just sure I was being detained.

I arrived at the baggage area, where my luggage was waiting. Someone brought me my passport, already stamped and approved. We then entered a waiting car. The driver was told to deliver me to the Hilton Hotel, where I was to check in for the upcoming conference.

For sure I had been given VIP treatment by the government of Kenya. What an astonished look came over the faces of my friends, standing in a long line, when they saw me already checked in at the hotel registration desk and picking up my key. "How did you get here so quickly?" several asked in unison. "We thought you had been arrested. We all looked for you after we cleared immigration and were worried about you."

I shouldn't have told them, since I knew some of them would spread it all over the American delegation that I was Mr. VIP, who had special privileges in Kenya. The fact of the matter was that I had not expected what had happened. I did say to them that receiving VIP treatment was the way to travel. We then went on to Meru.

The next morning Mr. M'Immanenie drove me to the church for the dedication and celebration. About a quarter mile from the church, we came to a dead stop. Completely filling the street were some 100 brightly dressed women, who began to dance, sing, and wave streamers as they stepped off in front of us. Seeing I was mystified, Mr. M'Immanenie smiled and said to me, "These Kaaga Church women are your escort to the church. They sing and dance to say you are welcome as the bringer of good gifts."

I was told more than 6,000 people had come for the celebration—including the minister of state, Mr. Anganine. He greeted me warmly and extended to me best wishes from President Daniel arap Moi. He then escorted me into the beautiful new building, where he and I, along with Bishop Imathieu, dedicated the facility "to the worship and glory of God."

Church dignitaries and high officials from the Methodist Church of England thanked First Church, Bartlesville, and me for the gift of the building. I must have shaken hands with every person in that 6,000-strong crowd. It had been a dizzying, almost euphoric day, which I could never hope to repeat.

The World Methodist Conference convened. I was elected to the executive committee for a five-year term. That particular conference made a worldwide statement of encouragement in facing down racism. Again and again I, like countless others, felt my heart "strangely warmed."

The week following my return to Bartlesville, we were notified that Dad had died. His six-year stint in a nursing home was over. We were all saddened, of course. Yet I could not regret his dying. Instead, my trust in God was strengthened by that lingering conversation we shared the last time we had talked. After the funeral the family sat together and talked for a while. We all realized that one era had ended and another had begun. We had become the "elder generation" of the Owen family

A month or so later Bartlesville experienced a devastating flood. The downtown area had been separated from the outer business sector. Hundreds of homes were damaged or destroyed. But like every other misfortune that had come against the city, the community rose up to meet it, endure it, overcome it, and eventually to make Bartlesville a better place to live in because of it.

A few weeks later still, we learned that E.W., my oldest sibling, had succumbed to liver cancer. Our oldest sister and brother had now passed away. The rest of us attended E.W.'s funeral in Louisville.

A historic day for First Church was celebrated the following week. We broke ground for the new building. Our goal was to have in hand $1 million by that time. The remaining $1.7 million would be borrowed and paid off as quickly as possible.

We had in hand more than $998,000 when the shovels turned the dirt.

Near the end of the year, three construction crewmembers were working in the deep ditch surrounding the foundation wall of the basement. They were sealing the wall with brushed-on chemicals. Since it was cold weather, they had a small heater in the ditch. The fumes ignited, and the heater blew up. Two of the workers were on fire when our custodian, Ben Suggs, heard their screams. Falling onto his stomach, he reached down and literally dragged the two burning men upward and outward onto the pavement. Then he stripped off their burning outer garments. He had saved two lives that day. He and the two men were taken to the hospital.

Later I found Ben in a treatment room with both hands under cold running water. The two men were hospitalized with severe burns. When asked about his ordeal, Ben simply replied, "I didn't think about anything but getting those two guys out of that ditch!" That was Ben. In a special ceremony before the congregation later, the church honored Ben with a sizable gift for being so thoughtless for his own safety and welfare.

Every week Weststar Bank hosted a town hall meeting for discussions of community concerns. I attended regularly. The mood at the time was rather somber because of the two Phillips takeover attempts and their lingering effects on the future. The more the subject was discussed, the gloomier the atmosphere became.

Finally someone declared, "Well, the Methodist Church must not be all that worried. Every day their new building keeps coming upward out of that huge hole." Laughter broke out, as did light applause.

I had heard earlier such gloom and doom addressed in a church meeting. Someone had said, "Building a multimillion dollar facility in these uncertain times is somewhat foolhardy. On any given day, Phillips could be relocated. Or worse yet, be taken over by a third hostile attempt."

Ray Steiner, one of the company's vice presidents, said softly in response, "Whether or not Phillips is here tomorrow or next year, the Methodist Church will still need to be here!

Let's get on with being the church and demonstrating what our strong faith and ministry is all about!"

His response defined the caliber of faith and spirit that carried First Church into 1987.

Instead of preaching a sermon on the first Sunday of my sixth year at First Church, I delivered what came to be called a "State of the Church" address. Over the preceding five years the congregation had grown stronger in every aspect of its ministry. Spiritual formation and personal devotional life were much more evident. Our membership had grown significantly as making disciples of Christ became our priority. Total giving was nearing $1 million a year. Attendance at worship services and Sunday school was steadily increasing. "Mission mindedness" reached out from the pews to across the world. Visible enthusiasm clearly defined the strategy of Vision 2000 for ministry to the end of the century. The congregation received the address as "compelling and appropriate."

While at a meeting of the district pastors the next day, Dr. LeRoy Sewell, our district superintendent, asked me how things were going. I shared with him the congregation's response to the address. He smiled and said simply, "I'm not surprised!"

Several days later Dr. Sewell was hospitalized in Oklahoma City. We assumed he would be there for only a few days. He improved some, then died rather suddenly.

His death was hard for me to take. For nearly my entire ministry he had been a close friend, worthy mentor, and insightful counselor. Perhaps most of all, he had been an encourager. I recalled the occasion some 20 years earlier when he said to me, out of the blue, "Ray, I see a future for you that you probably are not even aware of yet!"

I took his comment as yet another word of encouragement.

Though I was highly honored to participate in his memorial service, I felt a profound and long lingering loss at his dying. Few people were more devoted, supportive, and proud of their spouse as was Fay Del Sewell. Early in my pastoral ministry I heard it said, "If you can't love Fay Del, you can't love anybody." I had come to know LeRoy well enough to know those words were true.

The following spring my book *Listening to Life* was published. I had assigned proceeds to go to Dana's scholarship fund at Oklahoma City University.

That spring I also implemented a new policy regarding ministry with our shut-ins and those confined to nursing-care facilities. With so many of them, it seemed impossible to visit with any degree of frequency. Once a month the four pastors and as many staff persons as were available would take a day to visit every homebound and disabled member. In this way, these devoted and faithful members would see their pastors and staff persons regularly. That would be in addition to contacts made through the weekly newspaper, Sunday televised worship service, and "check ons" by the laity.

After the visitations were completed, we all gathered for pizza and to share reports about the visits. The stories were truly inspiring. I was so moved by the first visit that I wrote in my journal, "O God, help me to be your pastor more of the time, until I become yours all of the time."

Bishop Lawi Imathieu of the Kenyan Methodist Church preached at First Church. He thanked the congregation for providing the new building for Kaaga Church in Meru. He then challenged us to consider sponsoring one of the several new congregations planned for the western area of Kisumu. The amount needed for pastoral support, housing, and a tabernacle-type church was a significant undertaking for the Kenyan Church but really very modest for First Church. The bishop's challenge was accepted as a new part of Vision 2000's expanding mission outreach.

At the 1987 annual conference session, Russell Cheatham was appointed to the church in Stilwell. He had served well for four years at First Church and endeared himself to everybody in the congregation. Dr. John Welch, a longtime and valued friend, was appointed superintendent of the Bartlesville District. Certainly I felt fortunate in his appointment.

On the second ballot of the conference, I was elected a delegate to the 1988 General and jurisdictional conferences. William B. Oden was elected on the first ballot and led the delegation. The next day I was named the recipient of the conference's Human Relations Award. That was a special honor for me, in that the citation included my involvement with Paul's Chapel in Hugo.

Well into the year we still had not filled three key staff positions. Our search for the right persons had been unfruitful. Then suddenly our luck changed. Linda Muterspaugh came aboard as the director of children's ministries. She was a commissioned missionary. She knew the church; she knew her job; and she knew how to work with a large staff. Her competence, attitude, and experience verified immediately our wisdom in hiring her. She remained on staff until she retired in 2001 after having been ordained a deacon.

Ken Dossett came aboard as director of youth ministries and soon developed programs that captured the imagination not only of First Church but of the entire community.

Valdo Petter was hired as the director of Christian education. We had then filled all vacancies called for in Vision 2000.

In a joint venture with Oklahoma City University, the church sponsored Peter Kariithi's enrollment as a full-time student. He was the son of the M'Immanenie family in Kaaga Church. Peter was a fine student, who graduated with a business degree in less than four years.

That summer Lavelle and I traveled to Jamaica to attend my first meeting as a member of the executive committee of the World Methodist Council. I came away boggled of mind and challenged at the scope of Methodist influence and involvement in mission in some 70 countries of the world.

That fall the new building at First Church was officially opened for ministry. A unique feature was the relocation of the children's outside playground onto the flat rooftop of the new building. Every imaginable piece of outdoor play equipment for children was in place. Long before the building was completed the registration for daytime ministry for children overflowed into a long waiting list.

The church was located in downtown Bartlesville. Parents who worked for Phillips Petroleum in nearby multi-story buildings could see their preschool children happily at play on the highly secured rooftop. Without a doubt this feature demonstrated every day that "First Church downtown" was focused on ministry for children. The whole congregation was thrilled at the new look and convenience of First Church.

In the last month of the year, I witnessed signs of dark days ahead. I feared the situation might well endanger Vision 2000. My fears began as my leadership and authority as senior pastor was challenged by a person who represented a few local followers. During a meeting in my study, he accused me of surrounding myself with leadership of "weak lambs" who were not "spiritual" persons.

I was troubled greatly in my soul but not angry. I knew what had been said about me and others simply was not true. But at that point I believed it would be only a matter of time until I would exit the church. The seeds of discontent had already been sown. My only recourse was to retreat to my "prayer closet" to seek God's guidance in the coming days.

The situation broke open later at our annual charge conference, presided over by the district superintendent. Throughout the conference pointed questions came up concerning the pastor's authority and how leaders were elected, etc. Both the superintendent and the members looked baffled. One shot was taken at me personally during my pastoral report. I felt embarrassed for the whole body of the conference.

I went home saddened in heart and soul at the intensity of hostility shown by one person. The next day the chairperson of the staff-parish relations committee dropped by to visit. He had already figured out much of what had gone on the night before. He affirmed my leadership and advised me to "sit still." He assured me the congregation strongly supported my leadership. He said the whole matter would soon "die from the lack of oxygen." How helpful his visit had been for me personally.

I went about my business, and sure enough, the whole matter seemed quietly to dissipate. In time the one who had spoken so fiercely to me in my study sought reconciliation. We parted in peace, though our relationship never returned to what it was before the charge conference.

Vision 2000 was still on track and had survived its first and only threat for the rest of the time I was at First Church.

My journal entry for January 1, 1988, began with this observation: "I need to live above the many negatives I encounter in the church." Though worth attempting, that observation would soon prove difficult to practice.

Still another round of layoffs and job losses at Phillips Petroleum quickly squelched any rising sense of promising days ahead. The effects this time seemed much more pervasive than other rounds. The question, "When will these layoffs end?" became a common conversation startup in the church and community. "Negatives," therefore, were already difficult "to live above." Yet, with crumpled spirits, the congregation went on about its business of ministry.

Within days a man attacked one of our most beloved widows with a knife as she got out of her car in her own garage. She managed to escape into the house and to call the police. The man broke through the door and held the knife as if to stab her. The phone rang and the man fled. The police arrived and after an investigation said it was the same person who had been terrorizing other people in the neighborhood.

Less than a week later a man attmpted to rape a younger woman in her own household. She, too, was a faithful member of our church.

On top of all these "negatives," a bomb threat was called in to the director of children's ministry. Procedures for such emergency were implemented. The building was vacated in three minutes. The children were delivered to a safe place and remained there until authorities cleared the entire facility. Apparently the call was a "joke." Some joke!

Indeed, it was difficult for me as pastor to "live above negatives" when all these events occurred within the first 35 days of the new year.

In May Lavelle and I departed for England to participate in the 250th anniversary celebration of John Wesley's Aldersgate experience. The World Methodist Council sponsored the event. Queen Elizabeth had commissioned two trains—the John Wesley and the Charles Wesley—for the large group to trace the lives of the Wesley brothers from their birthplace to their deaths. Without a doubt it was a most informative and inspiring experience related to our roots as Methodists. The event came to its end as we all gathered in St. Paul's Cathedral in London. Queen Elizabeth and Prince Phillip attended the gathering and greeted us. Dr. Donald English, a distinguished member of the World Methodist Council, delivered a memorable sermon.

We went immediately from there to the place where John Wesley had personally encountered the grace of God, known as his Aldersgate experience, when he found "his heart strangely warmed, and that he had been saved from the law of sin and death." It was quite awesome to kneel and pray 250 years later at the very site of Wesley's experience.

The General Conference of 1988 met in St. Louis, Missouri. One item of business was to give permission to the South Central Jurisdiction to split the Dallas-Fort Worth episcopal area. That meant the South Central Jurisdiction would be electing three bishops instead of two.

The Oklahoma Annual Conference session convened in June. As I noted earlier, it was a special conference for me personally, since Dyton was ordained deacon on probation, and Darryl was ordained elder in full connection—both by Bishop John Wesley Hardt. I felt especially blessed to lay my hands on Darryl's head, along with those of the bishop and several other elders.

At that annual conference I had the privilege of nominating Dr. William B. Oden as Oklahoma's nominee for election to the episcopacy at the upcoming South Central Jurisdictional Conference in New Orleans. My nomination was soundly sustained with a standing ovation by those present.

At the jurisdictional conference in July, Dr. Oden was the first of three bishops elected. He was assigned to the Louisiana Area. Dr. Bruce Blake from Kansas was elected and assigned to the Dallas Area. Dr. Dan E. Solomon was elected from the Southwest Texas Conference and assigned to the Oklahoma Area—as our delegation had hoped.

The year was passing at seemingly flank speed. In the fall one of our young adults took her life in her apartment. She, her siblings, and their mother were all members of the church. Since I knew the family, I was asked by the chief of police to notify them of the sad news. Clint Purtell, the senior associate pastor, went with me. The mother and father had been divorced for several years, and the hostility still remained. That compounded the horror of the situation. I called the father, who came for the funeral and remained for several days. With help from a lot of our members and the pastors, the family made its way through the painful ordeal. That was but the first of three suicides over the next year. Neither of the other two was a member of First Church, but the impact of those deaths certainly affected the congregation.

As the year began with a number of "negatives," so it seemed it would end in the same manner. The person who had been angry with me dropped by to advise me that he and his wife were resigning as members of the administrative board. I thought we had reconciled our relationship during the past year, so I asked why. He was in a rush and would say only that he disagreed with the way I was doing things. When I pushed further as to what I could do to correct the situation, he shot back, "There's nothing you can do."

I regretted that the old wound had been opened again. Many years before, a district superintendent had said to me, "There are times, Ray, when all you can do with some people is to love them and leave them alone." It was time for me to take his advice. That's what I did for the remaining time I was at First Church.

The year apparently would end on a sour note for me. But the negative was overcome fully by the thrill of Dana LaRae's birth. She was named Dana after our deceased son and LaRae after Lavelle and me. Dyton and Deena had delivered to us a positive year-end gift of a second granddaughter. Even Christmas was made more joyful for us and certainly more meaningful.

Our staff retreat for planning the ministry of First Church for 1989 was especially exciting and productive. We were realizing the value of a unified and visionary group of highly qualified and motivated persons.

Early in the year Clint and I were drafted to make our acting debut in a drama about the lives of Peter and Paul. Clint was immediately excited about the whole thing. I was a bit hesitant but finally agreed, since the proceeds would go to the church's Mission Outreach Fund.

It was left to Clint and me just how we would dramatize the two apostles for about an hour. We decided to perform without a script. Everything would evolve as we spoke from our knowledge of the two characters. Indeed, we were taking an enormous risk. Three "silent" biblical characters were added to the cast to raise questions should Clint or I draw a blank during the performance.

Clint and I decided where we would start and end. Everything in between would be spontaneous. I was to play the role of Paul, and Clint would play Peter. The whole idea was scary for both of us.

There would be no rehearsal. How could there be, when neither of us knew what the other would say. The date for our debut was set. Tickets were printed. Publicity was significant. Certainly neither of us expected a large crowd. On the night of the big show, my study became the makeup and dressing room. Surprisingly, Clint and I looked much like the characters might have looked. Robes, belts, and sandals looked authentic, including makeup with lots of putty reconstructing our noses, cheeks and foreheads.

The opening scene would find the lazing, silent characters around a low table, waiting for Peter and Paul's arrival from the back of the audience. Clint and I made our way forward, chatting to each other through 350 people waiting to see the performance. Video cameras were ready to tape the drama for posterity.

It was amazing how well the whole thing went. Peter and Paul confronted each other, disagreed with each other, talked about where the infant church was headed, and how best to lead it. They dreamed of the church bringing the whole world to Jesus and bringing the kingdom of God on earth. It was humorous, informative, serious, inspirational, and a huge success. A sustained standing ovation thundered approval and appreciation.

All of us on stage were thrilled. A large amount of money was raised for mission. We learned later that the videotape had not turned out at all. There went our chance to prove ourselves worthy for some sort of recognition as actors. So the whole thing was rescheduled for those who had not been able to attend. Clint and I wondered how in the world we could do the same thing over when there was no script. How would we be able to capture the same spontaneity? We performed it again to a large audience. This time the tape was good and registered in the church's video library for the benefit of others for years to come.

Thus our acting career came and went after two productions. At least we had occasion to prove ourselves novice thespians. Vision 2000 added the category of religious plays and dramas as another spinoff ministry.

Francis and Monica M'Immanenie from Kaaga Church in Kenya arrived to speak to First Church on Mission Sunday. Five years earlier Kaaga Church had been the first recipient of funds from our Mission Sunday offering, more than $16,000. While with us, the M'Immanenies visited with their son Peter, whom we were sponsoring as a student at Oklahoma City University.

For six years First church had worked diligently to sponsor and bring to the community a Vietnamese family. Many government requirements had to be met. The family finally arrived and was received into the membership of First Church. It was a joyous day of triumph for our congregation. The Dong family added so much to the life of the church. Their kind and humble spirits, along with their commitment to Christ, simply inspired us to live up to their standards of discipleship.

Our district superintendent notified Mike Schlittler that he would be appointed to another church at the upcoming session of the annual conference. Mike had given First Church four years of splendid service. Paul Vickers succeeded him as associate pastor of evangelism and discipleship.

In mid-year Lavelle and I traveled to Switzerland to attend the executive committee's meeting of the World Methodist Council. We met at the Hotel Victoria, owned by the Swiss Methodist Church and located in a spectacular range of breathtaking mountain peaks. The whole area gave us an enlarged sense of reverence and the majesty of God. Plans were made for the 1991 World Conference in Singapore. "Jesus Christ, God's Living Word" was adopted as the theme for the event.

Spirit Rally '89 and our fall "Ingathering" effort to bring in new members were combined and launched in September. They breathed new energy into the congregation. Because of several downturns in the community, First Church was in serious financial deficit. The Ingathering brought in a sizable number of new members, which uplifted our spirits. Throughout the rest of the fall, the Spirit Rally continued to bolster our awareness that God was with us in those hard times.

For three years I had served as chairperson of the development committee for the Perkins Alumni Council. A major part of our committee's responsibilities was to raise funds for Perkins School of Theology at Southern Methodist University. With the help of Bishop John Wesley Hardt, bishop in residence at Perkins, we invited several business leaders in Texas and Oklahoma to join us for a "Partners With Perkins" luncheon in Tulsa. Several leaders attended. I made a brief presentation and asked them to become partners with the school of theology. We left it at that, after an extensive period of questions and discussion.

Apparently there was a notable response to the appeal, in which I am sure Bishop Hardt played no small part. During Ministers Week in January 1990, I received a citation at the annual luncheon for the work of the development committee.

On top of all the other downturn events at the Phillips Petro leum, a tragedy occurred in mid-fall. Its Plastics Plant in Pasadena, Texas, sustained a disastrous explosion. Several workers were missing. One woman who was badly burned was the daughter of the treasurer at First Church. I called all the officers I knew and prayed with them on the phone. When I called Glenn Cox, chief operations officer for Phillips, I was inspired to hear his calm words, grounded in his deep faith and trust in God. I watched the calm and confident way the company dealt with its latest setback. I had said it before and now was saying it again: "If I were not a pastor, I would want to work for Phillips Petroleum Company." The employees I knew from top to bottom were persons of deep and abiding faith and commitment to Christ.

All of this tragic news came right in the middle of our endeavors to underwrite the 1990 budget for the church.

Several years earlier Bethel AME Church had sold bonds to finance the construction of its present church facilities. Every year it became more difficult for the members to pay the required amount into the sinking fund at the bank, with which the bank paid interest to bond holders. The church was in default for several thousand dollars.

An officer of the bank informed me of the situation and sought my counsel on the matter. The bank certainly did not want to foreclose on the church. I asked for time to confer with the pastor and to explore ways First Church might be able to help. He told me to take whatever time I needed.

The pastor and I talked and decided to ask our two congregations to hold a joint celebration at Bethel Church. We planned the event and encouraged our members to participate. We told our members what we needed to raise and to come prepared to help lift this burden from the Bethel congregation.

I must say, it was wonderful to see so much cooperation for such a good thing. Before I realized it, I had been drafted to be the "preacher of the hour"—without right to decline. Every honorable objection I raised only stiffened the conspirators' decision.

From my experience of preaching at Paul's Chapel in Hugo, I knew how a black congregation could cause any preacher to preach better than he could preach.

The day came, and what a day it turned out to be! Bethel's sanctuary was stuffed way beyond full. Sure enough, with the congregation's encouragement, I preached way beyond my capacity. First Church members got involved at a level never before witnessed or experienced. I then explained the need of Bethel Church to pay off the bonds. I asked everyone present to make a gift that would make it happen.

The small table with two offering plates was brought out and placed up front in the aisle between the two rows of pews. The people came down the aisle singing as the pastor and I stood at the table. I was wringing wet with "preacher's sweat."

After all had come down and placed their gifts into the plate, more spontaneous singing broke out. It lasted until the offering had been reported. Some two thirds of the total was raised right there. Later that afternoon $500 more came in. Over the next few days, even more was received.

Several days later, I received word that only a small amount remained unpaid. I could believe the bank took care of that small amount.

That Sunday afternoon celebration, its purpose, and outcome really captured the attention of the whole community. For weeks I was teased about why I didn't preach at First Church like I had preached at Bethel. My response was, "First Church people, as yet, haven't responded to my preaching like Bethel Church did. When they are ready at First Church, I'll be ready."

To our amazement, First Church came to the close of 1989 on a high plane, meeting its entire budget for the year. It also had underwritten its budget for the following year in the amount of $1.036 million.

Clint received notice that he was being appointed to Asbury Church in Oklahoma City. He had done a splendid job for four years as senior associate pastor for administration. I particularly had been blessed by his labors among us.

Deandra Elise, daughter of Darryl and Denise, was born December 5. She was their second daughter and our third granddaughter. She added much joy to our family's Christmas.

The last days of December I spoke to more than 100 high school seniors and college students at "Decision '89" on the campus of Oklahoma City University. It was a good way to close out the year.

Another year of my journey with First Church had certainly tested my mettle and its maturation. Yet I could pray that the congregation felt as celebratory as I did.

Our annual staff retreat for 1990 lacked the usual energy, spirit, and anticipation. Much of its deflated spirit was because we did not have a senior associate pastor on board. Clint Purtell's appointment in Oklahoma City left a big hole in the staff's steadiness.

Dr. John Welch gave me permission to talk with the Reverend Jack Jordan about coming to First Church as the senior associate. Jack too was a quality pastor, highly regarded. Lavelle and I had a delightful time with Jack and his wife, Jerry, over lunch. Jack agreed to take the appointment, but it would be some time before the process could be finalized. Though hampered in its work, the staff planned a heavy but promising vision of ministry for the months ahead.

About this time I frequently did not feel well. My energy level took nosedives, leaving me depressed and anxious about my health. I had trouble sleeping at night. Headaches, sinus sieges, nervousness, and strange pains plagued my sense of well-being.

Finally I went to see Dr. Harris Moreland, a devoted member of First Church and a dear friend. He could find nothing major wrong with my physical condition. As a member of the staff-parish relations committee, he was well aware of the load I was carrying and the accompanying pressure. His prescription was not unkind. It was direct and emphatic.

"I can tell you," he said, "that you are working too many hours. You need to take frequent and regular days off and away from the church. You are headed for trouble. We all need your leadership but not enough to cause you a heart attack or some other physical problem."

I had come to the doctor for help and perhaps a bit of sympathy. I got a full load of the first and none of the second. Deep down I knew the diagnosis had been right. I returned to my office and reviewed my calendar for the rest of that day and the next. What I found gave evidence of the doctor's conclusion. I list here these items, not to curry sympathy, but to outline the kind of load most pastors carry:

- ❑ Help arrange for a family's son to gain admission to a mental health facility.
- ❑ Counsel a young man as he struggled with a "sense of call" to the ministry.
- ❑ Lunch with a husband and wife in crisis regarding their marriage.
- ❑ Two deaths. Follow up arrangements with the families and prepare messages for funerals later in the week.
- ❑ Hospital visits to two critically ill members dying from cancer.
- ❑ Talk with a single parent needing financial help to pay electric bill before scheduled cutoff the next day.
- ❑ Phone call from chairperson of finance committee for ideas to deal with financial deficit.

- ❏ Meeting of district pastors on church growth and discipleship.
- ❏ Prepare address for women's group about meeting specific needs of poor in the community.
- ❏ Work on "History and Heritage" lesson for prospective members for Sunday.
- ❏ Catch up on pressing administrative and staff matters.
- ❏ Find sufficient time for "prayer closet" and devotional life.
- ❏ Make time for family.

Having reviewed my calendar, I took my doctor's advice about taking time away from the church and being "unavailable." That time away was immensely invigorating. I would like to say I continued spending time away. Such was not the case.

Quite unexpectedly I was notified that I was to receive the Texas United Methodist College Association Award. It would be presented during Ministers' Week at Southern Methodist University in Dallas. A scholarship would be created at SMU the following year in recognition of my work and support for United Methodist colleges and universities in the South Central Jurisdiction.

I was surprised to be the recipient for two reasons: The honor of the award itself and that I was the only non-Texan ever to receive it. The presentation at the TUMCA dinner was a special time for the family members present.

Shortly thereafter, Bishop Dan Solomon called to ask me to come by his office the next time I was in Oklahoma City. The next morning I was on the road to see him. He asked if I would be willing to be appointed a district superintendent again at annual conference time in 1991. He assured me I could remain at Bartlesville First Church if I wished.

No matter how long a Methodist pastor has been in ministry, it is still a bit unsettling when the bishop or district superintendent talks about a new appointment. Before I could respond, Bishop Solomon suggested I spend time in prayer, talk to Lavelle, and consult leaders of First Church. That was a gracious act on his part. I was certainly willing to go wherever I was sent. That had been my response for more than 30 years. His giving me time to consider was deeply appreciated.

The timing of Bishop Solomon's conversation with me was interesting. Already the top leaders of First Church and I had planned to launch "Debt Free in '93." They felt I should stay. We were ahead of schedule and wanted to pay the building off. I spent time trying to discern God's guidance in the matter of moving at that particular time.

Lavelle and I talked about it. I met again with several leaders asking their counsel. We all agreed that it would be better for me to remain at First Church. Still, I could find no peace in the matter.

During this "seeking time" I left for El Paso, Texas. Don Forsman, a longtime and valued friend, had invited me to preach a revival at Trinity First Church for several days. While there, I quite thoroughly came to peace about Bishop Solomon's inquiry. I called him that very evening to say I preferred to stay at First Church. Bishop Solomon quickly agreed and even said that he felt good about the whole matter. His affirmation was just one more expression of his graciousness.

That spring and summer brought several highlights and joys for Lavelle and me. During Easter season my two brothers, P.J. and Doyle, along with their wives, Ruth and Rosemary, came for a visit of several days. We filled up many hours with laughter, reflection, and sheer enjoyment. We showed them Oklahoma sites, museums, and azalea festivals, and we ate too much.

A bit later the blessing of baptizing Deandra, our granddaughter, descended upon us all.

Dyton graduated from Perkins School of Theology and received an appointment back home in Oklahoma.

As a part of my getaway time, Lavelle and I departed on the World Methodist Conference's "Apologetics" trip through Turkey, Greece, and a four-day cruise to retrace the footsteps of the Apostle Paul's missionary journeys. Paulene Bohannon, Imogene and Dick Chambers, Tex and Juanita Ramzell, and Nadine Fontaine all accompanied us on the trip. Not only was the trip a fantastic experience, it fleshed out for all of us the eastern church's movement and influence. I came home far better informed as to the extent of Christ's church.

Still another wonderful highlight came when Dustin Michael,

son of Dyton and Deena, made his debut as our fourth grand-child and our only grandson. The blessing of his arrival was enhanced a month later when I baptized him.

In the fall Green Country Retirement Village opened its doors in Bartlesville. All of us on the executive committee felt pleased to see at last the dream of "Rich" Richardson now ful-filled. The entire community no doubt would reap benefits from this first-class facility's service to a large market area. All the frustrations, revisions, and unexpected delays now made the center's reality worth all our efforts.

As always, December arrived with its anticipation, struggles, and participation. We met entirely our $1.13 million budget for the year. On top of that, the church received a $100,000 designated endowment from the estate of a person who spent a lifetime loving and teaching children in public schools.

At Christmas time, as always, I volunteered to deliver food, clothing, and toys for the Salvation Army. Snow and ice made delivery very difficult, as it did for those lacking in so many basic human needs. At one older adult's home I found the kitchen faucet frozen because the back door would not close to keep the frigid air out. I arranged for a team of two from our Cadre of Concerns to take care of that critical need before night-fall. It was done. A widow in utter poverty thanked me at least a dozen times for the large bags of food and a box containing a winter coat for her.

Early Christmas morning I joined our usual group of men to deliver toys, clothing, and food to families who couldn't make ends meet. The Lions Club made this delivery an annual project and had been collecting for a year.

When 1990 had begun, I had expected tough going. Yet it ended with much cause for celebration. And much more cause for thanking God for the faithful people who made up the con-gregation of First Church.

At almost age 59 I had begun my 10th year as pastor of First Church, Bartlesville, in 1991. In one way the preceding decade had seemed a long time. Indeed, it had been more than twice as long as any other appointment I had served. In an-other way, those 10 years had passed so quickly. Little did I know that forthcoming upheavals, crises, bad news, surprises, and celebrations would make 1991 a truly memorable year.

The Sunday following Easter I received 28 persons into the church. Most came by profession of faith. It was the largest number received at one time since I was at Antlers 26 years earlier. Worship attendance that Sunday was a record of more than 1,600.

Then a series of terrible events rocked the church and community. A troubled young man murdered a lovely and vivacious senior high school student. She was reported missing when her abandoned car was found. The next day her body was found wrapped and stuffed into a culvert near our home.

The young woman was known for her devotion to God and a caring spirit. She was highly regarded among her peers for trying always to help someone. Her funeral took place in her church. I was among the several pastors who took part in the service. The man responsible for her death was convicted and sentenced to prison. He was the son of a fellow pastor, which compounded the tragedy.

Shortly thereafter a terrible tornado danced across southern Kansas and northern Oklahoma. In Copan, a town nearby, two people were killed.

Then came the horrible news that Ben Suggs, our former custodian, had taken his own life. He and I had talked about his alcohol binges. He was a gentle soul until he consumed liquor. Ben understood that his drinking jeopardized his job. In time we had to let him go. He understood.

Ben could do anything with his hands. Barehandedly he had pulled those two men out of the fiery trench at the construction site of the new building. In 1989 Ben had taken a scrap of marble left from remodeling the church foyer and made for me a beautiful desk pen base. Inscribed thereon was Proverbs 20:24. I have continued to use the base for my pen all these years to remind me to thank God for a good and special friend named Ben. I delivered the funeral message.

At the Oklahoma Annual Conference session in May 1991, I was elected on the first ballot to lead our 1992 delegation of 42 persons to the General and jurisdictional conferences.

Though I had been told I would be elected, I didn't think it would happen on the first ballot.

As soon as the ballot was read out, I had a compelling urge to slip out to the chapel to pray. It was an awesome feeling to know my colleagues in ministry had entrusted me with such a great responsibility. While I was kneeling at the altar, a friend who I thought might likely be elected first came and knelt beside me. He put his arm around my shoulder and congratulated me. In that moment I realized, in a much larger sense, the meaning of the Methodist term "connectionalism." Though that colleague and I held different theological perspectives, we both long before agreed to forget our differences and move to a deeper respect and friendship for each other.

Bishop Henry Belin of the AME Church came to Bethel Church in Bartlesville to burn the bond issue note we had already paid off to the bank more than a year before. His busy schedule had kept him from coming earlier. The bishop was most pleased.

He extended his blessings upon all of us for helping to make Bethel Church free of the bond debt. The bishop then invited me to be the guest preacher for his upcoming AME annual conference session in Muskogee, Oklahoma. I counted that a high privilege and still do.

A few days later Lavelle and I attended Bishops Week at Mount Sequoyah in Fayetteville, Arkansas. It was an annual retreat for spiritual renewal led by the bishops of the South Central Jurisdiction. It also served as the staging ground for prognostications as to who might be elected to the episcopacy the following year. Since six were to be elected, the predictions were numerous. My name was mentioned as likely to be elected. I was appreciative but also concerned about how such hearsay might affect the congregation.

Back home I expressed my concern to Joy Buell, the chairperson of the staff-parish relations committee. She invited Glenn Cox and Ray Steiner, who were former chairs, and me for lunch and discussion. I sat there amazed once more at the wisdom displayed as we talked. They decided that Joy should prepare a statement to the administrative board to clarify the election process and the church's response to my being talked about for election. The three then told me how grateful they were for the recognition First Church was already receiving.

"But if you are not elected," one of them said, "we will not have you coming back feeling you are a failure. We would want the bishop to know the congregation would want you to stay at First Church until you retire."

Joy's statement was presented to the board, including what the staff-parish relations committee wanted if I were not elected. The board gave a standing ovation of approval. That kind of support was so typical of First Church. Following is the letter:

Staff-Parish Relations Committee
First United Methodist Church
Bartlesville, Oklahoma
August 27, 1991

In order for all of us to know the fact, this is an official statement of information from the staff-parish relations committee to the administrative board.

Our senior pastor, Dr. Ray Owen, has been endorsed by the Oklahoma Delegation for the episcopacy. We are extremely proud of the honor his endorsement has brought to First United Methodist Church in Bartlesville. We need to keep perspective, however, as to what this endorsement means. Clearly, it does not assure Dr. Owen's election to the episcopacy.

At the Oklahoma Annual Conference session last June, Dr. Owen was elected on the first ballot to lead the Oklahoma delegation to the General and South Central Jurisdictional Conference in Fort Worth, Texas, in July 1992.

Six bishops will be retiring at the jurisdictional conference in Fort Worth. At least twelve candidates will be available to fill the six vacancies. These elections are somewhat like political elections in that they are difficult to predict. The possibility of Dr. Owen's election at that time as one of the six bishops is not a certainty. If elected, Dr. Owen would remain as pastor until September 1, 1992.

As a congregation, we rejoice in the recognition of leadership which his endorsement demonstrates. We fully and enthusiastically support the endorsement, which could lead to Dr. Owen's election. At the same time, should his election not take place, Staff-Parish wishes to go on record with fullest support for his return to First United Methodist Church as our *Senior Pastor*. Staff-Parish will keep the Board informed concerning steps in the process.

Prior to the Oklahoma Conference session last June, Dr. Owen shared his feelings on this matter with the staff-parish relations committee by stating, "I will not seek the episcopacy. If it comes to me, I will accept it as God's will." That possibility has now come. He has reconciled himself to the test of being endorsed as a candidate for election as a bishop in July 1992.

The staff-parish relations committee asks you to lift Dr. Owen and Lavelle in your daily prayers.

Joy Buell
Chairperson

That summer I experienced intermittent heart palpitations. Though not severe, they were bothersome. I spent a whole week taking a complete physical examination, a treadmill test, a Thallium test, and several other inconveniences. The cardiologist found nothing seriously wrong but did direct me to watch my diet, get plenty of exercise, and take more time off—all of which I had heard before but had a hard time, as a pastor, following through on.

At a district fellowship meeting one pastor kept needling me about numerous issues the Methodist Church was doing all wrong. One was pastors of large churches running the denomination and getting paid too much for doing so. On and on he went, subtly bringing me in on every complaint. At first I tried to inject some humor to still the tension most of us were feeling. Finally he blurted out something that made me angry. Before I realized it, I had hurt him and embarrassed several others. Immediately I was ashamed and sorry. Afterwards, several others came by to say the man deserved it. Though well intended, their words brought no comfort to my soul. How quietly and quickly indeed does sin lurk at the door. I certainly had not lived up to Paul's admonition to "be angry, but sin not." My conscience and soul were aflame with guilt and regret.

As soon as I got back to my office I wrote a remorseful apology to the recipient of my anger. It would have been far better had I apologized to him at the meeting, since I had disappointed all others present. So I sent a copy of the apology to each of those present. I asked the man to forgive me. I mailed all letters at the post office in hopes they would be delivered while the matter was still on our minds.

His letter of return contained only three words, with an exclamation point after each: "Forgiven! Forgotten! Forever!" Not only had I received a full measure of grace from him, I also had a new response to those who sought my forgiveness in the future. Every since, those three words have been my response to those hurting and seeking my pardon. The author of those three words and I are still close friends. We have never spoken since of the incident. How could we when his last word to me was "Forever"?

Later that same day, I was twice blessed as I visited two shut-ins. Age had enfeebled both physically but not mentally or spiritually. Both also were persons with very little means. As always, they were pleased that their pastor would take time in his busy schedule to visit them.

The first woman wept because medication cost increases meant she and her husband could no longer give to the church. I wept with her. For many years this woman had served as the church's secretary. As such, she became widely known as someone who was never idle in doing good for other people. The other woman insisted I take a tithe to the church from an unexpected check she had received. Knowing her need, I tried to object. She insisted. I felt unworthy in light of the love and devotion for church these two saints expressed.

In midsummer I attended the World Methodist Conference in Singapore. I was re-elected to the council's executive committee for another five-year term. From there I made an extensive tour of China. It was a dream fulfilled.

Our two sons, Darryl and Dyton, put together a Volunteers In Mission Project in Costa Rica. They wanted me to go before I was "lost to them as a bishop." How could I refuse? We spent more than a week working on prefabricated houses for victims of an earthquake, which had been followed by a flood. The team was blessed abundantly as we lived in "bivouac conditions."

Lavelle came down suddenly with a severe case of viral pneumonia. We almost lost her as her medical team worked feverishly to identify the culprit virus. Both lungs partially collapsed. She was in the hospital for a little over two weeks, with three different antibiotics dripping into her bloodstream. At last she took a turn for the better and came home. But before she could recover completely, she came down with a severe case of flu. I became alarmed but was relieved when the doctor showed X-rays indicating her lungs were completely healed. He added that the siege of pneumonia had not in any way made her susceptible to recurring pneumonia.

Near the end of the year the Phillips Petroleum implemented still another round of layoffs and early retirements. Its negative effects upon the church and community were significant but not to the degree rounds of the past had been.

The year ended with this notation in my journal on December 31, 1991:

> Cold, wet and dreary!
> Many hard hills have we climbed.
> Many valleys have we walked.
> But through every circumstance,
> We have found God to be gracious and faithful and true.
> So we live in gratitude and thanksgiving and excitement for the coming leg of our journey together!

As I considered all that was ahead in 1992, I became deeply concerned. The added responsibilities for leading our delegation to the General and jurisdictional conferences the following year, the numerous meetings that would be required for us to prepare ourselves, the weight of being endorsed and supported as a candidate for the episcopacy, the energy needed for being interviewed by 17 annual conference delegations, the significant investment of time and expense those interviews would demand, the continuing emotional drain throughout the entire process—all that made the coming months scary and possibly insurmountable. That was especially so when all these factors were piled on top of my already heavy standing agenda as senior pastor of a truly great church.

I concluded that if I were to prove adequate for what was ahead, I would need timely injections of physical, mental, emotional, and spiritual stamina. On several occasions during those months I did indeed experience profound spiritual renewal. Each succeeding spiritual interlude brought me to a higher awareness of God's presence and strength vitalizing my being.

The first experience came early in the year, following a retreat with some 20 high school youths. The purpose of the retreat was to raise their sensitivity as to what might be God's call to the ministry. All four of our pastors and our staff missionary shared how we had come to accept God's calling to ministry as our life's work.

That afternoon and evening the retreat turned out to be one of the richest and most rewarding events I experienced while at First Church. All five of us were amazed and impressed with the group's appreciation for the retreat. At the evaluation session most of the teens said they had already given thought to the call and that they were waiting to see where it all led.

As a result of that retreat, I was moved to reflect upon the progress of my own calling, such as how it all started, where it had taken me across some 33 years, what the ministry had made of my life, to what degree I had become the product of God's grace, the love and support of my family, the confidence of friends, the encouragement of mentors, and the priceless contributions of the local churches to my journey.

Consequently, I realized that every initial goal I had set in the beginning of my ministry and all the goals added along the way already had been reached. Most had been surpassed. No wonder, then, that I felt drawn downward upon my knees in my office to pour out to God the gratitude overflowing my heart.

"Oh, God," I declared, "I have received from you already more than enough for my lifetime."

As suddenly as that spiritual interlude had come, so it had passed. In its wake I was left with a vibrating sense that God was mixed up in all that was going on in my life, including my concern with the coming months. A sense of calmness and cleansing pervaded my entire being.

"No more fretting," I said to myself. "No more trying to manage what is not mine to manage." I was free and energized to move boldly into whatever lay ahead. Indeed, I had moved to a higher level of spirituality.

The interview process with annual conference delegations continued over nearly six months. Before long I actually looked forward to the interview sessions. My first two interviews were on the same day, with the Central Texas and the Southwest Texas conference delegations. Both interviews I felt went extremely well. In fact, I rather enjoyed the interchange. I was treated with every courtesy, kindness, and respect by the two delegations. I came home relaxed in knowing the spiritual encounter I had experienced a few weeks earlier had been confirmed.

The remaining 15 interviews were of much the same caliber. The last interview was with the North Texas Conference delegation in early summer. At the end of the interview journey, I felt good about the process and believed that I had presented myself with integrity. Certainly it had been a demanding schedule. I concluded there were outstanding delegates in every conference who were worthy of being endorsed as candidates for bishop.

To my distress, I woke up on my 60th birthday plagued by allergies and sinus discomfort, including headaches, sniffles, sore throat, chest distress, and general grumpiness from lack of sleep.

"How could one go from feeling on top of the world to the pits of misery in one day's time?" I moaned to myself.

I wrestled with my agony for two days. Then, right in the middle of my affliction, I felt an inflow of God's presence, peace, and even joy. It was every bit as soothing to my soul as that interlude several weeks before. It seemed the whole experience was a sign that life in its worst circumstance can also be life at its best.

In between interviews I spent time counseling, praying, and offering whatever I could to help those who had been laid off at Phillips Petroleum. This particular round of downsizing seemed to generate much more subsurface anxiety, anguish, despair, and anger than preceding rounds. In many ways I felt inadequate, if not unable, to help those in need. It was sad to see so many people struggling in the community.

As in previous situations, I preached to encourage faith, to counsel, and to lift up hope for the future. Several members each week indicated the preaching was helpful "during these tough times."

At the annual conference session in June, Dr. David Severe rose to a point of privilege to propose me officially as Oklahoma's nominee for election as a bishop at the South Central Jurisdictional Conference. The annual conference's standing response of approval touched me deeply. Only then did I realize the emotion my two immediate predecessors as nominees from Oklahoma, Bishops John W. Russell and William B. Oden, must have felt when they were so endorsed.

Blessings upon blessings were showering my life. Bishops Week in June at Mount Sequoyah in Fayetteville, Arkansas, was a special retreat for me. It served as the context for many expressions of best wishes for all of us who were candidates for the episcopacy.

On the following Sunday I had the special privilege and joy of receiving the 1,200th member to unite with First Church during my pastoral leadership. Truly, it was a thrill.

The following three weeks were filled with incoming calls, letters, and notes from across the jurisdiction—all giving best wishes and saying that prayers were being offered on my behalf. It was hard for me to keep focused on my pastoral responsibilities with all the comments and prognostications coming at me everywhere I went.

One really caring friend asked me, "Ray, how are you doing with all this swirling around you?"

Without forethought I replied, "I am trying to keep my head clear and my heart clean!" It was all I could say. Also, it was all that needed to be said.

The South Central Jurisdictional Conference convened July

14. The major item of business was the election of six bishops. All six were elected the same day: Alfred N. Norris from the Louisiana Conference, Joe A. Wilson from the Texas Conference, Ann B. Sherer from the Texas Conference, Albert Frederick Mutti from the Missouri West Conference; Joel Martinez from the Rio Grande Conference, and I from the Oklahoma Conference. The election had taken only nine ballots—a record, I was told.

My two former bishops, John Wesley Hardt and Dan E. Solomon, escorted me from the floor of the conference to the bishops' platform. Martha Hardt and Joy Solomon escorted Lavelle. Our two sons, Darryl and Dyton, and their wives joined us a bit later in a private room for some family time together before I was taken for a brief session with church and secular reporters.

I was assigned to the San Antonio Area in Texas. That area includes the Southwest Texas Conference and the Rio Grande Conference. The region covers 389,000 square miles and then had 121,000 Methodist members. We would move to San Antonio and assume episcopal responsibilities September 1, 1992.

The morning after the assignment was made, Lavelle and I had breakfast with a large number of people from the Southwest Texas and Rio Grande conferences. We had a lot of fun. Lavelle and I were asked to speak. As Lavelle spoke, one of her comments was, "What you see is what you get!" The crowd soundly approved. Already they must have known what they got in her was a whole lot.

July 16 I was consecrated a bishop through the hands of elder bishops laid heavily upon my head. Darryl and Dyton assisted in my consecration by escorting me to the chancel area to present me formerly to the waiting bishops. I was told there was no known occasion when two "elder" sons of a bishop had escorted their father to be consecrated. Another record, I suppose. Naturally it was quite an emotional experience for our family and for me particularly.

While the consecration was taking place, I sensed in my being a pervading presence. Later I shared this feeling with an elder bishop. Quite calmly he smiled, gripped my hand, and said, "Ray, most of us bishops could attest to what you felt."

Later another elder bishop asked how I was doing. I replied, "No day tomorrow will ever rival this today!" He too just smiled, as if he knew what I meant.

The following Sunday Bishop Dan Solomon introduced me to the First Church congregation as a new bishop. His splendid comments and sermon set the stage for a smooth transition of pastoral leadership. The congregation was very pleased with the bishop's helpfulness and graciousness.

The next day Joy Buell, chair of the staff-parish relations committee, ordered me and Lavelle to take the following week off—somewhere away from Bartlesville. We concurred with her wisdom and accepted it as one more indication of the quality of care by the congregation.

August 2, 1992, will live long in our hearts and memories. That day was declared by the mayor of Bartlesville as "Bishop Ray Owen Day," to be celebrated with a community-wide luncheon at the Bartlesville Community Center. A framed and impressive proclamation was read to the crowd and given to us as a memento of the occasion.

Present for the luncheon were members of other churches, fellow pastors, friends, community leaders, and city officials—all of whom conveyed their best wishes for our future.

Darryl and Dyton and their families were present. We were all deeply moved and honored by the city's outpouring of good words on our behalf. Never in all our lives did we imagine such an occasion. Yet the community's gift to us was but another example of Bartlesville's expressed grace, generosity, and appreciation.

In mid-August Bishop Earnest T. Dixon, my predecessor in San Antonio, arranged for a "get acquainted retreat" for Lavelle and me to meet the 11 district superintendents of the two conferences and their spouses. It was a gracious act on Bishop Dixon's part.

The purpose of the retreat was to make preliminary plans for our arrival in two weeks. What a marvelous time we had together. I shared with the superintendents my intentions of visiting every church in the two conferences, along with every related institution therein. I wanted to get started soon after my arrival so we could be finished by Easter the following spring.

Astonished looks came across faces. I then asked each superintendent to prepare an initial plan for the district so we could finalize how we were to visit nearly 500 congregations for a half hour meeting in each church. This endeavor would be a priority for getting acquainted with the 121,000 members of the two conferences. It would also provide for my challenging each congregation to develop a ministry vision for the future.

Upon our return Joy Buell, Superintendent John Welch, and several other pastors sponsored a "roast" for the new bishop. My brother Doyle and his wife, Rosemary, came all the way from Cleveland, Ohio, to join the proceedings.

While waiting in my study for the roast to begin, I scribbled the gist of a prayer, which I read as part of my final words to the audience. Below is the final version of that prayer as I faced the future as a United Methodist bishop.

Prayer of a Pastor
(Made recently a Bishop)
July 1992

> Come, Lord Jesus,
> stand by me.
> Forge me the man
> you see me to be.
>
> Take this life
> and let it be
> wholly healed
> and blessed by Thee.
>
> May ever your will
> be mine to seek.
> Your redeeming Word
> be mine to speak.
>
> May your piercing eyes
> be mine to see

the famished souls
a-hungry for Thee.

May your vigilant ears
be mine to hear,
the muffled cries
around me so near.

May your stilling voice
be mine to soothe
the troubled, discouraged,
who feel they lose.

May your inviting hand
be mine to raise
some stumbled pilgrim
your name to praise.

May your power of Spirit
be mine to share
with neighbor next door
your sustaining care.

May your strength in me
be mine to lend,
in selfless service
'til all I spend.

May your proven Way
be mine to walk,
the straight, the narrow
with Thee in thought.

May your gentle nature
be mine to embrace,
the least, the lost,
the whole human race.

Finally, Lord Jesus,

may your unmerited love
be mine to give,
'til your life in me
be my life to live!

The following Sunday I preached my last sermon as pastor of First Church to a capacity crowd. We hugged a lot of people and said goodbye with tears in our eyes to a lot of others. Our hearts pulsated with utmost joy. What a glorious 10-year-and-eight-month journey we had traveled, with an exceptional congregation named First Church, Bartlesville. Never before had I served a more committed, compassionate, caring, courageous, and generous congregation. The members had given us so much that left us with precious memories aplenty to bless us for the rest of our lives. Indeed, they had forged my mettle for all that was in store as a bishop for the final eight years of our ministry.

14

Journey in the Global Church

On August 26, 1992, Lavelle and I arrived in San Antonio, Texas, and moved into the spacious and brand-new episcopal residence. It was so new that all the furnishings were not yet in place. On September 12 I was "received" as the bishop of the San Antonio Area. Leaders from the Rio Grande and Southwest Texas conferences presented several symbolic gifts relating to my various responsibilities.

The four remaining months of the year were spent getting to know the two conference territories, their leaders, pastors, and congregations. I met with each cabinet and laid out preliminary plans and procedures for my leadership. The members of both cabinets were among the very finest leaders I had ever met. Immediately I felt the enormous respect these superintendents felt for me personally and for the office I held. My respect for them was equally felt.

In the course of those last four months of the year, I felt hurried but not in panic, scattered but not unfocused, eager but not impatient, appreciated but not pampered. We were all hard at work together and looking to eight years ahead.

In the midst of all this stir, Lavelle and I celebrated our 40th anniversary. With increasing joy we thanked God for the countless blessings we were receiving. Late in October we started visiting all the churches in the area. The Corpus Christi District was completed first.

One of my year-end prayers included the words "Lord, am I able to do this job?" Then I answered myself, "Of course I'm not!" Once again that plaguing flaw in my life showed itself. I had asked God a question and answered it myself before God could respond. I was still trying to run ahead of God. As a freshly made bishop, I still had a long way to go when it came to waiting upon the Lord.

Of all the ministry settings I would encounter during my eight-year tenure as a bishop, the most refreshing, rewarding, and invigorating for me personally would be my journey among the people of the Southwest Texas and Rio Grande conferences. Two especially delightful experiences I had while visiting the nearly 500 churches came as I met with two tiny congregations.

One was in the wide-open spaces of the San Angelo District. Since some of the churches were far apart, we had to move rapidly to get to the next church on time. On one occasion it was to Veribest Church. The day was really dreary and cold, made miserable by the wind. By the time we arrived, a peppery sleet was falling heavily.

Our meeting lasted less than half an hour. As we came out the door, we saw that the parking area, fields, and road literally were a sheet of ice because of falling temperatures. While we were dashing for the car, one of the members called out, "Bishop, you can now say you have gone from the Veribest to the very worst in less than half an hour!" Such fun loving from lovers of Christ is what I found in all the other 10 districts.

On a much later visit to the San Angelo District, Warren Griffin, district lay leader, in cahoots with District Superintendent Barbara Galloway-Edgar, invited conference Lay Leader Martha Etter, me, and all the spouses to a dinner at a fine restaurant in San Angelo. We were warned that the place would be crowded and that dinner might well consist of "scraps." In my mind that could mean leftovers or some specialty dish. I was not wrong.

When the eight of us sat down around the table, the waiter brought out salad, baked potatoes, onion rings piled high, and huge platters of beef tenderloin tips cooked to perfection with *au jus* at the bottom of the platters. Petit filet mignon!! Some "scraps!" Other customers at tables around us seemed to enjoy us first timers as we dealt with our "scraps." Every time thereafter when we were in San Angelo overnight, it was "scraps" or nothing.

The other tiny church we visited was in the Corpus Christi District. As we entered the sanctuary to meet with those gathered down front, a feisty 80-plus-year-old woman abruptly stopped me.

"Stand right there a minute!" she ordered.

Thinking she wanted to take a snapshot, I stood right there. She stepped back a bit and sized me up from head to toe. Since no camera appeared, I became fidgety as those down front looked on and waited. I was about to move forward when this woman declared rather loudly:

"I have never before in all my life seen a bishop, so I just wanted to see what a real live bishop looked like!"

A joyous and fun moment broke out all over the place. It was no surprise then that such meetings went well.

The brief time spent in those two tiny churches served to affirm that we were onto something very important in our visitation to every congregation in the two conferences. Consequently, I made myself a promise to be visible and present with the congregations in each district at least twice a year.

The spring visits became known as the District Confirmation Rally. The Shepherd's Visit would be made in the fall. At the Confirmation Rally we would show support and give congratulations and encouragement to the youngsters who were to be confirmed by their own pastors as full members of the church. My particular part in the rally was to extend the bishop's blessing upon each one, and to "yoke" each participant with a small wooden cross as a memento of his or her confirmation. In some districts more than 300 youths and adults would attend the celebration.

The fall Shepherd's Visits became district celebrations. They were annual occasions—eventually scheduled in the spring and fall—for all district congregations to gather and share a meal with the bishop. Then the Bishop's Exemplar Award would be presented to the person chosen by each district board of laity who had exemplified discipleship to Christ in special ways. Afterwards, there would be remarks and sometimes questions and concerns directed to the bishop. They were fun meetings, filled with the bishop's pronouncements, probings, problems, and a lot of laughter about who we were as United Methodists.

These two annual meetings gave all of us a sense of keeping in touch with one another. At some district celebrations more than 400 would be in attendance.

As I settled into the responsibilities of a bishop, I readily realized that much of my job was governed by "happenings" not on the agenda for the day. That was not altogether a surprise to me, since I had learned to cope with rapidly changing agendas as a senior pastor. What did surprise me was the ratio of time taken up with "happenings" that pulled me every day from basic work needing my attention.

At first I hoped for an occasional normal day and for time blocks so I could catch up on the beckoning matters piled up on my desk. "Catch up" never came. Neither did a normal day or free time. Neither was there such a thing as a dull day. Calls to be returned regularly inserted themselves in the midst of planned activities. Erupting problems, meetings, distractions, travel, emergencies—all became parts of an "ordinary" day in the life of a bishop.

One situation in particular was very disconcerting for Lavelle and me at first but later turned out to be rather funny. I was asked to give the invocation at an evening ecumenical event downtown to celebrate the life of Martin Luther King Jr. We were not yet familiar with downtown San Antonio, but we had verbal directions, which I had written down. The heart of San Antonio is extremely difficult to get around in, but it is worth the trouble once you get there. Very quickly the verbal directions became a lost cause. Lavelle and I drove around the meandering streets for well over an hour. At one point we lost sight of the city itself. All lights just disappeared. We never found the cathedral we searched for. Finally we made our way out of downtown and returned home. I felt awful because I had wanted to participate in the event.

Two mornings later I attended my first monthly meeting with all denominational leaders in San Antonio. I apologized to the group for never finding my way to the cathedral. Immediately, one of the new Roman Catholic bishops chimed in by saying, "I didn't find my way to the cathedral either, and it's one of our churches."

I was embarrassed until I heard those words. Another bishop stated that five other leaders of the dozen participating also hadn't shown up.

"The meeting," he said, "lasted more than three hours, which seemed like forever."

I felt better after these comments. When I returned home, I filed my "prayer never prayed," just in case I ever got invited again to offer the invocation at a celebration for Dr. King's life.

In the early spring of 1993, I called a Bishop's Convocation for each conference. Its purpose was to spend two days in a retreat setting with the pastors of each conference. Both events proved very productive in that they gave the pastors and me a forum for getting better acquainted and for interchange of ideas for our ministry journey together. I shared with the pastors what I felt would be the direction of my leadership. Since making disciples was the stated priority of the United Methodist Church, I established a "vital signs" report to be made to me each month. Those signs included membership changes, worship attendance, and giving.

The retreats began with a worship of "remembering our baptism" as the basis of our support of one another and our motivation for laboring together in calling others to join our journey of faith.

Another worship service was followed by conversations about whatever subjects the group wished to raise. It was here that I got a glimpse of the various theological positions of our clergy members in both conferences. I also got a glimpse of what great good these differences could make if they could be melded into a single passion for making disciples of Jesus Christ.

The retreats ended with a ritual of servanthood, expressed by a dry, simulated washing of one another's feet. Those rituals were powerful expressions of our lives together.

The two convocations apparently accomplished their purpose. Many pastors from both conferences commented on the clarity of the events as well as the clarity of my expectations. The convocations became yearly events during my remaining time in San Antonio.

Our two annual conference sessions in June went very well. "Write the Vision Anew" became the rallying cry for the years ahead. The Rio Grande and Southwest Texas conferences were the first two of the 17 in the South Central Jurisdiction to meet a special-asking goal for Lydia Patterson Institute in El Paso, Texas. Lydia Patterson is a high school owed by the jurisdiction that focuses on preparing poor, Spanish-speaking students for higher education. Many of the students walked across the Rio Grande bridge from Juarez to attend classes each day.

Most of the $127,000 four-year goal for the Southwest Texas Conference was raised on the floor of the conference, as was most of the $13,000 goal for the Rio Grande Conference. We felt good about that!

During the 1993 session the Southwest Texas Conference mandated a study related to the need for and feasibility of building a new United Methodist Center. Reports and recommendations were to be brought to the annual conference session the following year. Also, hundreds of individual church visions were filed with the conference, as I had requested.

With gratitude and high spirits the conferences ended. In my closing remarks I said to each session, "I am honored and pleased to be your bishop. You have made my first year among you not only notable but memorable. As a new bishop, I have made appointments. I have ordained, and I have presided. I am no longer a 'rookie bishop.'"

In both instances, the response was heartwarming.

Shortly thereafter, Lavelle departed for Tennessee to be with her mother, whose health was deteriorating rapidly. I departed for Lydia Patterson Institute for a two-week course in Spanish. It was a wonderful exposure to Mexican culture. We spent one weekend in Chihuahua, immersed in the language. I learned a lot but had to leave two days early because Lavelle's mother was not expected to live long. I returned to San Antonio and waited.

Lavelle's mother died several days later. She was a kind

and gentle person. Not once did I ever hear her say an unkind word about any person. She labored lovingly, whether in her kitchen or elsewhere. She was a mother-in-law of the highest quality. I said many times through the years that whoever came to visit in her home was as welcome the last day as the day of arrival—no matter how many days there were in between. It was a distinct honor for me to conduct her funeral.

In October the two cabinets and their spouses departed for a Volunteers in Mission project in South Texas and Reynosa, Mexico. We repaired and painted El Capote Church—an old Methodist church a few feet from what had been the Mexican border before the Rio Grande changed course. The church was established in 1874. One morning a Mexican man, Pedro Torres, showed up to help work on the church. He was quite amazed to see a group there restoring it.

Noontime came, and two members of our team took Pedro to lunch. He shared with David Chavez, a district superintendent, and Jose Galindo, a missionary, his desire to become a member of El Capote Church. The three of them talked and prayed together. Pedro accepted Jesus as lord of his life. He then asked if the two church leaders thought the bishop would baptize him and receive him into membership.

"At age 36," he said, "it is time for the prodigal son to come home."

Chavez and Galindo advised me of Pedro's desire and recommended I hear his story and confession of faith in Christ. He would be nurtured and mentored by the Reverend Jose Torres, pastor of a nearby church.

I accepted their recommendation and suggested we baptize him and receive him into the congregation at our closeout worship service, when the church would be completed and cleaned up inside and out.

When the time came, the only water available was the ice water we had to drink. I baptized the man with ice water. He shuddered, despite the warning. It was still a glorious experience for me, for him, and for all those on the team. That evening Pedro Torres met the Reverend Torres (no relation), the pastor whose church prepared our final dinner before we moved to the next stop on our trip.

The next day we were in Reyanosa, painting a clinic and preschool for children. An eight-foot wall surrounded the facility. Little children watched our every move. When the wall was finally painted, all team members covered the palms of our hands with paint and left imprints on the wall, with our names underneath. It was a lasting sign of our joy in the Lord and our love for the beautiful children.

By year's end I had only good feelings about all the work the conferences had done together. In appreciation, Lavelle and I hosted a joint Christmas dinner for the two cabinets, their spouses, and those on the extended cabinet. We recalled so many reasons in 1993 for being grateful to God. We reminisced concerning some of the special moments we had shared, like that painted wall displaying our palm prints.

My first 16 months as bishop had been an unforgettable period of progress for the two conferences and for increasing devotion to God.

Then I was reminded afresh that one who holds leadership responsibilities can expect forthright criticism. Such criticism can be beneficial when it is offered with genuine grace and respect for the recipient. When it comes as a scathing personal attack, however, it serves only to produce hurtful and destructive ends.

A large sealed envelope with an unsigned note attached arrived at my desk in January 1994. Inside was a published article that had already been distributed across the conferences. The note said the article totally rejected my leadership.

I decided not to read the article or respond to its author.

When the Southwest Texas Conference superintendents met with me the following week for our regularly scheduled cabinet session, they were upset by the article's personal attack on me. They suggested I demand an apology. Instead I asked that none of them respond. I hoped the entire matter would just die of inertia.

A few days later the author of the article sent me a "clarifying letter." He said everybody had misinterpreted the article's real intent. He said that if I felt an apology was due, he would apologize.

The issue was reborn but not long-lived.

I responded that since I had not read the article and did not desire to do so, I was in no position to determine if he should apologize. Since he had written the article, he alone had to decide if he should apologize. Soon the matter faded away, from a lack of further response, I suppose.

Not long afterward the South Central Jurisdictional College of Bishops traveled to the McAllen area of the Rio Grande Conference's Southern District for a previously planned "immersion experience" in Hispanic culture. The bishops were to visit several Rio Grande churches and assess how well we were reaching the Hispanic population. Further, we wanted to inform ourselves as to how better and more effectively our churches could strengthen our efforts to disciple increasing numbers of Mexicans moving into Texas, New Mexico, and the entire eight-state jurisdiction.

The bishops conversed with leaders of Rio Grande Conference congregations. We visited several ministry and mission projects. We prayed with the people. We sang hymns loudly. We clapped our hands to the beat of tejano music played by mariachi bands. The bishops watched colorfully dressed young dancers perform with precision. We ate more Mexican food than was advisable. We encouraged leaders about the church's opportunity to reach many people for Christ. We celebrated with gratitude our heritage as United Methodists.

Dr. Warren Hornung, superintendent of the McAllen District, and the Reverend Eubaldo Ponce, superintendent of the Southern District, hosted us with their typical graciousness and generosity. The immersion experience turned out to be a valuable and memorable event, which triggered two other endeavors related to strengthening the church's outreach to Hispanics.

A jurisdictionwide meeting was then called under the banner, "Our Future Together in Hispanic Ministries in Overlapping Conferences." It drew participants from all 17 annual conferences. The purpose was to strategize on how all 17 conferences more dynamically could engage in Hispanic ministries. One vital key to a more productive ministry was the Rio Grande Conference itself. Because of its membership size (about 15,000), very limited resources, and an area of some 380,000 square miles to serve, the idea of folding the Rio Grand Conference churches into overlapping conferences came up. That had real value, since one Rio Grande Conference district overlapped five conferences in Texas alone. The notion was considered, but soon the meeting moved on to how individual Hispanic and Anglo congregations in the same community might more closely work together toward common goals.

Later the jurisdictional College of Bishops set into motion a another aspect designed specifically for the Rio Grande Conference. I was directed to form a blue-ribbon committee to produce a strategy of growth for making the Rio Grande Conference self-supporting. Over several months the Committee of 13 worked diligently at its assignment. We designed and refined a 13-point reasonable and workable strategy. If implemented, it would move the Rio Grande Conference far up the road to reaching self-support in five to eight years.

I presented the promising plan to the next meeting of the College of Bishops for perusal and response. Before the plan could be implemented, the college had to adopt it. The response was positive, and the college expressed appreciation for the plan's comprehensiveness. The college then "received" the report. The strategy was never implemented.

After some 18 months in the episcopacy, both Lavelle and I caught a passing case of gloominess. In one conversation, she expressed our honest, mutual feelings.

"This is the most awful time we have ever had in the ministry," she said.

I agreed. Some 550 miles cut us off from family, young grandchildren, and former friends—all of whom had been our source of comfort and encouragement. Having bared the face of our blues, we moved on.

On the heels of our down-ness I received a call from a developer asking me to meet with him the next day regarding a piece of property about three miles from the episcopal residence. A few conference leaders and I met on a 3.5-acre piece of choice land.

"My partner and I," the developer said, "want to deed the property for our new conference center! In addition, all utilities and environmental requirements have been completed and approved. Also, we will pay for all closing costs and related expenses!"

The site was a perfect place for our new United Methodist Center. We had already located a smaller site a bit further away and had planned to present it for purchase at the upcoming conference session. Both the donor and his partner were dedicated and involved members of a United Methodist church. What a gift! Not only would we be able to forego a $250,000 outlay, we were receiving free a larger and much better site valued at almost three times as much.

That's often the way it is in the ministry. About the time you feel so low you don't want to get up, God brings by some unexpected blessings. For me at least, the blessing of land was an effective "blues chaser."

On Palm Sunday 1994 I was scheduled to preach at all three worship services in University United Methodist Church, San Antonio. Long before daybreak rapid palpitations of my heart awakened me. My heartbeats felt more like quivers than distinct beats. It was the most distressing feeling I had ever experienced. Luckily, our primary care doctor lived across the street. Lavelle called him, and he said to rush me to the emergency room at Southwest Texas Methodist Hospital. He would call the cardiologist on duty to stand by, and he would join us at the emergency room in a few minutes.

While we waited in the emergency room, I asked Lavelle to call Dr. Steve Wende, pastor of University Church, and the dean of the cabinet, Jerry J. Smith, to advise them of my situation. I was examined, given medication, sent to a room and kept overnight.

I was relieved when the doctor said that a few "painless" tests would be done to determine appropriate treatment. In the meantime, I could go on about my responsibilities while taking prescribed medication. I thought that meant I would be back to normal in a week or so. I was wrong. It would take many months for me to feel normal for any length of time.

The various medications were all powerful. The side effects were intolerable. All of these side effects were going on at the time of our two annual conference sessions. The medications made me listless, tired, and unable to concentrate well on the business items of each conference. I certainly was not up to my standard alertness. The Southwest Texas Conference moved forward with strong support for constructing a new United Methodist Center on a new site in the developing area of northwest San Antonio. Despite my own feelings about my part in the conference, everyone seemed pleased with the outcome.

The afternoon following the Southwest Texas Conference, a terrible accident occurred. David, the younger son of Janice and Bob Huie, was killed in a go-cart accident on a school yard in Austin. A second boy was seriously injured, but recovered. Upon hearing the horrible news, Lavelle and I rushed to Austin to offer our prayers, support, and love. At the time, Janice was serving as superintendent of the San Angelo District, and Bob was serving in the counseling ministry.

The death of David brought back the memory of our Dana's accidental death. We knew firsthand what a jagged hole had been torn in Bob and Janice's hearts. We knew from experience that hole would never completely close, but by God's grace and help, it would heal. The whole conference seemed to be present for the funeral as a sign of deep sorrow and loving support.

Erratic heartbeat, new medication, and more tests overshadowed the summer months. I was in no pain, but I felt periodic weakness when sieges of palpitations returned. Having continuing side effects from the medications added to my frustration and aggravation.

In the fall I departed for my first episcopal visitation, to the Caribbean area for 17 days. I visited churches, colleges, hospitals, and mission projects related to the Methodist Church in five countries. Dynamic and productive ministry was going on in Antigua, Dominica, Panama, Puerto Rico, and Costa Rica. The Cuba leg of the visitation had to be canceled because of a political squabble between President Bill Clinton and President Fidel Castro.

While in Panama I visited a church in the impoverished area of Bocas del Toro (mouths of the bull). A recent earthquake had added severely to the Indians' suffering. The district superintendent and I visited mission projects. We were received with humble and genuine welcome. After two days I prepared to board the small plane back to Panama City.

My host held my hand, looked deeply into my soul, and said to me, "Bishop, you have come among us to greet us in the name of Jesus. You have shared with us your faith, your love, and your life. You have eaten our food. You have prayed and worshipped with us. You have seen our many needs. You have offered us Christ. You have been a blessing to us. Now, we wait! We wait to see what all God will make of your visit."

I remember his words regularly. They still move me to pray for those faithful followers of Christ—as I promised to do. Under heavy handicaps, the Methodist people of Bocas del Toro are still carrying the love of Christ to an area of the world not even known by most of us.

While in Puerto Rico, I met District Superintendent Juan Vera Mendez. We became instant friends. A while later he was elected a bishop in the autonomous Methodist Church of Puerto Rico.

Upon my return, my medication once more had to be changed—the sixth time in seven months. I hoped this change would be the last and would deal with side effects. It wasn't, and it didn't.

The campaign to raise $3.5 million for the new United Methodist Center was launched. I conducted "pacesetter" dinners in every district of the Southwest Texas Conference. The endeavor consumed my time during the fall of 1994, but it was worth the time and effort. Foundations were approached for grants in the same time period. By the middle of December, a significant portion of our goal had been pledged.

The Reverend Harold Burkhardt and Jack Rodgers gave superb leadership in coordinating and managing the campaign. They kept me focused and pointed me toward other possible donors. When I grew tired, I leaned on the words of Paul to the Galatians, "Be not weary in well doing, for in due season you shall reap, if you faint not!"

In December 1994 a called session of the Southwest Texas Conference convened to consider a joint venture between Southwest Texas Methodist Hospital in San Antonio, which was related to the conference, and Columbia-HCA Healthcare System. The new entity would be named "Methodist Healthcare System." If approved, all indebtedness of Methodist Hospital (about $25 million) would be paid off, and a church-related corporation would have half ownership of Columbia's six hospitals and healthcare clinics. The Methodist half of the joint venture would be designated "not for profit" and named "Methodist Healthcare Ministries."

As the bishop, I had stipulated that two aspects would have to be accepted by Columbia before I could give my support: (1) Columbia would have to pay for a full-time, full-fledged and comprehensive chaplain's ministry at all seven hospitals in the joint venture; (2) The foundational and constitutional documents establishing the joint venture would include the United Methodist Social Principles as the value system by which the entire venture would conduct its business.

Columbia not only agreed to my two "essentials," it welcomed them as reasonable enhancements of the entire venture. After some debate on the floor of the conference, the joint venture was approved with fewer than 25 negative votes. Jerry J. Smith, superintendent of the San Antonio District, played a significant role in bringing the joint venture into reality.

In 1993, "stand alone" Methodist Hospital was able to appropriate about $250,000 to healthcare for the underserved of the area. In 1995 the joint venture generated more than $1 million for distribution. When I retired in 2000, that amount designated for medical care for the underserved was around $10 million a year, channeled through some 30 Wesley nurse facilities and other Methodist medical clinics.

Certainly, it was gratifying to see so many Methodist Healthcare ministries meeting so many medical needs for so many people who otherwise would not have had adequate access to basic health services.

My yearlong journey had been filled with ups and downs, rounds and rounds. Yet it had been a most productive year. I had grown and matured some more. I had come face to face with my own mortality. Through it all, I could declare, "God is good, indeed—all the time."

Regular sieges of atrial fibrillations continued into 1995. I could sleep only a few hours before a new siege would set in long before daybreak. For several days I would feel fine, followed by several days of intermittent fibrillations. I was discouraged when my cardiologist told me we were running out of different kinds of medications. He and I were both frustrated. Since one medicine was keeping my blood thinned, I was told there was little danger of a stroke. Such words were of some comfort to me.

While all this fibrillation was going on, Lavelle departed for Tennessee. Her father urgently needed surgery. We were both emotionally strung out. It seemed everything was going wrong. Even the campaign to raise funds for the new conference center was moving at a snail's pace.

I visited a person of much means about his participation in the campaign. I had information about his generosity to other church-related campaigns. His pastor set up a meeting for us to visit in his home. We were optimistic.

It quickly became apparent that he did not want to spend much time with me. He made it clear he had little interest in the building campaign. He objected to the project, suggesting the building was not needed. The visit went downhill from there. With biting words he spoke his displeasure for the "bureaucracy" of the church.

"I'm going to give $1,000 this year and next year," he said. "I won't let a bishop come to my home without making a contribution!"

As a bishop, I had not felt complimented. In fact, I felt a bit embarrassed that the man was grudgingly making a contribution only because a "bishop" had come to his home. I felt the entire visit had been an imposition on the man and our effort a failure. We left.

I got myself back on track, however, as I remembered Cecil Smith's words back in Antlers nearly 30 years earlier.

"You will make a sale one out of three tries," he said.

I smiled and was inspired to get away from there and to the next prospect.

That very weekend, Harold Burkhardt and I visited a trustee of a large foundation. Having heard our presentation, the man seemed impressed and indicated our building project was certainly within the guidelines of the foundation. He thanked us for coming and said he would recommend approval of our application.

Making the sale hadn't even taken the three tries. Surely Cecil would be smiling if he had known of our visit.

A week or so before the Southwest Texas Annual Conference session convened, I suffered the agony of a severely infected tooth. What next? The timing could not have been worse.

The United Methodist Building on Bandera Road was astir with preparation for the session. A backlog of administrative urgencies on my desk was already being covered over by new "stuff" even more urgent. It felt like the whole building was the arena for a county rodeo. We didn't know what would happen next, but we knew it was coming with intensity. With my tooth pulsating, I said teasingly to my secretary on my way out, "Well, at least surgery on my tooth will give me a two-day respite from this rodeo!"

At the annual conference session we moved forward in providing a much needed assistant to the episcopal office. Several other matters were presented, discussed, approved, and implemented. A few highly emotional issues related to leadership of the conference Council on Youth Ministries were raised and dealt with. Also, 1995 was election year for delegates to the 1996 General and jurisdictional conferences. That served to prompt spontaneous periods of posturing by some candidates seeking election. Except for occasional flashpoints and volleys of disgruntled fire across the bow of the ship called "the church," we were moving forward in the work Christ called us to do—and having fun, most of the time, along the way.

In the summer, I took part of my renewal leave for about six weeks. Never had I been so long away from the daily routine of ministry, and never before had I been in such need for getting away.

Following Bishop's Week at Mount Sequoyah, we went to Lake Tanneycomo at Forsyth, Missouri, for several days of relaxing, reading, gathering materials for my upcoming series of lectures at Mount Sequoyah, and fishing for trout. We saw several shows at Branson.

I instructed my secretary that she was not to call me unless it was to hear from the foundation about the grant we applied for or some extreme emergency. Sure enough, midway through our stay, she called with the good news that the foundation had approved the grant. That meant we had reached $2.468 million. The news was released, and celebration broke out all over the episcopal area. What once had looked like an insurmountable sum had been reached with the large grant. Even Cecil would have said again, "Life is good!"

The rest of our renewal time was spent visiting our two sons and their families, a trip to Tennessee to visit with our folks, and a stay at Prude Ranch near Fort Davis, Texas. We were there at the same time as a youth group that came every year. Horse riding was a main focus of their camp.

The Prude family were longtime Methodists who for many years had provided the camp for kids to learn more about life and how to live it for God. Decades earlier, Mr. Prude, 90, started referring to youngsters by the name of the horse each rode. The kids loved it, and so did we as we rode several times with them. By week's end, youths unfamiliar with horses were riding well and even participated in the wrapup rodeo.

While eating lunch with Mr. Prude, I asked him if he had any idea about how many kids had gone on to live for Christ as the result of their experience at Prude Ranch.

"Hopefully, the vast majority of them," he answered.

In August the Methodist bishops all over the world were invited to gather in Korea by Bishop Sondo Kim, president of the Council of Bishops for the Korean Methodist Church. It was indeed a historic event when more than 100 bishops from 34 countries took part in the conclave.

At the first session, I was deeply moved. I asked myself, "How can it be that 35 years after I was here in Korea as the chief chaplain's assistant of the Pusan Area Command, I would return as bishop of the church?" Indeed, journeying with God takes us to unbelievable experiences and heights.

We gathered for our first worship service at Kwang Lim Church with 5,000 in attendance, a 250-voice choir, and a 52-piece orchestra. Bishop Kim preached. What a day!

Ambassador James T. Laney, former dean of Candler School of Theology at Emory University in Atlanta, invited us to his home for a buffet reception. Having served as a soldier in Korea in 1947 and having returned as a Methodist missionary in 1959, he helped us all understand just how influential the Methodist Church in America had been upon Korea — the fastest growing area for the Methodist Church worldwide.

The president of South Korea, Kim Young Sam, invited us to the presidential residence—the "Blue House"—for a reception. Each bishop had opportunity to meet and greet the president and his wife. He arranged for a photograph of us with him. He then gave each a copy and welcomed us to Korea.

We were taken to Panmunjom—a village along the dividing line between North and South Korea where the July 27, 1953, Korean War armistice was negotiated. The building in which the talks were conducted had a white line across the floor. The line marked the border between the two nations. Sentries outside at opposite ends of the building still stared at each other in glare-eyed readiness to challenge any suggesting encroachment.

Bishop Bob Fannin described the extreme tension in the air when he was stationed at the Demilitarized Zone in the late 1950s.

Bishop Roy Sano of the Los Angeles Area in the United States preached the sermon for our final event of the trip. It was attended by 30,000 worshippers. The experience was indescribable, especially when a large number of "Pigeons of Peace" were released in the domed public arena where we met. We all departed the next day filled with praise, hope, and recommitment to Christ.

Before I left First Church, Bartlesville, we had set into motion a centennial jubilee for the church. Soon after arriving in San Antonio, I was invited to give the centennial message in September 1995 at the large community center. I accepted.

The time had quickly come upon me after three years. The celebration design was impressive. Every living pastor was invited back and asked to preach on a specific date during the year. All kinds of special events were scheduled during the entire weekend.

Some five or six former pastors were still alive. But, eerily, two of them died before their date arrived. My turn came in September. Receptions, meals together, and special events were all scheduled. Lavelle and I arrived to find so many expressions of love and appreciation for us. It was almost overwhelming. A part of my responsibilities during the event was to dedicate the History Room, which had been set aside after the remodeling during the new building phase.

On display were numerous items and artifacts related to my nearly 11 years of ministry there. We dedicated the special area as the "Ray Owen History Room" in honor of Lavelle and me. I was invited to deposit whatever else I wished to be stored there, including papers, letters, and mementoes gathered over the years.

Emotions made it difficult for me to speak the dedicatory liturgy. Over and again, the church had given me an honor and gift for which I could never repay. The next morning (Sunday) I preached to some 1,100 people in the community center. It was the final segment of the centennial celebrations for what has to be one of the greatest churches in United Methodism.

The aura of that event has hovered heavily upon my life ever since. Our visit was capped off by spending time with Dr. David Thomas, pastor, and his delightful wife, Patty. They had been friends from the beginning of my ministry.

A bit later Lavelle and I celebrated our 43rd anniversary, made even more memorable by the dinner we had that evening. We went to a new steak house in San Antonio. A fine looking young man came to take our order. Half teasing because the restaurant was new, I asked, "Is this really a good place to eat?" Unperturbed, he quickly answered, "Oh yes, my wife and I celebrated our first anniversary here only a few days ago!"

"Well," I responded, "we are here to celebrate our 43rd anniversary!"

With wide-eyed wonderment, he stepped back. His mouth gaped open.

"Really?" he said. "How have you lived together for that many years?"

Now unguardedly enjoying the situation, I blurted out, "Well, it hasn't been easy!"

He laughed!

Immediately I realized I should have rephrased my answer.

I had to work hard from there to get back into Lavelle's good graces. I was helped by the waiter's bringing us a huge double-sized frozen chocolate sundae with pecans, big enough for four persons. By the time we overate most of it, there was no more desire to take my response further.

In November we broke ground for the new 22,000-square-foot United Methodist Center on Huebner Road. It was a high occasion for those who doubted it could be done and by those who worked hard to see that it was done. We were still raising money for furnishings and for interest on borrowed money. Yet we knew the rest of it would come, and it did.

That same month the five United Methodist bishops of Texas sponsored a statewide summit meeting in the State Capitol on the welfare of Texas children. The purpose was to raise the awareness of state legislators and Governor George W. Bush of the dire need to increase spending on the needs of the children, especially nutrition and healthcare. Several hundred people participated. With that summit as a backdrop—and the help of several legislators and Governor Bush, an active United Methodist—allotted funds for children doubled over the years ahead. I was pleased and privileged to join the other four Texas Methodist bishops in a letter of appeal to the governor.

The intermittent atrial fibrillations had made 1995 a hard year for me. I was no further up the road to any kind of improvement than I had been at the beginning of the year. I had simply lived with the problem. I had been dealing with it long enough. My cardiologist and I talked over my situation. I inquired about a pacemaker's ability to control my heartbeat: How risky was the procedure? How soon could we get it implanted? How long would I need to recover? What was his advice for me?

He said the procedure would take about 45 minutes; the pacemaker would control the heartbeat rate. I would notice complete normalcy upon waking from the anesthesia. I would have no pain and no recovery time. I would walk out of the hospital and go about doing whatever needed to be done. The batteries would have to be changed in six to ten years.

He said I could indeed leave the hospital and celebrate late Christmas with our son and his family in Abilene.

We set the date for December 29. I was in the hospital overnight. Everything turned out precisely as the doctor had described. I was "regular" of heartbeat. No pain. No aftereffects.

Upon my dismissal from the hospital, Lavelle was there with Christmas gifts in the car, and we left for Abilene to meet Darryl and his family at a motel to have our late Christmas. We returned home the following day. Everything had gone as the doctor had said it would. I have had no serious problems since.

The year ended on a note much higher than it began. I, most of all, had reason to rejoice after 21 months of irregular heartbeat sieges and frustrations. Life flow takes us onward in a day-to-day trek into new possibilities through uncharted waters. To the extent we trust God's providential care and sufficiency, we are able to embrace the waiting mysteries the future holds in store.

Sometimes it takes the better part of a life's journey to reach the level of authentic trust in God. At 64, and halfway through my fourth year as bishop, I was still saying with Paul, "I am learning to be content with whatever I have."

Having lost ground on a few edges of my physical fitness, I lived in the contentment of Paul's additional words, "We do not live to ourselves, and we do not die to ourselves. If we live, we live to the Lord, and if we die we die to the Lord; so whether we live or whether we die, we are the Lord's." Like spiritual balm, those words applied daily brought resilience to my soul.

The spring meeting of Huston-Tillotson College's board of trustees convened in Austin. It was the first anniversary of my chairmanship. The college had taken its name decades earlier from the merger of Samuel Huston College (Methodist) and Tillotson College (United Church of Christ).

Its history and heritage are rich indeed, in that Tillotson College was the first school of higher learning in Austin. As a predominantly African American college, it stood tall and proud. Certainly, I felt honored to serve alongside a dedicated faculty, staff, and student body. As with most private schools of higher learning, financial stability was always a struggle. Still, the ethos of the board and campus was that of pride in its past, unity in its present, and high hopes for the future. My involvement with Huston-Tillotson College was one of the most gratifying responsibilities I had as a bishop.

Dr. Prenza Woods, a retired Southwest Texas Conference leader, was my immediate predecessor as chairman. His predecessor had been Bishop Ernest T. Dixon. Both of them had graduated from Huston-Tillotson and become lifelong best friends. Also, both of them had become prominent and revered leaders of the Southwest Texas Conference. I sought Dr. Woods' insight and counsel on several occasions. He became a trusted and revered friend.

While we were on vacation in Tennessee, Bishop Dixon died quite unexpectedly. Having just recovered from surgery at Methodist Hospital in San Antonio, he received word that he was being discharged. As he was dressing, he collapsed and died. We were all shocked and grieved at his sudden passing. I returned home immediately for the funeral at University Church.

Ernie Dixon was a lovable, gentle, and kind instrument of God. I had known him for a long time before I was elected a bishop. There was no hesitancy on my part, therefore, to seek his counsel many times. Always I felt he was there for me. We met for lunch on occasion. I invited him to our annual conference sessions and to assist me in ordaining deacons and elders. He accepted. He and Ernestine dropped in on business sessions to the delight of conference members. I asked him to preside twice so that I might have a break. Conference members thoroughly enjoyed his time in the chair, which allowed for a little banter and laughter from "leftovers" of the past. I enjoyed his presence as a "real bishop."

Ernie became a treasured friend whom I came to love and highly respect. His passing was as gentle as his living. Nearly all of the South Central Jurisdictional bishops were present for his funeral. On the way to the cemetery, I said to Dr. Austin Frederick, then the Victoria District superintendent and later the assistant to the episcopal office, "I shall miss Bishop Dixon a lot!" And I did.

The South Central Jurisdictional Conference in July 1996 met at Kansas City. Only one bishop was to be elected. After several ballots, Dr. Janice Riggle Huie was elected from the Southwest Texas Conference. At the time of her election, Bishop Dan Solomon and I shared the honor of escorting her to the bishops' platform. Joy Solomon and Lavelle escorted Dr. Robert Huie to join his spouse, now a bishop-elect. What a wonderful moment for the church.

The new General Commission on United Methodist Men convened in October in Nashville to organize as mandated by the 1996 General Conference. I was elected president of the commission. Dr. Joe Harris from Oklahoma was elected later as the general secretary. From the outset, he gave outstanding and inspiring leadership, along with the dedicated members of the commission.

A few days later, in November, we moved into the new United Methodist Center, an elegant facility. It had been almost exactly two years from the time we launched the finance campaign to raise the $3.6 million total cost. In 1998 we gathered to dedicate the building. It had been truly a miraculous finish of four years.

The new building stood as a testimony to the San Antonio Area's truly "writing the vision anew!" The best proof was the increasing membership of both conferences. Not only were we fulfilling the church's mission "to make disciples," we were enabling those new disciples to make the two conferences what God envisioned them to be.

Years earlier, I had heard Corrie Ten Boom say about her concentration camp experience at Ravensbrook under the Nazi regime, "When the worst has happened to you, only the best remains!" It might follow in one's mind that when the *best* had been reached, the *worst* would be waiting ahead. That was not the case for us in the following year—1997. We would see the *best* bettered in many instances.

After many hours of working together, the bishops' "Initiative on Children and Poverty" really got underway. I, for one, was inspired by the scope of its vision. The initiative boldly called every local congregation worldwide to engage in proactive ministries on behalf of children and those struggling in poverty.

The call immediately generated excitement, energy, and

support, even before some of the written guidelines and resource materials could be published. Having heard the initiative was forthcoming, the San Antonio Area went about developing strategies for carrying out the overall vision.

For example, a local congregation in the Rio Grande Conference had already put into place a "Sidewalk Sunday School" ministry. It served later as a catalyst and sparked several other ministry projects for children. The Sidewalk Sunday School located itself in a densely populated area of apartment complexes.

I visited the site and found the ministry reaching out effectively not only to children but to constituent families as well. Its tentacles were already finding additional target areas for developing other programs in addressing needs of children. This "sidewalk" concept soon attracted national attention and subsequently served as a model for the larger body of the church.

I left the site deeply impressed with the vision seen by the sponsoring local church. I was inspired by the dedicated volunteer staff members who were meeting needs of children from the wellspring of genuine love for Christ in their hearts.

I endeavored to develop an ecumenical thrust of the initiative by inviting judicatory heads of other denominations to link up their local churches with ours, so as to meet the needs of all children in every local community. They agreed. An impressive Charter of Commitment was developed and signed by eight heads of denominations. The media picked that up, too, which further enhanced public awareness of children in need in South Texas.

Private agencies like Any Baby Can and Methodist Healthcare Ministries arranged for a citywide rally in San Antonio at the Alamo Plaza. Its purpose was to heighten further public interest and support for the plight of children in our city of 1.3 million residents. Never before had I seen such an ecumenical endeavor in which so many private and secular groups worked so well together to address a common need.

As the rally day drew near, I was informed that I would be the presenter of the major address. Surprised and reluctant, I wanted very much to say no. Several outstanding professional leaders of childcare were far more qualified than I to speak on the matter. Before I could even register my objection, I was informed any objection I might raise was already unacceptable. The rally went off very well and furthered public awareness of children's needs. Once again, the media did a fine job lifting up a key community concern. I was rewarded with a video tape recording of the rally. Indeed, it was reward enough.

In many ways the day-to-day work of a bishop is like any other supervisory job. It has its up and down days—and many days of both. In the remaining days of 1997, I enjoyed a season of decisions and events that kept my spirit fired, encouraged, and gratified.

At the annual session of the Southwest Texas Conference, a truly courageous commitment was made to overhaul, upgrade, and expand the Mount Wesley Conference Center in Kerrville. The work was sorely needed. It included rerouting and paving roads into, out of, and throughout the entire campus. Commitment was made to raise $7.8 million for the project to be done in stages. I was particularly pleased and proud that Mount Wesley's future was secured and that its key role in "making disciples of Jesus Christ" would be greatly enhanced.

Another event of very special meaning to me happened as I delivered the lectures on "The Witness We Make" during Bishops Week at Mount Sequoyah in Fayetteville, Arkansas. The experience served as a double source of blessing to me. One was the sense of relief that the responsibility of preparing the talks was over. The other was that the lectures were apparently well received by those who heard then.

Since the lectures had dealt with the fundamentals of personal witness through one's heart, hands, and head, a suggestion came that they be published as a resource for training laity in witnessing to others. At the encouragement of Communications Director Doug Cannon and other leaders of the Southwest Texas Conference, we set forth to publish the lectures in book form for distribution to clergy and lay members of the 1998 annual conference session. As typical of the communications expert Doug Cannon was, he had already certified the value of the lectures by using them as the resource for a six-week study in his own Sunday school class.

Back in the early 1950s, Walter L. Underwood served my home church (First Methodist) in McKenzie, Tennessee. He moved from there to Texas, where he was elected a bishop in 1984. What a thrill it was for me as a delegate to support his election. Since First Church, McKenzie, had played a part in his ministry, Walter and his wife, Billie, were invited to return for a worship service. After that service his episcopal portrait would be hung in the vestibule of the church.

In late spring of 1997, the church invited Lavelle and me to return for a similar occasion while we were home on vacation. I was asked to preach at the worship service. Certainly, the church had contributed immeasurably to my eventual entry into ministry. Members, teachers, leaders, and friends had modeled before me the characteristics of Christian living—all of which helped me to respond to God's call upon my life.

Of course, we accepted the invitation. After a delightful lunch at the church, my portrait was displayed on the opposite end of the vestibule, "for balance," as someone commented. Someone else remarked how the foyer area was taking on "quite a historical look" for visitors and future generations. Another person said, "Not many churches the size of McKenzie First Methodist have seen two persons vitally connected to its history elected as bishops."

I suppose such comments of the church taking on a historical look had some credence. Standing at the outside right front of the vestibule was another marker noting that Bishop Holland Nimmone McTyeire's visit had historical significance to First Church, McKenzie, in the late 1800s.

Another aspect of my "season of spiritual highs" came while we were still in Tennessee. My brother P.J. and I were able to spend more time together than usual. Much of it was spent driving over the territories of our growing-up years. We revisited homesites. Names and faces of several saints and a few sinners we had known flashed through our minds. We assessed again their influence upon our lives. We stood at tombstones of relatives in cemeteries. There we gave thanks to God for the stories they lived and told to our delight as children. Their examples of decency, honesty, and hard work had helped to mold our characters. New Valley Church stood conspicuously silent, as if waiting for us to report in on where our faith journey had taken us over the decades. And to what it would lead us in the future.

We both realized the leg of our faith journey yet to be traveled was much shorter than how far we had come. Neither of us raised an objection to the difference in the two. Nor did we express any word or wish to make the journey again.

Later, I reflected on those hours we spent together. It all seemed to amount to yet another rite of passage. At his age, 71, and my age, 65, we both seemed very much at peace with calm assurance that life is ever forward until it reaches "home" with God. What times P.J. and I have had together since have been more reflective and certainly more precious.

When Lavelle and I returned home to San Antonio, two special letters of blessing were waiting for my response. The first was from Dr. Robin Lovin, dean of Perkins School of Theology at Southern Methodist University. It contained an invitation for me to serve as bishop-in-residence after I retired. I was deeply touched and honored to receive the invitation. Its coming from a friend I highly admired and respected made the invitation significant. To serve as bishop-in-residence behind Bishop John Wesley Hardt made the offer even more appealing.

The presence of a bishop on campus made visible the connection of the church and the university. The position also put the face of the church in connection with the university. It gave students classroom time with the bishop so they could see that teaching was one role of the office.

Dean Lovin graciously consented to my taking time to consider the matter. I really wanted to accept the opportunity, although Lavelle and I had already planned to retire in Oklahoma to be nearer our sons and their families. I continued to have health problems, so I waited in prayer for guidance. In the end, we both felt it was best for us to follow through toward retirement.

Dean Lovin, as usual, was gracious and understanding of my decision, which gave me even one more reason to call him friend and to enhance my admiration for him. Though I believe we made the right decision, I still wish I could have accepted the invitation.

The other letter related to my "season of good days" had to do with Bishop Ernie Dixon. The Texas Department of Transportation had approved designating a section of U.S. 87 southeast of San Antonio as the Bishop Ernest T. Dixon Memorial Parkway. I was invited to be a part of the dedication service. State legislators, dignitaries, and other officials were present, along with many leaders from the two conferences. Speakers expressed their affection and appreciation for Bishop Dixon. I knew Ernie had grown up in San Antonio and had served his last 12 years as bishop of the San Antonio Area. I did not know how deep and ranging his influence and labors had been in south Texas. Truly, Ernest T. Dixon was a great man and servant of the Lord.

As the bishop of the San Antonio Area, I was asked to host a tour of some 200 people to the Holy Land. As the departure date drew near, new threats of war between Iraq and the United States rose to dangerous heights. Cancellation was likely. Tensions eased three days before departure time.

This trip was my third to the Holy Land. In all three instances, there was tension and uneasiness. By the time we arrived in Israel, the environment seemed safe. Our son, Dyton, accompanied me and was of great help to the group because he had been there before. Getting to know the members of the tour made this particular trip so very rewarding.

In the spring of 1998, six new churches were launched in the Southwest Texas Conference. That was in addition to several new churches already up and running. It was at this point that the cabinet proposed a list of 18 sites where United Methodist churches should be launched in the future. Already, both the Rio Grande and Southwest Texas conferences had been growing at a notable percentage rate for the past six years running.

At the Huston-Tillotson College commencement service in Austin, I received the honorary doctor of divinity degree. The citation by President Joe McMillan was so laudatory and commendatory that I was embarrassed. At the next board meeting, one of the trustees said to me jokingly, "Bishop, we didn't know you were such a superstar. Perhaps we should elect you for another term as chairman!"

The group responded with laughter that gave me time to think what to say.

"Remember," I responded, "I am presiding. No motion to that effect will be entertained."

I was so startled at President McMillan's citation that I asked him for a copy to read about once every week when I needed to believe big in myself. He told me he had not written it down and doubted he could recall it. What a spontaneous and erudite mind he possessed, even if it could not recall what had been said only an hour or so earlier.

One of the most inspiring and enduring moments in my entire ministry came as I was "yoking" new confimands during one of the annual confirmation rallies. The youngsters came and kneeled at the chancel rail. One boy with a disabling disease had to be held up on his knees by two adults. His name was Dylan. As I came to him, Dylan looked up and smiled at me as I yoked him and laid my hands on his head to utter a blessing upon him. As he was being helped to stand, he smiled again and said softly to me, "Thank you, bishop!" Apparently, in a matter of seconds, he had received a blessing far greater than the one I had pronounced upon him. I kissed him on his forehead and thanked him for the blessing he had extended to me. If ever I have seen the face of God in a human, it was in that young boy's face.

The Southwest Texas Conference made visible the Bishops' Initiative on Children and Poverty by way of an "Undie Sunday" rally on the eve of the 1998 annual conference session.

All 357 of its congregations were encouraged to collect and bring children's underwear, socks, and other items of clothing to a beachside public park in Corpus Christi, where the rally was to take place. Wesley Community Centers and other United Methodist agencies would do the distribution to children later.

The response of the churches was overwhelming. None of us imagined the degree of commitment the congregations made to the appeal. Truckloads of filled boxes were unloaded in the park. The thousands of packaged items created a huge mound.

We had an open-air worship service as passengers in cars on the street looked on quizzically. We worshipped. We praised

God. We gave thanks for the outpouring of love wrapped in those packages. The initiative was launched anew. Excitement heightened as the media picked up the event and reported the essence of Undie Sunday to the public.

The 1998 conference also heard about plans for the Great Methodist Gathering, a major evangelistic rally scheduled for October 9, 1999, in San Antonio's Alamodome. Preparing for that event would take the time and energy of a great many people over the next 17 months.

While on my way to Nashville for the General Commission on United Methodist Men, I stopped in McKenzie to see my brother P.J. That evening, my lifelong friend, Charles Thompson, and his wife, Betty Sue, and I had a catfish dinner together. We had a wonderful time. Our time turned out even more special as he asked if I would like to stop to see "Aunt Fannie."

At 96, she was still alert and glad we came by. She and her husband had rented their small cabin to Lavelle and me as our first home. I had known her quite well over the years. We reminisced for a few minutes about days long passed. Our brief visit was capped off when she remarked, "Raymond, when you were living in our little rent house, I saw you several times sitting in the yard swing reading the Bible."

I had no idea she had seen me. It was while we lived there that I decided to read the Bible from cover to cover for the first time. We moved before I had read it through.

"I knew then God had something special in mind for you," Aunt Fannie continued.

I had a difficult moment before responding. Finally, I was able to say in response, "And I'm sure you prayed for me to that end."

She smiled but did not answer.

Sometimes, and quite unexpectedly, pure manna from heaven falls upon us in such abundance that gratitude to God, and to saints like Aunt Fannie, cannot adequately be expressed.

Soon after returning home to San Antonio, I departed with a group of bishops for a visit to Angola and Mozambique for two weeks. The trip was to be even more enjoyable in that Bishop Bob Fannin and I were assigned as roommates for the duration. This visit would be my fourth and final one to parts of Africa.

Arriving in Lisbon, Portugal, we rested up, visited sites in the city, and refreshed our memory about Vasco de Gama's place in Portuguese history. It was de Gama who found passage to Angola, Mozambique, and Brazil, which he had claimed as Portuguese territory some 500 years earlier.

Before departing for Luanda, Angola, late the next afternoon, we were informed of the bombings of our embassies in Nairobi, Kenya, and Dar es Salaam, Tanzania. The General Board of Global Ministries immediately notified our families that we were safe and a long way from either country.

Our gracious host, Bishop Emilio J.M. de Carvalho of the Western Angola Area, met us at the Luanda Airport. What a welcome! We started our tour at the Aligrea Methodist Ministry Center. I delivered to Bishop de Carvalho a "love gift" for the school from the Southwest Texas Conference. The center's school for beginning grades was doing a remarkable job in spite of critically few resources.

In one classroom of children in the second grade, I saw two persons in their late teens. I assumed they were assistants to the teachers. I was told the two were so determined to get an education that they had enrolled in the second grade. We found eagerness beyond belief among children wanting an education.

We visited a second Methodist school that had dirt floors, no desks or chairs, and a chalkboard that consisted of a black painted rectangle on the wall. There, too, the efforts of United Methodist teachers were no less than heroic. The $12 million call across the church on behalf of "Hope for the Children of Africa" was certainly timely and critically needed.

On Sunday, I preached at Boa Esparanza Church and was told 927 were in attendance inside and outside the church. Later Bishop de Carvalho told us Angola's basic needs were for infrastructure in transportation, commerce, communication, education, housing, roads, and development of natural resources. We were informed Angola had wealth in gold, petroleum, and diamonds, which could help lift the country's economy out of chaos if there were peace.

"Above all," he said, "We need lasting peace! ... No more mercenaries! We need big power to demonstrate interest in assisting Angola and all of sub-Sahara Africa. Finally, we need reconstruction of buildings, hospitals, schools, and medical healthcare centers!"

From there, we went to the province of Malange, Angola, where Bishop Moises D. Fernandes hosted us. Rebel forces some 30 kilometers away were still fighting government forces. We had to be escorted by a military detachment to visit the destroyed Kessua Methodist Hospital several miles from Malange. Here were ruins of one of the finest former hospitals and medical centers in all of Africa. The complex had included a sanatorium for tuberculosis patients, a nursing school, a seminary, a school for children, a church, and housing. The words of Bishop de Carvalho about the need for reconstruction of hospitals had certainly not been overblown.

We received encouraging words at the hospital site from Dr. Randolph Nugent, general secretary for the General Board of Global Ministries, that the Methodist facilities there would be rebuilt, if and when ongoing peace was established. I delivered to Bishop Fernandes a gift from the Southwest Texas Conference.

Back in Luanda, we were received by the U.S. ambassador, who briefed us regarding U.S. and Angolan relations. Later, the acting president of Angola received us for an hour or so. He told us about the yet unrealized hopes and dreams for the country. We were all emotionally touched to learn many of the high government officials had attended or had been connected to Methodist schools and mission centers over their lifetimes. The United Methodist Church was praised everywhere we went for its commitment to the needs of the people.

The most moving experience I felt over the entire trip was our visit to the Slave Museum. Bishop de Cavalho explained to us where and how some three million slaves had been taken from Angola over 200 years. They were shackled, baptized, drugged, and driven through a tunnel onto a waiting ship to transport them into slavery. By the time they were alert from being drugged, they were on the high seas. Our singing "We Shall Overcome" was never more poignant for me personally. All of us bishops joined hands and sang that song.

That evening we departed for several days in Mozambique. Bishop Joao Somane Machado directed our visit to his episcopal area. The following day we were received by the U.S. ambassador to Mozambique, who explained the growing relationship of the United States and Mozambique. That evening Bishop Nkulu Ntanda Ntambo from the Republic of Congo, traveling with us, was notified of a widespread and severe uprising in the Congo. He and his wife were distressed at not being able to contact their family members. They left us to return home after we all prayed for them and the church of the Congo.

The next day we visited Chicuque Rural Hospital Complex. It included a fine medical facility, a teacher training center, and a school of nursing—all United Methodist operations. We went from there to the church at Masinga, where the first Methodist mission in Mozambique was founded. A large crowd had waited many hours to greet us, feed us, and sing with us in celebration. Because we were late, a large number of the crowd had to leave before we arrived to get home before dark. All of us in the group were saddened at their not being able to join in the celebration and meal.

Back in Maputo the next day, the president of Mozambique received us for a briefing. He, too, had past connections with the Methodist Church. He spoke to us of Mozambique's achievements, dreams, and challenges. Afterwards, he offered us soft drinks, coffee, tea, cookies, and conversation around several tables. A few of us lucked out as the president sat and talked to us a bit at our table.

On our last evening, Bishop Machado called a rally of the people to honor our group. He preached, and we sang a lot more. Afterwards, he asked each of us to come forward to receive a beautiful ebony cane.

"This is a bishop's cane," he said. "When you raise it, the people will be quiet to hear what the bishop has to say!"

The audience enjoyed the laughter. When I got back home, I discovered why the people laughed. Raising the cane didn't work for me, either.

Shortly after I returned home, a devastating August flood

hit Del Rio, Texas. A small creek overflowed and roared across several areas of the city. Several people lost their lives, and several others were missing. The United Methodist Committee on Relief immediately sent an initial grant at my request. Then the Southwest Texas Conference disaster-response coordinator went into action to follow up with assistance to victims. A state trooper arranged for me to take a helicopter ride over the devastation with Doug Cannon, our director of communications. Curves in the creek were littered with household goods of all sorts, appliances, and even cars. It looked like a war zone. The United Methodist assistance was still going on to get victims onto their feet a year later.

In October 1998, 14 inches of rain fell on San Antonio. Many more lives were lost as two rivers simultaneously swept over banks through cities and towns to wreak havoc and destruction. Again the United Methodist Committee on Relief and our disaster-response coordinator continued bringing victims back to recovery a year later. A full-time flood recovery office for South Texas was set up in our United Methodist Center.

Ministers Week at Southern Methodist University has always been a favorite and "must attend" event for me. The week offered time apart for further education, reflection, relaxation, and rekindling friendships among the pastors.

During the 1999 Ministers Week in February, I was doubly blessed. At its annual breakfast, the Texas United Methodist College Association bestowed upon me its TUMCA Award for the second time. This time I was indeed a resident of Texas. Then at the opening luncheon of the week's activities, I was greatly honored to be named "Distinguished Alumnus of Perkins School of Theology." Dean Robin Lovin's introductory words on my behalf made the distinction even more meaningful to me.

Upon my return to San Antonio, we formerly dedicated the new $3.6 million United Methodist Center and declared it debt-free. We recalled John Wesley's words upon seeing the rapid growth of the infant Methodist Church when he said, "Look what God has wrought!"

At the spring 1999 meeting of the South Central College of Bishops, I finished my term as president and passed the gavel to Bishop Joel Martinez. This particular gavel held an interesting meaning. While in recess at the Southwest Texas Conference session back in 1995, my gavel, its pallet and my small desk clock mysteriously disappeared from the table at which I presided. At first I thought it was some sort of prank. In fun, I offered a reward for the items' return. They did not reappear. I then doubled the reward. They never showed up. As a result, several finely crafted gavels and pallets were sent to me from talented craftsmen. I gave one of those sets to Bishop Martinez with an inscription explaining its unique origin and requesting that it be passed on to succeeding presidents, since there was no known official gavel already in play. As I passed the gavel, I said, "Surely, this gavel among bishops is safe from disappearance!"

By this time, the national elections were heating up. Governor George W. Bush of Texas was in the thick of things. His pastor, Dr. James Mayfield of Tarrytown United Methodist Church in Austin, helped to arrange a meeting for me with the governor. As the resident bishop, I wanted to present Governor Bush a copy of the United Methodist Church's *Book of Resolutions*. My presentation would be on behalf of all five Texas United Methodist bishops.

Doug Cannon, our director of communications, worked out details for the meeting. On the same day, Lieutenant Governor Rick Perry had already invited me to pray for the Texas Senate at its opening session. Both occasions went extremely well. I was much impressed that both the governor and lieutenant governor were known to be active worshippers at Tarrytown Church. In a speech concerning social issues, the governor's response carried clear nuances of language in the *Book of Resolutions*. It was evident he had read the United Methodist Church's position on the subject at hand.

The day before the 1999 Southwest Texas Annual Conference session convened, I suffered a terrible allergy attack, which produced sniffles, headaches, sore throat, and general grumpiness. I could think of no word for my ailment other than "misery," and it wasn't adequate. By taking Tylenol, drinking water and juices, and eating cough drops, I apparently managed to deceive conference participants to some extent.

The session went well. We elected delegates to the General and jurisdictional conferences for the following year. My book, *Each One Disciple One,* was distributed to each member of both the Southwest Texas and Rio Grande conference sessions. This book was a follow-up to use in conjunction with *The Witness We Make.* Also, the Southwest Texas Conference approved the establishment of an Academy of Discipleship to equip disciples of Christ to become *disciplers* for Christ. The academy not only would train those who finished the curriculum; it would steadily reinforce the *premise* that until a disciple *of* Christ becomes a discipler *for* Christ, true discipleship has not taken place. The curriculum for the academy included some 20 courses. Dr. Austin Frederick, assistant to the episcopal office, gave outstanding leadership to the design, development, and implementation of the academy.

In late summer of 1999, the Russia Initiative Team had scheduled a visit to the United Methodist church in Vologda, Russia. The church was sponsored and supported by the Southwest Texas Conference. Team members were the Reverend Scott Somers, the Reverend David Semrad, the Reverend Beth Gustafson, and Julie Wiley from the conference communications office.

Katia, our Russian interpreter, greeted us with a warm welcome to Moscow. The drive from the airport to the hotel gave us a wonderful opportunity for a ground-level view of the city. Katia checked us into the Hotel Rassia in the heart of Moscow. After a brief rest, we had an early dinner several stories above the street. From there, we enjoyed a panoramic view of Moscow's expansiveness. It was truly a beautiful metropolis. We then visited nearby Red Square, St. Basil's Cathedral, the Kremlin, and Lenin's Tomb. We stood on a flat metal plate that served as the point from which every city, town, and hamlet in Russia was measured in kilometers.

Early the next morning, the Southwest Texas team met with Bishop Ruediger R. Minor, resident bishop of the area. Staff, faculty, and several students from the new United Methodist seminary in Moscow joined us for a discussion about the school's pressing future. It was inspiring to see the newest United Methodist seminary struggling heroically to become an outstanding school for training and equipping Russia's future ministers and leaders.

We then visited the War Memorial for much of the afternoon. The memorial denoted the defeat of Napoleon's army. The entire area carried the very aura of world history. At the memorial marking the Holocaust carried out by Hitler's Third Reich, we all stood silently. I shall never forget the haggard faces of life-sized statues of Jews holding the hands of their children as they were marched to their extermination. The adjoining area was almost unbearable to see. The team stood stunned. We wept around a large area of preserved toys, caps, shoes, skates, ball bats, and children's playthings left behind. The memorial starkly reminded us of what horror, havoc, and evil a single madman can wreak upon humanity when he is let loose in the world.

That evening the team boarded a train for an overnight trip to Vologda. Vera Agapova, the pastor of the church, and several members met us, hugged us, and welcomed us to Vologda. Vera had responded to her call to ministry and was appointed to the Vologda Church after her pastor-husband had been killed in an automobile accident. Vera and her son graciously hosted me in their home while I was in Vologda.

The team visited the orphans home and received handmade gifts from the beautiful, happy children. We gave each child a gift, sang with them, and were blessed by the love we received from the hard-working staff members.

The following morning we were invited to meet city officials. They thanked us and expressed deep respect for the Methodist ministry in Vologda. Especially, they thanked us for "adopting" the orphans home of some 60 children. We had lunch with Father Constantine at this Orthodox Church. We learned of his heroic efforts to keep alive the faith for more than a half century. He knew about the Methodist Church and blessed us for our efforts on behalf of children.

The worship service the next day touched and inspired us. The small church seated only about 30. Nearly twice that many managed to crowd in. Following the pastor's sermon, I was asked, as the bishop, to bless the building and the people present. What a privilege! Afterwards, I was notified that a government official had been in attendance and wanted to speak to me. She thanked me for blessing the church and for the ministry the "Methodists from America" were doing for the congregation and the children. Certainly, I was impressed that she had made a point of expressing the government's appreciation.

The metropolitan Orthodox bishop of Vologda invited the team to lunch. He, too, profusely thanked us for what we were doing in Russia. He told all those present that I was the first and only denominational church leader he had ever met from the United States.

I spoke briefly of our gratitude for being invited to have lunch with the metropolitan bishop of Vologda and said I counted it a high privilege to meet him and other Orthodox leaders present. The bishop and I exchanged gifts. Our "leaving" took quite a bit of time from needing to shake hands with all those present.

We boarded an overnight train to St. Petersburg in a pouring rain. I think every member of the church, and a lot of others who had heard of us, stood on the open platform to see us off. As I neared the steps onto the train, a young man named Dimitri stopped me. He was a member of the church and served as one of the interpreters. I turned to meet his piercing eyes. We shook hands as he said to me through tears, "Bishop, I will never forget you. Your visit with us has shown us the love of Christ."

I grabbed him and hugged him as the pouring rain soaked us even more. I was so touched I could hardly speak. I finally managed to say, "Dimitri, I will never forget you, either, nor this moment you and I have shared in this place!"

I have never forgotten him. Many times since, I have thought of Dimitri and offered prayers of thanksgiving for that special moment.

After all the team got aboard, we let down the windows of our Pullman car to say goodbye again and again to those standing there in the deluge. We begged them to get out of the rain, but they just stood there, singing, saying goodbye, and thanking us for visiting them. Finally, the train pulled out, and the entire team was dripping wet, not only from the rain but also from tears of gratitude and joy for what the people of Vologda had deposited forever into our lives.

We arrived early in St. Petersburg—a city known for its beauty and its welcoming spirit. My stay was for only a few hours, since I had to leave for Helsinki, Finland. There I would await the arrival of several other bishops to begin our episcopal visitations to the Northern Europe and Baltic conferences of the United Methodist Church. Scott Somers saw me off at the airport. It was a thoughtful gesture on his part. He and the team had indeed taken good care of me during my stay in Russia. I arrived in Helsinki and had until the next afternoon to rest before joining up with the other bishops who would be arriving.

Helsinki, too, is a beautiful city. The people were very friendly and most helpful to visitors on the streets. I took a long walk through the area and had an early dinner at a Chinese restaurant. The Chinese waiter welcomed me and asked if I had ever visited China. That set into motion a chat throughout the meal about his former country. It had been a good day. I wrote a bit in my journal and went to bed. I slept soundly for the first full night's rest since departing San Antonio.

The next morning I strolled along the open-air market in the harbor where friendly merchants sold all sorts of fresh foods. I was welcomed to Helsinki a number of times by people on the street. I boarded one of the hydrofoil vessels and skimmed across 70 miles of water to Tallin, Estonia. The entire city seemed to be abuzz with construction and refurbishing now that Estonia was no longer a part of the Soviet Union. I visited several sites, including the huge cathedral downtown. I returned to the port to spend time enjoying a panoramic view of the city from the tall harbor facility while waiting for the hydrofoil's return to Helsinki.

That evening the other bishops arrived. It was homecoming time. Bishop Hans Växby, our host bishop, met with us the next day for a briefing on his episcopal area. It was enjoyable, helpful, and certainly interesting. We all had lunch at a farm, which had been in one family continuously for more than 500 years. We were given an overview of its history. We visited a long-standing horse-riding school. Children were riding with perfect posture and in impressive rhythm with the horses. I was much intrigued and impressed.

The next day we all scattered to our assigned areas of episcopal visitations. My area was Norway. Ouyvind Helliesen, district superintendent, met me at the Stavanger Airport. He drove a long loop along the coastline of his district. The verdant meadows were occupied by cattle and sheep. We drove into the mountains and through long tunnels to reappear at several spectacular waterfalls cascading down into breathtaking fjords hundreds of feet below. Already I had fallen in love with Norway.

That evening we had dinner of fresh cod, boiled potatoes, and fresh vegetables with a pastor and his family en route to Stavanger. What a meal! I would find Norwegian hospitality unrivaled anywhere in the world I had visited. Already I was finding Norway's natural beauty matched only by its friendly and fun-loving people.

The next day I was asked to spend time with several pastors to discuss the church's role in its global context and to respond to questions. We had a lively and delightful encounter with one another. Sunday came, and I preached at the church in Stavanger. The congregation again and again welcomed me. That afternoon, I participated in the formal opening of a new church.

The following day we met with the Lutheran bishop and his staff. He had requested our visit. The occasion was another highlight of my time in the Stavanger area. Afterwards, Ouyvind and I strolled among the streets and shops of downtown. We "people watched" and chatted as he sipped his favorite beverage—a soft drink from McDonald's.

Late that afternoon I flew to Harstad via Oslo for the second leg of my visitation. Superintendent Lief Hansen met me at the airport and delivered me to Solton Methodist School, where I was quartered for my time in Harstad. Lief was an engaging and dedicated person.

Jenny Annerson, 88, asked Lief to bring me to her house for a weekly prayer meeting with several other elderly and saintly women. I was glad to go. What a delightful and vibrant spirit filled the group. They quizzed me about the United Methodist Church. They also refreshed my soul.

That afternoon Lief took me on a tour of several churches and sites. He guided me through the coastal gun emplacements built and operated by German occupying forces during World War II. The artillery guarded the narrow waterway into the harbor area. The whole area, now preserved, still created a chilling atmosphere.

That evening I met with a group of United Methodist Men for a talk and dinner. There were, somewhat to my surprise, several young men in the group. The older men had managed to get them involved in the life of the church. As usual, lots of good-natured banter was going on between the age groups.

The next morning Lief and I departed on a large Hydofoil for Finenes to visit a church well north of the Arctic Circle. As we glided over the water along the shoreline and fjords, I must say I had never seen a more tranquil and beautiful area. Breakfast along with that view was a double treat. We then retired to the lounge and plopped down in overstuffed captain's chairs for three hours of drinking in the wraparound view.

The next afternoon we went deep-sea fishing for cod and saith fish. The boat owner was a member of the church and invited the director of the Solton School to come with us. We fished by hand and straight line in 100 feet of water. I caught a fairly large codfish. In a short while, we had hauled in a tubful of nice-size fish of both species. They were our dinner at 10 p.m. in the home of the school director. The occasion was simply relaxing, filling, and enjoyable.

The next morning Lief and I spent the day meeting church leaders and enjoying our time together. Early the following day I left for the Porsgrunn-Oslo area for the final leg of my episcopal visitation

Superintendent Arne Ellingsen met me at the Oslo Airport. We went by the conference headquarters to meet the staff and for me to be interviewed for a story in the conference newspaper. We then visited the Methodist hospital. From there Arne drove me to Porsgrunn and checked me into the hotel. We stopped at a retreat to meet district leaders in a planning session. Then we went to Hamm Singa to visit "troll land," where a giant troll guarded the entrance. I was informed that Norway was the home base of the troll culture that had spread all over the world. Children in Norway, to their delight, are still told the troll stories.

The next day I preached at the church in Oslo and had dinner that evening with Bishop Ole Borgen (retired) and his wife, Martha. It was definitely a delight to visit the enormous Methodist Library Bishop Borgen had collected and cataloged in the full basement of his home. Arne then drove me around the Oslo area. We saw a huge water tower that had been remodeled into luxury apartments. Unusual! We toured the ski area, where competitive games took place each year.

The next day Arne and I sat on the railway station platform and talked of the church, our parts in it, and our personal walks with Christ. It was a special time for our last hour together. The train arrived at Porsgrunn and delivered me to the Oslo Airport entrance gate, where I boarded my plane to San Antonio.

In all, I had spent 21 days abroad visiting churches in six countries by way of nine aircraft, three trains, two hydrofoils, and numerous motor vehicles. My time traveling and visiting truly had been a memorable experience.

It was good to be home for one full day before flying to Nashville to preside at the five-day fall meeting of the General Commission on United Methodist Men.

Three weeks later the Great Methodist Gathering was upon us—after nearly two years of planning. Some 12,000 Methodists from the Rio Grande and Southwest Texas conferences converged on the Alamodome in San Antonio for a six-hour celebration on who we were as Methodists and to launch an areawide effort to make disciples for Jesus Christ. What a day! The dream of a mass public rally that Bill Ault, a San Antonio layman, had shared with me nearly three years before had become reality. Taylor Boone's tireless leadership as chairperson of the planning committee event had paid off in great proportions.

A massive choir broke forth to lead the crowd in singing. Bishop Leontine Kelly preached—even beyond her capacity. She captured the hearts of those present that day. Several laypeople witnessed as to their relationship with Christ. More singing and praise. Dr. Eddie Fox, director of World Evangelism for the World Methodist Council, lifted our spirits even higher. He called us individually to rededicate our lives to the awesome responsibility of inviting others to claim Jesus as lord and savior. I had never seen that many people in one place so inspired about their faith and witness.

After lunch Dr. Kirbyjon Caldwell, pastor of Windsor Village Church in Houston, challenged us to move into the masses of the poor to "offer them Christ" and to join in their struggle for justice, hope, and opportunity. By that time, the spirit of God was apparent among us.

I took the closing part of the Gathering. We had distributed to each person a silver-dollar-sized coin that said on one side, "The Great Methodist Gathering 10-9-99." On the other side were the words "Each One Disciple One—My Commitment!"

I lifted the coin and explained its meaning. I said, "When I lift this coin as far upward as I can reach, and say, 'Each one disciple one,' you raise your coin and say to God, '*My* Commitment!'"

My words were spoken, and their response made. I think the Alamodome must have quivered a bit. The event closed with a sustained "Praise the Lord!" of approval. I offered the benediction, and the crowd went forth to make disciples.

The excitement must have equaled that of those 83 pastors at the Christmas Conference in 1784 at Lovely Lane Chapel in Baltimore when they "leapt through the windows" in a hurry to get back home to make disciples of Jesus Christ.

Year 2000 arrived right on time. The Y2K Bug never showed up to bother our computers and shut down society. All that hype was for naught—just like most of our time worrying.

The arrival of the new year did not cause me to dwell on my journey in the global church as a bishop being just nine months from completion. I was not saddened by that fact. Nor was I ecstatic. I simply was at peace and ready for the completion when it came.

Four months later I reached my 68th birthday. By that time, I naturally gave frequent thought to my approaching retirement. We had to finalize plans to move into Epworth Villa Retirement Community in Oklahoma City. We had to buy furnishings and take care of many details. All these matters had to be delayed because Lavelle had to spend time with her dying father. He died in April after nearly 80 days in the hospital.

Lavelle and her sisters gave constant comfort through their presence at their father's bedside.

To our surprise, Dr. Austin Frederick, the assistant to the episcopal office, along with Superintendents Harold Sassman and Jon Lowry, flew in from San Antonio to bring the family at the funeral their condolences and love on behalf of Methodist people in my area. Their taking the time and expense to be with us was just one more expression of why I felt so fortunate to be their bishop.

The 2000 General Conference convened in Cleveland, Ohio. United Methodists from the Ohio East Area outdid themselves in welcoming the bishops and later the nearly 1,000 delegates.

The Council of Bishops met for several days before the General Conference. That gave Lavelle and me some time to spend with my brother Doyle; his wife, Rosemary; and their family in Cleveland. Doyle and Rosemary gave us a delightful tour of the city's many elegant and historical buildings—not the least of which was the completely restored Depression-era Severance Hall. There the following week several choirs from United Methodist colleges in Ohio would perform a special concert. The bishops and their families would be seated in the upper level for a spectacular view of everything.

We had dinner with Doyle and Rosemary in their lovely home. Charles, their son, and his wife, Dumont, joined in a sumptuous meal prepared by Rosemary. We sat at the table for quite a time, talking and reminiscing of days past, the present, and life as it was coming at us from the future. It had been a special day for us.

On Sunday I preached at the Church of the Savior in Cleveland Heights. It was for me a high compliment to be invited by the senior pastor, Dr. Charles Yoost. Doyle and Rosemary are much involved in the life of the church. The reception later reinforced the notion that the congregation was warm and excited about their church.

Doyle and Rosemary hosted a late brunch for the two of us that included several leaders of the church. Their daughter Polly; her husband, Ned; and their four children joined us at the table. The children were very bright, loving, and certainly engaging in conversation. I appreciated the few wisecracks about Doyle made by some of the leaders—all in fun, of course, and for my benefit.

Later, a supper and reception by the Ohio East Area was given for the bishops and their spouses at the National Rock and Roll Hall of Fame. We all stood in line for more than two hours, greeting delegates from all over the world. It was a whopping success, despite the pouring rain that came down the whole time.

At the evening session a service of "dust and ashes" was conducted as an act of repentance for the mistreatment of slaves and black people in the past. The service was indeed moving as black bishops from other Methodist denominations participated and approved the act of repentance.

The next morning, I served as the liturgist for the worship service. As I looked out upon those nearly 1,000 delegates from all over the world, I thought of how far the United Methodist Church had come and how far we yet had to go if we were to "reform even this nation."

Shortly after my return to San Antonio, the Southwest Texas and Rio Grande Annual Conference sessions were upon us. Members of each session found at their seats a copy of my latest book, *Second Thoughts*, given in deep appreciation for what the two conferences had given me over eight years.

Both conference sessions went well, with notable highlights. When I commented later on how well the sessions had gone, someone remarked, "Well, Bishop, that's because the two conferences didn't want to make it hard on you this last go-round!"

I let his words go at that, for fear he would explain more than I wanted to hear.

One highlight in the Southwest Texas Conference was bestowed upon Martha Etter. She was given the Bishop's Exemplar Award in recognition of her tremendous leadership for eight years as conference lay leader. After she was elected in 1991 to head the Southwest Texas Conference delegation to the General Conference in 1992, the conference Board of Laity needed revamping to be in compliance with the *Book of Discipline*. Bishop Dixon had suggested she undertake that endeavor. Thus, Martha was elected in 1992 as lay leader and chair of the Board of Laity.

In her eight years as lay leader, she and the board connected lay leadership from the smallest congregation to each district Board of Laity and then to the conference board. Not only that, the board pushed for training in job responsibilities for lay leaders at all levels. Her leadership simply revolutionized the laity's strength and influence in the conference. No wonder lay leaders from across the South Central Jurisdiction elected her as 1996-2000 president of their regional association. Indeed, it was a high privilege to present to her the Bishop's Exemplar Award. The members of the 2000 Southwest Texas Annual Conference session stood to confirm the appropriateness of the recognition.

One very special highlight of the Rio Grande Conference session was the opening of the Getsemani Community Center in Georgetown, where Southwestern University is located. For many years the tiny Getsemani congregation had struggled to keep the church alive. Then Superintendent Rodolfo Barrera worked with the leadership of the Central Texas Conference, which includes Georgetown, in a joint effort to expand the church's ministry by developing a children's care center. Funds were raised from several sources for Volunteers in Mission to remodel and expand the structure. On the eve of the annual conference session, a large crowd arrived to celebrate the opening of the center, which included a refurbished home for the pastor. It was a victory celebration. The new facility was bound to attract new members to Getsemani's ministry as well as be a presence on weekdays for meeting needs of children in the community.

Upon my return to my office, I found a letter that gave my spirit a real lift. For a few years I had corresponded with Don, a convicted felon in prison. I had come to communicate with him as a result of a letter I had received from his mother years before. Don had hoped for parole "sometime in the future." All indications were that he was a model prisoner. I had suggested the best way for him to prepare for the future was to get a college education while doing time. He took my advice and enrolled in college courses. We paid what costs were over and above what the state paid. Officials kept me informed of Don's progress. I was amazed at his eagerness to learn and the grades that were confirmed by the program reports. He proved to be well above average in his studies.

In our correspondence, we discussed the possibility of a sponsoring church helping Don secure a job when he was released. One of our larger congregations took up the challenge. I was able to tell Don he had a job waiting for him and a congregation to support him once he got out.

Don continued his studies and received his degree. He then asked me to write a letter of support to the upcoming Parole Board meeting. I had done so. It was Don's first interview. Members of the board were much impressed but suggested Don continue his time. He was disappointed but not discouraged. He informed me he had enrolled in a master's degree program and asked for my continued financial support over and above what was not paid for him. I considered his decision to be evidence of his sincerity about getting an education and agreed to continue to help.

His letter on my desk this time was a "Hallelujah" letter. Don wanted me to know that he would be released after several weeks of processing and reorientation to "life on the outside." He was happy to know he had a job waiting and an understanding congregation to stand alongside him in his new journey. Immediately, I wrote him my congratulations for his remarkable achievements. His promise to me was that he would pursue his intentions to finish his master's degree.

I had never met Don face to face, nor had I ever talked to him. I retired before he was released on parole. Yet few things in my life gave me more satisfaction than knowing I had played a small part in the life of a convicted felon who had turned a corner into the winds of a prepared and productive life.

When the South Central Jurisdictional Conference convened in July in Albuquerque, New Mexico, I had the honor and privilege of preaching the memorial sermon.

The agenda called for the election of four new bishops. Dr. Rhymes Moncure from the East Missouri Conference was elected on the first ballot and assigned to the Nebraska Area. Dr. William W. Hutchinson from the New Mexico Conference was elected and assigned to the Louisiana Area. Dr. D. Max

Whitfield from the North Arkansas Conference was elected and assigned to the New Mexico/Northwest Texas Area. Dr. Ben Chamness of the Texas Conference was elected and assigned to the Central Texas Conference. Certainly the jurisdictional conference had elected four outstanding leaders of the church.

With only six weeks to go, Lavelle and I became preoccupied with retirement. We had yet to do so many things, like arranging to move to Epworth Villa in Oklahoma City and buying those furnishings. Suzanne Delamain, my area secretary, was so helpful in sorting, packing, and shipping archival material and documents for permanent storage. By August 1 everything seemed to be falling into place.

On the evening of August 4, our entire family was picked up by those two limousines and delivered to the downtown Hyatt Regency Hotel. More than 600 people had gathered there for our Retirement Celebration. Bishop John Wesley Hardt was the keynote speaker. He so graciously lifted up our ministry in such a marvelous way. He and his wife, Martha, made the celebration complete.

Dr. Robin Lovin made a presentation to me in recognition of our support of the scholarship fund at Perkins School of Theology. He said that more than $120,000 had been received in our honor.

Lavelle made a delightful impromptu speech to the full enjoyment of those present. At our very first meeting with the area delegates, she had said to them, "What you see is what you get." Eight years later the two conferences could say, "Indeed, what we got was a whole lot!"

It was then time for me to share my "Reflections as the Bishop" for eight years. The fun I had in delivering my reflections was apparently enjoyed with equal fun by the audience. The family was then transported home by the two limousines, where all 10 of us crashed. It had been a day unforgettable for all of us.

On August 18, Lavelle and I welcomed Bishop Joel Martinez and his wife, Raquel. I introduced them to both cabinets and asked Dr. Austin Frederick to introduce the new bishop and his spouse to all the staff members at the United Methodist Center.

Lavelle and I departed for Oklahoma City, thus essentially ending my eight-year term as the episcopal leader of the San Antonio Area. I had arrived as a new bishop with a great deal of excitement and anticipation. After eight years, I could say I had learned the scope of responsibilities expected of a bishop. In so many ways I had been blessed and uplifted in my spirit. Also, I had "grown some new wood" in my learnings and leadership. We had painted a vision for the coming eight years, and for the most part, we had brought that vision to birth.

It was fully time, therefore, to move into that experience and opportunity called "retirement." In that setting, too, we would move forward into the long shadows of living. And as always, God would become increasingly real in that leg of our journey as well.

15

Journey of Reflecting, Recording, and Recycling

Soon after we were officially retired, Lavelle and I, along with Bobbie and Jack Lyons, made a return trip to Highland Park Church in Lawton. We wanted to reminisce a bit about our beginnings in the ministry and to enjoy each other. We expected to find a dilapidated building that had long been condemned. Instead, we found a completely restored facility with an expanded fellowship hall, classrooms, and a paved parking area. It was a beautiful sight to behold.

We were thrilled that an active congregation was still present in the community. The Oklahoma Indian Missionary Conference had certainly put life back into that church.

The front door was not locked, so we went inside. Though remodeled, the interior was still familiar to us.

I sat for a few minutes in a pew near where I had said, "I will" in response to Brother Herman Snodgrass' question, "Who will take my place?" Those few moments sitting there recaptured the sense of God's nearness to me. We all relived our days there some 40 years earlier, and we were immensely blessed.

Reflecting! Recording! Recycling!—These are among the vital factors figuring into the equation of retirement. We take strength and perhaps pride in recalling where we began and how we got to where we are. We continue, with joy and gratitude, to record life as it is arriving daily. We are ever adapting as we understand more clearly the value of the approaching future.

While en route to a luncheon a few days later, a longtime friend asked me, "Well, Ray, what do you intend to do with all the time you now have on your hands in retirement?"

Quite quickly I responded, "I don't intend to be idle, absent, or invisible from the scene and drama of life."

Still, because the flow of my life has changed, I am reminded daily that I am indeed retired. No longer do I have to board, bleary-eyed, that express before daybreak to fly me across country for a meeting that will last so late I will have to board the "red-eye" express to fly back in time to make it to an early breakfast meeting the next morning. No longer, too, does my volume of mail take big chunks of time to decipher, discern, and work to the bottom, so I can then start on the stack of callback phone messages awaiting.

To keep from being idle, absent, and invisible to the scene of life, I brought to retirement my two ink pens to wear them out writing what I want, beginning with my autobiography. From there, I have a few partial manuscripts to finish—or not.

I preach when I want to, teach what I already know, go where we want to, and come home when we *decide* it's time. Our agenda is changeable but not liquid. We can go to bed early and rise late—as soon as I can break my lifelong habit of going to bed after midnight. We have sights yet to see, travels yet to take, and laughter to share on the way. We may become bent a bit in stature with the passing of time but not bored in the meantime. Life to this point has been too precious to bankrupt in the future with fear, caution, and retreat. If in time we need to lose weight, we hope to achieve it by less eating rather than less ease.

After my first full decade of pastoral ministry, I was besieged with the notion of writing a much-needed book. Its title would be *The Edge of Urgency*. I thought it was high time congregations more fully understood and appreciated the stalking urgency that accompanied the daily life of the pastor.

I wanted to lift up those dimensions of urgency that rose out of the pastor's comforting the dying; consoling the bereaved; counseling the troubled; meeting the needs of the poor; advocating for justice among the marginalized; conciliating disputes; smoothing the ruffled feathers of members; visiting the sick and shut-ins; supervising staff members; making time for strengthening family ties and relationships; nurturing one's own spiritual life; guarding physical health; getting involved in community affairs; preparing sermons and lectures; preaching, teaching and speaking; and seeking all the while to excel in one's "calling" of never being caught up.

Such a portfolio of responsibilities—many of which are unscheduled—hold every pastor in the grip of urgency. Any given day does not bring relief. Rather, it brings merely a brief respite before the pastor has to plunge immediately into another dimension of urgency. As one observant layperson and friend asked me, "How in the world do pastors keep their sanity when they have to grapple daily with a dozen highly charged emotional situations?" His question only reinforced my notion that it was indeed high time for congregations to recognize the stalking force of urgency felt by the pastor.

Alas! I didn't get very far into writing that "much needed" book. Very quickly I realized I was also besieged with equal proportions of naiveté, ignorance, and brash presumption. I simply was not capable of addressing such an enormous subject. Quietly, therefore, I filed the outline and related material under the general heading, "Someday...Maybe."

Now, after four full decades in ministry, I have, in some measure, written two books. One is the account of my journey as I experienced it. The other is the account of my journey as I have expressed it for others to assess.

The time has come, therefore, for me to say what that district superintendent in Bocas del Torosaid to me: "Now I wait! I wait to see what God will make of my twice-taken journey."

While I wait, I ponder some related words of John Jay (1745–1829), first chief justice of the United States. While in his 80s, Jay was asked how he was occupying his great mind. He replied, "I have a long life to look back on and eternity to look forward to."

In a way, the chief justice alluded to his twice-taken journey. More importantly, in mentioning "eternity" he added the third dimension of journey we all make. That aspect of the journey merits our expressed attention, since we will take no titles earned or honors bestowed as we pass into that timeless zone of being home with God.

Quips that Quickened the Quest

It's never far from the acceptable to the exceptional.

Pens never run out of ink at a convenient time.

Never answer an anonymous letter.

Contentment is never where you are not.

Little multiplied by many equals much.

Oneself: the best source of laughter.

Baggage is as essential as destination.

Betterness is the antidote for bitterness.

No "best breed" in human show.

Much of limitation resides in the mind.

Rejection can be a form of affirmation.

Secret giving buys joyous living.

Guilt is the forerunner of grace.

Right doors are as important as right keys.

Luck is the offspring of labor.

"Miser" is but four letters from "Miserable."

Virtue points not to its lack in others.

Pessimism and persimmons are double cousins.

Standard of living and quality of living are not mutually exclusive.

Many stumbles are over self.

Almost good is but a bit better than bad.

The light we follow is the end we find.

Forgiveness is nobler than fairness.

Words are never just words.

A wink can wound as deeply as a welt.

Our greatest fault is to see not one's own.

My way plus your way still might not equal right way.

Mettle is measured by heat and hammer.

Doubt genuflects in faith's presence.

What we bring to the moment often influences the hour.

Today's dream feeds the taproot of tomorrow's drama.

Bias bears the birthmark of insecurity.

Choice: the maker of character as well as chaos.

Risking and governing: twin measures of meaning.

Trash: the spent residue of untried possibility.

Children are much our own echo.

Coasting usually is costly.

Fear can drive us to fealty.

Writing and erasers: both are essential.

Worship in arrears equals life in arrears.

Laughter lightens life.

Eyes on the past teaches us only what we already know.

Volume seldom determines value.

Worry is an inside robbery.

Bottom is for visiting, not staying.

Titles are no more than just that.

We are muchly the dividends of others' deposits.

There you are, wherever you are.

Waste is the worst end of effort.

Minuses carry value as well as pluses.

Change is permanent.

Good is found where you make it.

The highway of life is also a toll road.

Urgency revises the value of a minute.

Life is rife with risk.

Success floats upward. So does scum.

One tongue can exhaust a host of ears.

A clear head and a clean heart will get you far.

Stuff answering stuff is still just stuff.

You can't lead where you won't go.

Cabinet Colleagues:

District Superintendents with Whom I Served

Southwest Texas Conference

Gregory A. Robertson

Tom O. McClung

Shirley D. Hill

Warren G. Hornung

J. Gordon Talk

*Jerry J. Smith

*Austin Frederick Jr.

Malford C. Hierholzer

William B. Henderson

Jon D. Lowry

Frederick B. Waters

Janice Riggle Huie

Harold G. Sassman

Barbara Galloway-Edgar

Robert E. Hall

Harry G. Kahl

William B. Sandberg

Fred. E. Martin

J. Keith Wyatt

Rio Grande Conference

Roberto L. Gomez

David Chavez

Eubaldo Ponce

Jose Salas

Rodolfo Barrera

Jesus Bermudez

Michael R. Dobbs

Ruben Salcido

Francisco P. Estrada

Eutimio Gonzales, Jr.

Miguel A. Albert

Edgar Avitia

*Served also as assistant to the episcopal office